# Stone Wondrously Hewn

## The Cathedral of St. John the Evangelist

John J. O'Hagan

Excerpts from the English translation of *Dedication of a Church and an Altar* © 1978, International Commission on English in the Liturgy Corporation (ICEL); excerpts from *Documents on the Liturgy, 1963–1979: Conciliar, Papal, and Curial Texts* © 1982, ICEL, excerpts from the English translation of *The Roman Missal* © 2010. All rights reserved.

Copyright © 2014 by John J. O'Hagan

No part of this manuscript may be reproduced, stored in a retrieval system, or transmitted in any form or by any means; electronic, mechanical, photocopying, recording, or otherwise; without the prior written permission of the author.

Published 2017.

Printed in the United States of America.

ISBN: 978-09977753-3-4

Cover Design: Paul Huber

Cornerstone Photo Credit: Paul Huber

Layout/Editing: Gina Burns

Printer: The Caxton Printers, Ltd., Caldwell ID

This book is dedicated to Charles Hummel.

You have for so long been such an important aspect of the history of St. John's Cathedral. Your love, not just for the building but for the Church, is obvious. We have the monument we have today in large measure because of that love, and your work.

Certainly, I have this book to offer only because of the many hours you were willing to spend with me. You have been unstinting in giving me access to documents, material, and most of all your personal recollections. A peripheral benefit of working on this book was spending so many pleasant afternoons visiting with you and listening to you, and learning so very much from you.

Thank you.

### *From the rite for the blessing and laying of a foundation stone:*

*Father, the prophet Daniel spoke of your Son as a stone wondrously hewn from a mountain. The apostle Paul spoke of him as a stone firmly founded.*

*Bless this foundation stone to be laid in Christ's name.*

*You appointed him the beginning and end of all things.*

*May this work begin, continue and be brought to fulfillment in him, for he is Lord forever and ever.*

*Amen*[1]

*"Catholics live in an enchanted world, a world of statues and holy water, stained glass and votive candles, saints and religious medals, rosary beads and holy pictures. But these Catholic paraphernalia are mere hints of a deeper and more pervasive religious sensibility which inclines Catholics to see the Holy lurking in creation. As Catholics we find our houses and our world haunted by a sense that the objects, events and persons of daily life are revelations of grace."*

Reprinted with permission: *The Catholic Imagination.* Reverend Andrew Greeley. (Berkeley, University of California Press. 2001.)

# Table of Contents

**Chapter 1**
*In the Beginning* .................................. 1

**Chapter 2**
*Bishop Gorieux Puts His Stamp on Idaho* ...... 13

**Chapter 3**
*The Cornerstone is Laid* ..................... 21

**Chapter 4**
*The Lower Level: The Cathedral's First Sacred Space* ................................. 27

**Chapter 5**
*Bishop Gorman Takes the Reins in Idaho* ...... 35

**Chapter 6**
*The Basques Get Their Own Church* .......... 49

**Chapter 7**
*Gorman Finishes the Cathedral* .............. 55

**Chapter 8**
*Bishop Kelly Introduces an Era of Austerity* ... 61

**Chapter 9**
*The Building They Gave Us* .................. 67

**Chapter 10**
*A First Look at the Architecture* ............. 73

**Chapter 11**
*A Step Inside* ............................... 79

**Chapter 12**
*A Closer Look at the Nave* ................... 89

**Chapter 13**
*The Transepts* .............................. 97

**Chapter 14**
*The Apse* .................................. 107

**Chapter 15**
*The Sanctuary* ............................. 113

**Chapter 16**
*A Plan to Renovate the Cathedral* .......... 117

**Chapter 17**
*The Renovation* ............................ 127

**Chapter 18**
*He Who Sings Prays Twice* ................. 135

**Chapter 19**
*No Great Building is Ever Finished* ......... 143

**Chapter 20**
*History is Not Dates; History is People* ..... 155

**Chapter 21**
*The Future is Mestizo* ...................... 167

**Chapter 22**
*Quo Vadis?* ................................ 173

**Appendix A**
*Glossary* . . . . . . . . . . . . . . . . . . . . . . . . . . . . . . . 175

**Appendix B**
*Bishops of the Diocese of Boise* . . . . . . . . . . . . . . 181

**Appendix C**
*Pastors/Rectors of St. John's Cathedral* . . . . . . . 193

**Appendix D**
*Myths/Mysteries of St. John's Cathedral* . . . . . . 195

**Appendix E**
*Key Facts About St. John's Cathedral* . . . . . . . . 199

**Appendix F**
*Timeline for St. John's Cathedral* . . . . . . . . . . . . 201

*End Notes* . . . . . . . . . . . . . . . . . . . . . . . . . . . . . . 207

# Acknowledgements

With special thanks to:

Paul Huber, for his work on the book's cover design.

Gina Burns, who gave her professional time and talent to the layout of this book.

Michael Brown, former editor of the Idaho Catholic Register, who rendered unstinting assistance and selfless time in getting me information from the diocesan archives.

All of the staff at the offices of the Diocese of Boise, who were always gracious as I imposed on their schedules.

All of the parish staff at the office of St. John's Cathedral, who helped in everything from accessing musty archives to crawling around in dusty attics.

Father Jerry Funke, who suggested, "Why don't you write the history of the Cathedral?"

# Introduction

July on the western Snake River Plain can be a brutal time. Other than cottonwood trees, marking the course of the Boise River as it winds its way to join the larger Snake River, sagebrush is the most common endemic plant. People unfamiliar with the area are surprised to hear of summer temperatures in the 90's and 100's, unabated day after day. If any rain should fall from July until October, it would be the rarest, and briefest, of events. This is the western edge of the "Great American Desert," and it is an anvil for the hammer of the sun in what Ernest Hemmingway would thirty years later describe as "high blue windless skies."

July of 1906 was typical: highs in the 90's and 100's; weather records from that time confirm that the average temperature for the month was 92.5, with consistent temperatures in the very high 90's or over 100. A dry, searing heat.

In that heat, a group of men were working in an open pit 10 feet below ground level. Their excavation provided no shade, and unfortunately blocked any breeze. The sandstone walls surrounding them trapped and reflected the heat.

Despite the harsh circumstances they were glad of the work. Digging, grubbing, pulling, and toiling defined their lives. It was work such as this which provided them a living they never could have imagined. It will probably come as a surprise to most people in "Right to Work" Idaho of the 21st century that labor was very well organized, and very powerful, in the early 20th century. It was a condition of employment for the two major projects at the time, the Idaho State Capitol and St. John's Cathedral, that skilled workmen be hired from the Labor Temple. From 1910 to 1922, the average hourly wage of building trades workers more than doubled from .50¢ to $1.08

*Page ix*

*Stone Wondrously Hewn*

an hour.[2] At the same time, the average work week declined from 48 hours to 43.

Besides a day's work and a day's wages there was one other consolation as they dug and sweated, broke fingers and tore limbs. The work they were engaged in now with pick and shovel would be the foot, the cradle, the beginnings of a monument, not just to their labor, but to their faith. Those now anonymous laborers—mostly new immigrants, if not to the United States, certainly to Idaho—were largely Irish and German and certainly Catholic. Many of them had followed the army west, after the Civil War, but it wasn't a military fort they were working on now. They were preparing the ground for a cathedral for the newly created Roman Catholic Diocese of Boise.

"Cathedral." The term derives from the Greek *kathedra*, seat. A cathedral is a bishop's church; it is where his chair is. It is literally the bishop's seat, and it is the seat of ecclesiastical authority in a cathedral's diocese.

A Catholic church, certainly a Catholic church built at the beginning of the 20th century, was never meant to be simply a place of worship. It was meant to be a place of grandeur and awe, a reflection on this earth of the wonders and glories of God. Catholic ritual is rich in symbols and complex in practice. The places where it is celebrated are rich in art and visual reminders. None of the art, though, is art for art's sake. There is nothing accidental in liturgical art; virtually every piece and placement has a meaning. We will visit that theme time and time again in this book. The interior of a Catholic church is not just a place for people to gather, nor even a repository for beautiful art. It is a sacred space. "The very nature of a church demands that it be suited to sacred celebrations, dignified, and evincing a noble beauty…"[3]

All who view it should be struck with that sacredness. This is doubly so in the case of a church which is also to be designated a cathedral.

In the eyes of certain critics Catholic churches are places of excess. It is a common criticism of Catholic churches that they are money wasted, the predictable complaint being that "the money could have been better spent on the poor." It is not just a common criticism, it is an ancient one. Jesus himself faced it with the woman who poured expensive oil on his head. His response was a straightforward one 2,000 years ago and is still valid today: "The poor you will always have with you" (Matthew 26–11). Catholics hold very firmly to the belief that a church is the reflection on earth of the glory of God's promise. A Catholic Mass can be celebrated under almost any circumstances. Masses have been said on the hood of a Humvee or a rock in the desert. Given the opportunity, though, to establish a permanent place of worship Catholics will establish it with love, and yes, sacrifice for their God. Catholicism has been described as a very "sensual"

*Introduction*

religion. It is one which gives its followers much of its impact and import from the senses. Money saved in limiting decorations would be money soon spent and soon forgotten on other items. Money invested in richly adorning God's house will be appreciated by generations to come.

It is important to keep in mind that in Catholic usage "the Church" is first of all a term describing not a building, but the people of God. The people *are* the Church and to suggest that they should scrimp on the adornment of the place they gather to worship God is to suggest that they should dress themselves in rags for that worship.

It is this mindset, the idea that we are building something not for ourselves, but for God and for future generations, which will be constant throughout this book. We will see how, through one-hundred-plus years, the work of these early laborers has not just persevered, but has grown and expanded. We will see that the work on the cathedral was not finished when the final stone was emplaced, nor when the first Mass was celebrated. The Cathedral, as a Church, as the living, growing, "people of God," is an ongoing project. As late as 2015 major artistic enhancements were being added to the Cathedral of St. John the Evangelist. It will *never* be completed.

It is not obvious to the casual observer, nor considered by most people, that virtually none of the great cathedrals in the world were finished in a single generation, nor are necessarily completed yet. Notre Dame, Nantes, Chartres, St. Peters, took hundreds of years to build and are constantly being improved. The artists who designed them and the workers who built them knew without a doubt that they would never live to see the finished monument. That sure knowledge, though, diminished not at all the commitment and dedication they put into these edifices, which future generations would enjoy. We can see that same commitment and the same ongoing work at St. John's. As an example, while the cathedral was begun in 1906 and dedicated in 1921, the massive carved oak doors which define the front entrance were not added until 1973. The stained glass windows which grace the lower level on the south side were done in 2015. Other enhancements are planned.

It is likely that lofty considerations such as these were, at best, passing thoughts to the men laboring in the summer heat. They were there for the job. The privilege of putting their stamp on what would turn out to be a soaring monument to their faith was probably not a driving motivation. Still, it had to have occurred to them. The early 20th century was not a friendly time for immigrants to the United States, and particularly not for Catholic immigrants.

Up until about 1840 the United States was largely a Protestant country. Starting about 1846, the devastating potato famine drove literally millions of Irish, virtually

*Page xi*

*Stone Wondrously Hewn*

all Catholic, to immigrate to the United States. Political and social upheaval throughout Europe soon drove more millions of German, Italian, Polish and Eastern European Catholics to join them. Suddenly the solidly Protestant United States looked not quite so solid. In 1850 Catholics made up only five percent of the total population of the United States. Fifty years later, they comprised seventeen percent.[a] Catholics suddenly became the largest religious denomination in the country, a position they continue to hold today. These "foreigners," almost none of whom spoke English, flooded American cities and workplaces.[b] They not only spoke different languages, they practiced a decidedly different religion. In fact, the rites of that religion were conducted in yet another language, Latin! Suspicions toward these newcomers manifested themselves in language unfortunately familiar in the 21st century, i.e. "they are lazy, they are dirty, they are taking our jobs," and the now fantastical, but then very popular, fear *"they are the pope's army and their only allegiance is to a foreign power, the Vatican."*

These newcomers, without exception, had been despised, marginalized, and exploited for fifty years. They had fought, in large numbers, on both sides in the Civil War. Now, at the dawning of a new century, they were ready to assert their rights, and claim their places in the new order. *We have arrived. We are part and parcel of this muscular new land, and we are planting our presence here, now, for all generations to see.* One hundred years ago, the undertaking of such a project was a tremendous leap of faith. One hundred years later, it remains a tremendous monument to faith.

This book will examine the architectural and artistic edifice which resulted, and how it has changed. It will examine in some detail that architecture, and that art. To the casual observer, the cathedral and its artistic embellishments are certainly beautiful and even awe inspiring. As we examine these embellishments, we hope to bring more than just the overall beauty to the fore. We hope to point out some, perhaps, never noticed features: features which will demonstrate the thought and personal emotions which the planners and artists put into their work. *"Nothing in liturgical art is accidental."* That premise will be demonstrated over and over again in these pages. Art, though, is not all that the cathedral has to offer. A sense of the sacred, and the importance of earthly reminders of that sacredness and the lives of the very human people who imparted it, are all very present in this building.

This book, then, is an examination of the people and the history of the Cathedral of St. John the Evangelist in Boise, Idaho.

---

[a] Today, Catholics comprise approximately 25% of the United States population. This increase is still largely driven by immigrants now not from Europe, but from Mexico and Central America.

[b] The Irish, although they suffered plenty of discrimination on their own, had one distinct advantage over almost all other immigrant groups. Their language, thanks to centuries of domination by Great Britain, was English.

## Introduction

Having stated what this book is, let me state what it is not.

This book is *not* a history of the Diocese of Boise, nor even of the parish of St. John's. It is intended to recount the history of a building. In doing this, we will, of necessity from time to time, invoke the history of some people and of the parish, and even of the diocese, but this is not a history of any of those entities. With particular regard to the bishops of Boise, it should be obvious that, for the first 25 years of its existence, the bishop of Idaho, with his seat in the Cathedral of St. John's, was a virtually daily presence in the cathedral. As the state grew, and as churches were added, this became less and less true. Always, though, the cathedral is his church, though his involvement with its day to day routine has become less and less through the years. Thus, some of the bishops, particularly the earlier ones, will get a more extensive treatment than some of the later ones, and some of them will get only a passing mention. This is not a slight on any of the bishops; it is simply a recognition of the roles they did, or did not, play in the history of St. John's Cathedral.

In its formative years, of course, the history of the Cathedral *was* the history of the diocese. St. John's was the only Catholic church in Boise from 1876 until 1937,[c] when St. Mary's was founded —

---

c    As a matter of fact, in 1919 the Church of the Good Shepherd was opened in Boise, but that church was a "mission" of St. John's.

with much criticism because it was "so far out in the country," at 28th and State Streets! The letter creating St. Mary's parish is an interesting view of how important geographical boundaries were to a parish in the twentieth century. The bishop, in detailing the new parish to the pastor of St. John's, was very clear where the boundaries would be. The letter informed Father O'Toole of St. John's that he was having withdrawn from his parish:

> ***"… all that part of Boise beginning at and including Fifteenth Street and west and westerly thereof including its environs; we also withdraw all that part across the river which is called the Bench, west of Roosevelt Avenue but so that Roosevelt avenue south of Alturas Street belongs to the Cathedral Parish and Roosevelt Avenue north of Alturas Street belongs to St. Mary's parish."***[4]

Of course, many of these lines were further adjusted when subsequently Our Lady of the Rosary, Sacred Heart, St. Mark's, and Risen Christ parishes were established. History, though, is never a linear progression. It stops, starts, and takes unexpected changes of course. Any recounting of it has to follow the same discursive path.

If one is looking for a definitive overview of the Catholic Church in Idaho, it will not be found here. In that regard, I can only suggest the work of Right Reverend Cyprian Bradley O.S.B. and Most Reverend Edward Kelly, D.D., Ph.D.

*Stone Wondrously Hewn*

*History of the Diocese of Boise, 1863–1953.* It cannot escape observation that that work is now over half a century out of date. Perhaps someone should consider updating it.

A note on directions in describing the church building: When we refer in this book, to the "right" or the "left" we are referring to the congregation's perspective as they are facing the altar. The "front" of the church is the end with the altar in it. The "back" of the church is the end with the choir loft and ironically, the "front doors" in it.

In chronicling the history of the cathedral, there is no escaping the fact that its beauty is, in large measure, due to the generosity of benefactors. Art work, exquisite construction materials, and beautiful furnishings are major features of the cathedral's beauty. None of these would have been possible without the generous gifts of many people. In almost all cases, the names of these people are available in the historical records. In almost all cases, I have chosen to leave the names unchronicled. Partly, this is an excess of caution: if twenty people are named and two are left out, the twenty will not be particularly honored, but the two will certainly be offended. Mostly, though, it is in deference to one of Jesus' lessons.

*As he looked up he saw rich people putting their offering in to the treasury; then he happened to notice a poverty-stricken widow putting in two small coins, and he said "I tell you truly, this poor widow has put in more than any of them; for these have contributed money they had over, but she, from the little she had has put in all she has to live on."* (Luke 21:1–4)

The Cathedral of St. John the Evangelist was built, is maintained, and continues to grow through the generosity of its people, rich, poor, and in between. If any acknowledgement is to be given to people who have made the cathedral what it is, it would have to be:

**To the people of God who believe in the promise, and who are committed to its fulfillment, now and forever. Amen.**

# Chapter 1

*In the Beginning*

Contrary to a commonly held belief, what is now the state of Idaho was not part of the Louisiana Purchase. The western limit of the Louisiana Purchase was the western slope of the Continental Divide. Idaho's eastern border is generally, although not totally, west of that line. Lewis and Clark on their Corps of Discovery expedition went well beyond the area included in the Louisiana Purchase, and crossed the northern third of Idaho using the Clearwater and Columbia Rivers for a major segment of their trip all the way to the Pacific Ocean.

*Stone Wondrously Hewn*

The area now covered by the state of Idaho was at various times claimed by Russia, Spain, Great Britain, and the United States. First to fall by the wayside was Spain, in 1819, under the terms of the Adams-Onis treaty. That treaty, named for the American Secretary of State, John Quincy Adams, and the Spanish Foreign Minister, Don Luis Onis, was primarily effected to define the borders of the Spanish Territory in the southwest United States. By the terms of that treaty, the United States relinquished its claims to the area of Texas west of the Sabine River. (That inconvenient accommodation would be completely forgotten 20 years later.) In return, Spain ceded its claims to the Oregon Territory north of 42 degrees, approximately the latitude of the current northern boundary of the state of California.

In 1824, Russia abandoned its claims to any territory of the western North American continent south of 54 degrees, 40 minutes north, which was essentially the southern limit of Alaska. Subsequently, in 1867, the United States purchased Alaska from Russia for approximately 7 million dollars.

Finally, in 1846, the United States and Great Britain entered into the Oregon Treaty, which effectively terminated Great Britain's claims. Thus, by 1846, the United States had gained sole possession of what was generally called the Oregon Territory, encompassing the current states of Washington, Oregon, Idaho, and parts of Montana and Wyoming.

The designation of the area and its boundaries changed several times over the next several years. Originally, the entire area encompassing present day Wyoming, Montana, Idaho, Oregon, and Washington was referred to as the Northwest Territory. In 1848, the Oregon Territory, consisting of Idaho, Oregon, Washington, and parts of Montana and Wyoming was created. In 1853, the Washington Territory was carved out of the area. It was made up of Washington and parts of southern Idaho and western Wyoming. Ten years later (1863), gold discoveries in Idaho gave that area enough importance to be declared its own territory. That first "Idaho Territory" extended into what are now Montana and Wyoming. In 1890, Idaho became a state.

Not only the political boundaries, but the ecclesiastical ones changed repeatedly during this time. At various times, various parts of the current diocese of Boise were under the jurisdiction of the Diocese of St. Louis, the Diocese of Nisqually (now the Archdiocese of Seattle), the Diocese of Oregon City (now the Archdiocese of Portland), and the Archdiocese of Quebec.

The contention that Idaho was at one time under the episcopal authority of our neighbor to the north is one of those intriguing, if now unimportant, historical enigmas which keep academics busy. From 1839 to 1843, both St. Louis and Quebec had some ecclesiastical authority in different parts of the Oregon territory. When Quebec might have exercised, or

*Chapter 1*

lost, any authority it had over the territory which became Idaho is undeterminable. The problem is that when these matters were being settled in Rome, neither the United States nor Canada had agreed on where the boundary between them lay. Thus, the indult creating the Vicariate of Oregon, which included Idaho, in 1843 simply referred to the territory "commonly called Oregon." In 1843 no one was quite sure where the northern boundary of the territory lay. That question was not resolved until the Oregon treaty of 1846, when the 49th parallel was accepted by both Canada and the United States as the demarcation line. Rome may have spoken in 1843, but it wasn't entirely clear just what Rome had said—certainly not the last time Catholics have been faced with such a dilemma.

The first official Catholic presence in the area probably dates from July 11, 1840. On that date, Father Pierre-Jean De Smet, S.J. set up a camp near present day Driggs, Idaho and began evangelizing the local natives. July 23, 1840, is generally given as the date of the first mass celebrated in Idaho, at the head of Henry's Lake, by Father De Smet. Two years later, Father De Smet and the Jesuits established a mission near Coeur d'Alene, Idaho, and the first Catholic church, Sacred Heart Mission, was built in 1842 near the St. Joe River. Because of flooding, that church was moved, in 1846, to a hill higher up above the Coeur d'Alene River. A new church was built there between 1850 and 1853. That church, the oldest building in Idaho, is now part of Cataldo State Park.

**Cataldo Mission: The oldest building in Idaho**
*(Photograph from the author's collection)*

As for Boise, the future site of St. John's Cathedral, despite the fact that it is now Idaho's capitol and by far the largest city in the state, for many of its early years it was a relatively unknown crossroads. In the early 1860's, the largest city—not just in Idaho but in the entire Northwest—was Idaho City, with a population of over 7,000. (Idaho City today has a population of less than 500.) Idaho City was where the gold and the action was. Boise City, as it was then referred to, was important only as the junction of the road from Idaho City with the Oregon trail.

On July 4th, 1863, Major Pinkney Lugenbeel established Fort Boise at this juncture.[a] The Army Reserve Center

---

[a] The first "Fort Boise" was established in 1834 by the Hudson's Bay Company near the confluence of the Boise River and the Snake River, about 40 miles west of Boise City. It was moved several times and abandoned in 1854. The United States Army never occupied that Fort.

*Stone Wondrously Hewn*

now located at the site is named after Major Lugenbeel. The establishment of the fort and its location was prompted by increasing problems with the natives resisting settlers along the Oregon trail, which generally follows the Snake River as it crosses southern Idaho. Substantial gold deposits had been uncovered in the Boise Basin, where Idaho City is located, just the year before. The United States now had two reasons to establish a military presence in Boise: 1) to protect immigrants on the Oregon Trail; and 2) to protect the rich mines which would help finance the Civil War. That war, like virtually every war in history, was turning out to be much longer and much more costly than anyone had anticipated.[b]

In June and September of 1863, Archbishop Blanchet of the Diocese of Oregon City sent the Reverends Toussaint Mesplie and Andrew Zepeherin Poulin to the Boise Basin to minister to the miners there. These two priests established churches at Idaho City, Placerville, Centerville, and Pioneerville. With the exception of Idaho City, none of these areas has a church today. Both fathers Mesplie and Poulin traveled in and out of the territory, back and forth to Portland, for the next five years.

---

[b] Popular Idaho lore claims that gold from the Boise Basin financed the Civil War for the United States Government. It is true that the gold discoveries in Idaho, 1862–1868, very closely tracked the dates of the Civil War, 1861–1865, but the best estimates of the financial cost of the Civil War to the United States is 5.2 billion dollars, while all of the mineral wealth ever taken out of Idaho is about 3.4 billion dollars.

The Army at that time had a significant population of Irish soldiers, and Irish soldiers were Catholic soldiers; thus, the Catholic presence in the area very closely followed the official U.S. presence. The first Catholic mass celebrated in what is now the city of Boise was probably one celebrated in the cabin of John O'Farrell in the autumn of 1863.

John O'Farrell was born in Ireland in 1823. He was of a somewhat privileged class; his father was an officer in the British navy. At fifteen, John was enrolled in naval school. He sailed to the Far East, the east coast of the United States, and around Cape Horn to Monterey, California. John O'Farrell liked what he saw in California and decided to stay. Timing is everything, and O'Farrell's decision to take up residence in California, just as it was changing hands from a Mexican territory to the United States, was a fortuitous one. As a resident of the territory, he automatically became an American citizen when the United States gained possession of it.

O'Farrell seems to have had a knack for meeting and establishing relationships with famous people. En route to California, he met a young lieutenant of Marines, William Tecumseh Sherman, who 20 years later would inscribe his name in infamy with both the citizens of Georgia and the Nez Perce of Idaho. "War is hell," Sherman is famously quoted. He set out to prove that with his March to the Sea in 1864, and in 1877 he was cruelly

## Chapter 1

adamant that the defeated Nez Perce not be allowed to return to Idaho.

Once he arrived in California, O'Farrell took up with both John Sutter and William Marshall. Those two apparently infected him with a "gold fever," which would eventually bring him to Idaho. Before that, though, O'Farrell continued to display an adventuresome streak. Although he was now an American citizen, he volunteered for the British army in 1853, saw action in the Crimean war, was wounded at Sebastopol, and decorated for valor. Recovering from his wounds, he returned to the United States and began prospecting in Colorado in 1858. He tried his luck in several places, including Louisville, Kentucky, where he met his wife, Mary Ann Chapman Lambert. Mary Ann was herself an immigrant from Ireland, and a divorced woman with a daughter. John married Mary Ann and adopted her daughter in the fall of 1859. In 1863, after Idaho had become a territory, they joined a wagon train headed to the territory. They built the first white settler's home ever in the Boise area.

It was one room of approximately 200 square feet and it eventually held seven people of the O'Farrell family. It was made of cottonwood trees, which were the only trees in any abundance along the Boise River plain. Cottonwood seldom grows as a straight tree and O'Farrell worked mightily to accommodate the crooked material by flattening it with a broad axe and using large amounts of clay to chink the resulting spaces. Mary Ann covered the interior walls with fabric to give them a somewhat smooth and uniform aspect. The floor was packed dirt. This humble abode sheltered the O'Farrell family for seven years.

The O'Farrell cabin is not only significant in the history of Boise, it is significant in the history of St. John's. Seemingly not at all dismayed by the cramped quarters and stark furnishings of her home, Mary

**The O'Farrell cabin**
*(Photograph from the author's collection)*

Ann offered it to Fathers Mesplie and Poulin to celebrate the first mass ever in Boise, in 1863. Eventually O'Farrell, now a successful businessman, had a commodious, two-story house built at 5th and Franklin Streets in Boise. That house is still standing.

O'Farrell's cabin was used for services for several years, and is still in existence, near the corner of Fort and 6th Streets in Boise.

*Stone Wondrously Hewn*

It is maintained as a historical monument as the earliest residence and place of worship in Boise.

In 1868, Father Mesplie shifted his base of operations from the now declining Boise Basin to Boise City. In January of 1869, he announced his plans to build a church in Boise on land donated by the O'Farrells. On Christmas Eve of 1870, Father Mesplie dedicated Boise's first "real" Catholic church on the block bounded by State, Washington, 4th, and 5th Streets. That block is now occupied by the Pete T. Cenarrusa Office Building. The lot was donated by John O'Farrell. Much of the money which had been collected for the building was from the soldiers from Fort Boise and miners from as far away as Montana. Both of those groups were heavily Irish and so the first Catholic church in Boise, not surprisingly, was named St. Patrick's. St. Patrick's burned down just two weeks after it was dedicated. It would be six years before Boise once more had a Catholic church. In

**St. John's Cathedral and St. Patrick's Hall at 9th and Bannock**
*(Photograph courtesy of Idaho State Archives #71-162-5)*

*Chapter 1*

the interim, services were held in hotels, the courthouse, and at Fort Boise. While Father Mesplie was very effectively, and under difficult circumstances, handling matters on the ground in Idaho, ecclesiastical lines shifted as often as political/geographic lines did. Essentially, the Vicariate Apostolic of Idaho was carved out of the Oregon Territory in 1868, re-defined in 1883, and designated as a diocese in 1893.

The Reverend Louis Aloysius Lootens, a Belgian priest, was elevated to bishop and named apostolic vicar for the Vicariate of Idaho in 1869, the year after it was created. Bishop Lootens served in Idaho until 1875. In 1875, due to the decline of the mines and the effective pacification of the Oregon Trail, those two large groups of Irish — the army and the miners — were declining. Bishop Lootens found himself in a vicariate with a disappearing population. In addition to the problems of a declining Catholic population, Bishop Lootens faced issues of his own failing health. He requested retirement in 1873. A recalcitrant Archbishop (Blanchet) would not allow him to leave the territory until its debt had been retired. This Lootens could not manage. Despite his best efforts, approximately $4,000.00 in debt hung over his declining territory. Finally, despairing that he would ever escape the burdens of the office, Lootens apparently just gave up and left in October of 1875. His resignation was finally accepted nine months later. Lootens lived another 25 years in retirement in Canada. At Lootens' retirement, the Vicariate of Idaho was assumed by Archbishop Francis Norbert Blanchet of Oregon City. Archbishop Blanchet appointed Father Mesplie as Apostolic Administrator of the Vicariate.

The indomitable Father Mesplie aggressively took up, again, the pursuit of a church in Boise. He picked the location of 9th and Bannock streets. Six years after St. Patrick's burned down, Father Mesplie was able to celebrate the opening of a new church in Boise in December of 1876 at the corner of 9th and Bannock streets. The new church was named St. John the Evangelist.

Why the name of the church was changed from St. Patrick's to St. John, and in particular John the Evangelist, we do not know. A search of the archives of both the Diocese of Boise, and the Diocese of Portland (Boise at the time was part of the Diocese of Portland) has yielded no clues.

Father Mesplie, in addition to his other duties, was a chaplain in the United States Army. From time to time in the period of his service in Boise, the army sent him to Utah, Oregon, and Washington. One assignment had him involved in the peace negotiations with the Umatilla Indians during Chief Joseph's famous flight from the United States Army.[c]

Virtually all of Father Mesplie's work as a chaplain was as a volunteer and without

---

[c] Chief Joseph's campaign was used for many years in classes at the United States Military Academy at West Point as a classic example of a fighting retreat.

**Interior of St. John's: Christmas 1900**
*(Photograph courtesy of Idaho State Archives #82-135-1)*

pay. In August of 1872, after twenty-three years of volunteer service, he received a commission as a United States Army chaplain, at $1500.00 a year. Archbishop Blanchet did not approve of the appointment. "Don't be so simple as to let yourself be caught in this trap," he wrote, "They shut your mouth with a vain title, to get the souls of our Indians."[5] Bishop Blanchet would prove to be a better judge of things military than Father Mesplie.

Father Mesplie's military career would culminate with him earning the dubious distinction of being the only priest in the history of Idaho (likely the only priest in the history of the United States) to this day, to be court martialed and convicted by the United States Army. This sad situation came about probably because of what several of his contemporaries describe as two of Father Mesplie's very prominent personality traits. One, he was an outspoken critic of the treatment of the Indians in the Northwest; two, he was a terrible record keeper and businessman. Those were not traits which engendered great success in the military bureaucracy as it was wrapping up the unpleasant business of the "Indian Wars." In 1882, Father Mesplie was granted a leave of absence from the army for five months

## Chapter 1

to return to his native France for a visit. Unfortunately, at the end of that time he did not return and, in fact, overstayed the leave which had been granted by four months. Equally unfortunate was the fact that before he had left on his trip he had submitted warrants for his pay while he was gone. As Governor Woods, writing a letter attempting to defend Father Mesplie put it that "…puts him in an awkward relation to the United States Army."[6]

Father Mesplie was court martialed and convicted by the army of being absent without leave and of submitting fraudulent warrants for his pay as a chaplain. He was dismissed from the service with no pay or retirement on January 15, 1884. Despite the efforts of perhaps two of the most famous generals in the history of the United States Army, William Tecumseh Sherman and Phillip Henry Sheridan, to have him restored to the retired list, the dismissal stood. Father Mesplie had served as an army chaplain for almost thirty-five years, twenty-three of them as a volunteer without pay. After his dismissal from the army a disheartened Father Mesplie never returned to Idaho. He died in Grass Valley, California, at the home of his nephew on November 20, 1895.

With the departure of Father Mesplie, the Vicariate of Idaho remained under the aegis of the archbishop of Oregon City until 1885, when Alphonse Glorieux was named the second vicar apostolic of Idaho.

Bishop Glorieux was a native of Dottignies, West Flanders, Belgium, born on February 1st, 1844. While still undergoing his seminary training in Courtrai, (Kortrijk,) Flanders, he had committed himself to a life of missionary work when he affiliated

**Bishop Alphonse Glorieux**
*(Reproduced with permission of the Diocese of Boise)*

with the American College at Louvain. When he had completed his studies, he was specifically ordained for the Archdiocese of Oregon. He arrived in Portland on December 8th, 1867. He served in a variety of assignments in the territory, ranging from parish priest to the president of St. Michael's College in Portland. It was while he was serving in this position that he was recommended for the position of Vicariate of Idaho. On April 19th, 1885, Father Glorieux was appointed to the position of vicar apostolic of Idaho. He actually took up residence in Boise on June 12th, 1885. Upon his arrival, the Idaho Statesman, at that time a tri-weekly newspaper, commented on his easy manner, rhetoric, and delivery. His new position, while it elevated him to the episcopate, left him as a servant of the Archdiocese of Oregon City.

That was the situation until August 25th, 1893, when the Diocese of Boise was created and Bishop Glorieux named as its head. Thus, while Father Glorieux was the *second* priest to be named a bishop for Idaho he can claim the honor of being the *first* bishop of the *Diocese* of Boise.[d]

---

[d] The Diocese of Boise originally encompassed the entire geographic area of the state of Idaho, and a very small piece of western Wyoming. When the state of Idaho was created in 1890, the boundaries of the state became the boundaries of the diocese.

**Bishop's residence at 9th and Jefferson: Bishop Glorieux is standing, with an unidentified priest sitting.**
*(Reproduced with permission of the Diocese of Boise)*

*Chapter 1*

Idaho, in the waning days of the 19th century, was very much a frontier area, and the position of bishop was anything but a simply administrative function. Bishop Glorieux traveled extensively throughout the territory almost from the first day he arrived. By stagecoach or on horseback and in every kind of weather he visited virtually every area of his diocese in his first year. He not only visited, he performed priestly services. Records from the time show him performing services in homes, boarding houses, bunkhouses, and railroad section camps. His name is on baptismal records not just in Boise, but in Caldwell, Mountain Home, Hailey, Bellevue, Shoshone, Payette, Silver City, and Glenns Ferry. Service in the Idaho Territory was not for the indolent, and Bishop Glorieux was anything but indolent.

Eventually, having surveyed his diocese, Bishop Glorieux took up residence in Boise, at St. John's Church, an unprepossessing wood framed building at the corner of 9th and Bannock Streets. Eventually a residence was built for the bishop a block north of the Church at 9th and Jefferson Street.

With Bishop Glorieux's residence there, that church became a cathedral. The citizens of Boise collected $100.00 and had a cathedra, outsized for the modest building, installed. Father Joseph Van der Hayden, one of the priests assigned to St. John's, aptly described the new cathedral.

> *... in the pompously so-called Cathedral there were neither wax-candles for the altar nor vegetable oil for the sanctuary lamp and that the Mass wine used was manufactured from Boise grapes by an honest non-Catholic resident, who guaranteed its purity. The candles we used were the stearic wax candles in great demand by the miners.*
>
> *Kerosene oil lamps did duty as sanctuary lamps and the Mass wine which we bought at the rate of 75 cents the demi-john, was fetched from up town by one of the altar boys. It was hardly a temptation for them; for the wine was tarter than a sour apple.*[7]

Bishop Glorieux was open, unpretentious, and gregarious. Father Francis Hartleib was, at that time, the resident priest at St. John's. Rather than disturb Father Hartleib at the modest dwelling the church owned, Bishop Glorieux took up residence at a boarding house on Warm Springs Avenue. He took his dinners at the "Spanish Restaurant" where he could get a punch card, good for twenty-one meals for $4.00. Breakfast and lunch were simply bread and cheese, or cold meats eaten as he went about his duties.

Bishop Glorieux was an avid walker and became a familiar figure on the streets of the capitol city, striding about at all hours of the day and night. In his flowing clerical garb he would walk about the developing downtown, fingering his rosary or reading his breviary. He was well known and regarded by the owners of the various business establishments he passed. The story is told that one night he was walking past an "Irish saloon" when the bartender, apron around his waist, stepped out the door and unceremoniously threw out a dog which had wandered in. "And stay out ya son of a bitch!" he shouted. As he turned to go back in, to his horror, he saw the bishop of Idaho observing the scene. His apologies couldn't spill out of his mouth any faster or more profusely. Bishop Glorieux, with a smile, assuaged the man's fears. "That's alright, son," he said. "I've been in this territory for almost twenty years, and I've heard that term plenty of times, but I think this is the first time I've ever heard it used properly."

It wasn't long before the inadequacies of both the building and the site became obvious to the new bishop. Two additions to the original building had been made and a third was under consideration to accommodate the once again growing Catholic population of Boise. The capitol city and its business district were rapidly encroaching on the church environs.

# Chapter 2

## *Bishop Glorieux Puts His Stamp on Idaho*

Bishop Glorieux, once he had toured the territory and discovered the paucity of church buildings, embarked on an aggressive program of building churches throughout the territory. In 1894, he authorized the building of St. Anne's Church in Bonners Ferry, near the Canadian border; and between then and his death in 1917, eighty-one Catholic churches were built, covering every area of the state. There are, at the present time, 52 Catholic parishes and 27 "missions" in Idaho. The decline is due to a decrease in priests, not a decrease in Catholics.

There are an estimated 180,000 Catholics in Idaho, but only 47 priests. In addition to churches, Glorieux oversaw the establishment of eight grammar schools, a high school, and five hospitals.

Bishop Glorieux was one of a generation of American bishops who made the conscious decision to step out of the cloistered halls of the church establishment and establish themselves as public figures in the political scene. He had received his appointment to the episcopacy at the Third Plenary Council in Baltimore. It was that council which had declared, among other things, that the era of a docile Catholicism, the atmosphere which had inspired the "Know Nothings" to demonize immigrants and Catholics — and in the mid-1800's, they were one and the same — was over. Catholic immigrants of the 1840's, primarily Irish and German, had served on both sides in the Civil War. Because of the circumstances of where they had settled, primarily the industrial North, the vast majority served the north, but many served the south as well. The Irish Brigade, formed of troops from New York, Massachusetts, and Pennsylvania, lost over half of its men at Antietam and Fredericksburg, and by the time Gettysburg was over had been reduced to regimental size.[a] The *Pastoral Letter of 1884* which the council promulgated was a ringing affirmation of the sacrifices Catholics had made in the Civil War, and notice of the full participation of the Catholic Church in the American political process.

> **We repudiate with equal assertion that we need to lay aside any of our devotedness to the Church, to be true Americans;... to argue that the Catholic Church is hostile to our great Republic... is evidently so illogical and contradictory an accusation that we are astonished to hear it advanced by persons of ordinary intelligence. We believe that our country's heroes were the instruments of the God of Nations in establishing this home of freedom; to both the Almighty and to his instruments in the work, we look with grateful reverence; and to maintain the inheritance of freedom which they have left us, should it ever—which God forbid—be imperiled, our Catholic citizens will be found to stand forward, as one man to pledge anew 'their lives, their fortunes, and their sacred honor.'"[8]**

Bishop Glorieux clearly took these exhortations to heart. He became heavily involved in Boise's and Idaho's civic affairs. He was one of the first Boise residents to order shrubs and trees for his residential lot and to plant flowers around the edges. A beech tree, now 106 years old, which Bishop Glorieux planted in 1910 is still shading the southeast corner of the rectory building. Boise, as has been mentioned, is located in an arid high desert. To get trees and plants established was a labor intensive, year round chore

---

a    In the Civil War era, a *regiment* was typically 1,000 men and a *brigade* was three to six regiments.

of watering, pruning, and mowing. The frugal bishop did it all himself. Glorieux was one of the founding members or the Boise Board of Trade and Chamber of Commerce. He was appointed to the board of the Oregon Short Line Railroad when it decided to extend its business to Idaho. One of the earliest relationships he developed was with James H. Hawley. Hawley was an Idaho attorney who had first come to the territory in the Gold Rush of 1862. He never made it as a gold miner, but he became an attorney, district attorney, U.S. attorney, mayor of Boise, and governor of the state. Hawley and Glorieux developed a close relationship. Though Hawley was not a Catholic, he did not hesitate to open his home as a temporary shelter for a group of Holy Cross Sisters who arrived unexpectedly at 2:00 AM one morning. The nuns stayed at the Hawley home for a week. Hawley donated the original baptismal font for St. John's Cathedral in 1921 and he himself was baptized a Catholic at it in 1929.

Bishop Glorieux was appointed by Governor John Morrison to serve as chairman of a committee which was charged with implementing a reform school system for the state. He exhorted Boise Catholics to support the Spanish American War, and he preached repeatedly against the violence and lawlessness which was paralyzing the northern part of the state in the Coeur d'Alene mines. Bishop Glorieux was invited to speak at Boise's Fourth of July celebration in 1899. This was not just an opportunity for the leader of the once maligned church to be an important part of the city's prime celebration of "Americanization." It put the bishop in the position of addressing one of the frequent charges lodged against the Catholic church; that is, that Catholics could not be "good Americans."

The labor strife and violence which had been plaguing the Coeur d'Alene mines in northern Idaho gave Bishop Glorieux the platform he needed for his speech. A large percentage of the miners, engaged in a protracted struggle with the mine owners, were Irish and Catholic. Notwithstanding the involvement of his flock in this difficult issue, Glorieux used the occasion of his speech to ask for, "...*Divine Guidance for those trying to stamp out lawlessness in North Idaho, and that the influences at work for law and order might prevail in that section of the State, so long cursed by anarchy's rule.*"[9] With what had to be an unpopular statement to the miners, Glorieux was demonstrating that the Catholic Church was throwing its moral support to civil authorities.

Bishop Glorieux was one of the first contributors to the Boise Symphony Orchestra. When all of the Boise churches combined their choirs for a performance of Handel's *Messiah* in 1897 at Sonna's Opera House, Bishop Glorieux was accorded the honor of wielding the baton during the stirring Halleluiah Chorus. Northwest Magazine, in 1906, gave him a glowing accolade.

*Stone Wondrously Hewn*

*He has been a good Captain at the helm of his ship, a tender father to his wayward children, a loving almoner to the poor and needy, a faithful servant to his Lord and Master. Respect and admiration he claims from all of our citizens, love from all who know his kindness, his charity, and his worth, and from us, who have grown up beneath his tender care, a filial affection which we willingly, joyfully accord him.*[10]

While addressing his civic duties in the state and the needs of Catholics throughout his diocese, it didn't take Bishop Glorieux long to agree with Father Van de Hayden's dim assessment of Boise's cathedral. It was totally inadequate as the cathedral for the Diocese of Boise. It was in the replacement of that wood-framed church that Bishop Glorieux created his most lasting and impressive monument: the Cathedral of St. John the Evangelist.

Bishop Glorieux began this project in 1902, with the purchase of the entire block bounded by Hays Street to the south, Fort Street to the north, 8th Street to the east, and 9th Street to the west. At that time, Fort Street was the northern limit of the Boise township. Glorieux paid $12,000.00 for the property—as was his habit, in cash. For the next several years, plans were developed but no improvements were made, until 1906, with construction of a rectory on the southwest corner of the lot.

The rectory was completed and opened on April 19th, 1906, in time for Bishop Glorieux's 21st anniversary as a priest. When it was finished, the rectory contained the chancery offices, two parlors, the bishop's private office, study, bedroom, and bath. There were four guest rooms, two rooms for other priests, and a chapel. Dining room, kitchen, and servants' quarters rounded out the building. The rectory, characterized by the Idaho Daily Statesman as "of Elizabethan style architecture" is a beautiful and imposing building at the corner of 9th and Hays Streets. It is still part of the cathedral complex and older than the cathedral it supports.

Even while the rectory was being built, Bishop Glorieux formed a committee and

**Rectory, St. John's Cathedral.**
*(Photograph from the author's collection)*

*Chapter 2*

began discussions of "the erection of a new Cathedral." Several proposals were made, and in 1904, the firm of John E. Tourtellotte & Company was engaged to begin plans for the new cathedral. Charles F. Hummel, a "de facto" partner of John Tourtellotte, was given the assignment of designing the new cathedral. While things were still in the planning stage, the decision was made to move the church at 9th and Bannock to the new site at Fort and 8th Streets, and this was in fact undertaken, beginning in July of 1905. In August, after a month of preliminary work had been done, and just as the actual moving was beginning, the building caught fire and was destroyed.

Initially, the likely cause of the fire was given as a small boy and his cigarette:

> *The origin of the fire is a mystery, but it is charged to some careless boy and a cigarette."*[11]

Subsequently, the anonymous and errant young man seems to have passed from the story. It is generally accepted now that the demise of St. John's church was more likely caused because the church, while it was being moved, came into contact with one of Boise's newly installed overhead electric lines, caught fire, and was destroyed. Between the insurance payment and the sale of the property at 9th and Bannock, the church had enough money to build a new, temporary structure at the southwest corner of 8th and Fort Streets.

Plans for a new cathedral continued. The Idaho Daily Statesman, on May 3rd, 1905 reported that:

> *… the architects completed taking the soundings. Now that this data has been secured, the plans for the foundation can be completed and it seems probable that excavating will be commenced in a few days."*[12]

Excavation must have indeed started within a few days, because by July of the following year a contract was let for:

> *Furnishing, setting and backing up with stone laid in cement mortar, of water table on top of the present basement walls of the new St. John's cathedral. All walls except brickwalls (sic) and walls around Sanctuary, to be laid on a level with top of water table."*

*That is it!* A contract of less than 50 words begins the work of building a cathedral!

Excavation of the site began at an interesting point in the history of American construction. The United States had taken on the completion of the Panama canal just two years earlier, and the Panama Canal and William Otis of Philadelphia were about to forever alter how major excavation was done in the world. Otis had patented the first steam powered shovel in 1839, but it wasn't until the early 20th century that the technology was perfected to allow

*Page 17*

a somewhat mobile excavator available at construction sites where the scope of the project justified laying iron rails to accommodate the huge machines. The first Bucyrus steam shovel arrived in Colon, Panama on November 12th, 1904, two years before the cornerstone of the cathedral was laid.[b]

Particularly intriguing to the curious historian is that both projects were begun with animal power and finished with steam. Exactly when that transition took place we do not know, but sometime in this era (1905–1910) the unnoted but significant change was made from horse drawn equipment to powered equipment. There are actually photographs of Boise's major construction projects at the time — the capitol building and the cathedral — with a team of horses working next to a puffing steam shovel.

One Saturday evening, though, after a day's work, the horses were brought to their stable, rubbed down, and put away, never to be taken out again. The world of construction had made the transition from animal power to power generated by the burning of fossil fuels. It was not a flawless transition. No one had considered the problems that would arise in a Boise winter, when a piece of equipment operating with hydraulic pistons was exposed to freezing temperatures. An immediate, if temporary, solution was to fill the pistons with whiskey instead of water. Problem solved. Whiskey was never going to freeze in a Boise winter. How many steam shovel operators might have found themselves as the most popular men on the job site is not recorded.

When the actual "above ground" work of raising the cathedral walls began (around 1910), machines on crawler treads, which obviated the use of rail tracks, and booms capable of swinging in a 360-degree arc were in common use. Eventually, internal combustion engines replaced the cumbersome steam as the power source. Other than that, though, the essential elements of these labor saving devices has not changed very much in the one hundred years since.

There were three major projects underway in downtown Boise at the same time. The state capitol building was being built between 8th and 6th Streets, the Episcopal cathedral (St. Michael's) was being built at 8th and State Streets, and St. John's Cathedral was being built at 8th and Hays Streets. The same architectural firm, Tourtelotte and Hummel, was overseeing both the capitol building and the Cathedral of St. John's. In fact, the records confirm that not just workmen, but equipment, was from time to time shared between the two sites.

Now, with the old cathedral a charred ruin and a new cathedral a very long

---

[b] Eventually, over 100 steam shovels would be employed to build the Panama Canal. The obviously much smaller excavation needed for the cathedral site was, just like the Panama Canal, begun with horse drawn scoops and completed with steam shovels.

way from reality, provisions had to be made for the celebration of Mass in Boise. The church had been insured, and payment for the tragedy allowed a temporary structure to be completed at the new site. A church was constructed on the southwest corner of 8th and Fort Streets—the gymnasium of St. Joseph's school occupies that site today.

Thus, the first two buildings built on the site were on the two diametrically opposite ends of the block. Bishop Glorieux was "nailing down" the extremities of his new property. The tower and the bell of the old church, which had been moved separately and thus survived the fire, were used on the newly constructed church. That church was Boise's next cathedral and was used for the next six years while the current cathedral was being built. When the cathedral's lower level was opened for services in 1912, the old church was converted to classrooms for St. Joseph's school, and eventually remodeled yet again as a gymnasium. Finally, in 1941 the building was demolished, and in 1948 the current gymnasium built there.

# Chapter 3

## The Cornerstone is Laid

Ground work and excavation for the subterranean areas of the cathedral was already underway when the earliest surviving contract for work on the cathedral was signed. The agreement for foundation and walls of the basement was actually signed by Mr. Hummel's son, Frederic, who was at that time an apprentice in the office. The acceptance of this contract was a huge undertaking for the firm; they almost simultaneously took on an even more ambitious project, the construction of the Idaho State Capitol

*Stone Wondrously Hewn*

building just five blocks south of the cathedral.

It is obvious, by the terms of this contract, that the foundation work had already been done. The contract refers to the "…top of the present basement walls." No contract prior to this one seems to have survived. Surely, though, the process of establishing the footing for the new cathedral was not done without detailed and specific plans.

Under whatever the circumstances, progress on the building was not dependent solely on the energies of the men toiling in the excavation. The Idaho Daily Statesman noted in early September of 1906 that

> Work on the handsome new St. John's cathedral on Eighth street is being delayed on account of the failure of the stone columns which are to support the lower stone rail of the building to arrive from Omaha. The workmen have been waiting nearly two months for the arrival of the columns and it cannot be ascertained how much more of a delay will be necessary."[13]

Despite delays, on November 11th, 1906, work on the cathedral had progressed to the point where the cornerstone could be laid. Laying the cornerstone, generally seen as the seminal event of every great building, was conducted with all proper pomp and circumstance. The Idaho Statesman ran an article full of the florid phraseology common to the era:

The day seemed made for the impressive ceremonies, the glorious sunshine adding much to the splendor of the occasion as it fell on the brilliant gold-embroidered robes of the priests and bishops. Long before the appointed hour the platform seats, with a capacity of 1200, the aisles and the streets below, were crowded with an eager throng who came to witness an epoch-making ceremony in the history of Boise and of Idaho, a ceremony full of rejoicing and thanksgiving. It was estimated that more than 3000 people were present. Promptly at 3 o'clock as the solemn strains of the pontifical march were heard the procession left the bishop's palace and slowly approached the entrance to the cathedral over which a temporary arch had been erected which was handsomely draped in the national colors. First came the cross-bearer with two acolytes, then the pupils of St. Joseph's and St. Teresa's schools, followed by the visiting priests. Then came the visiting bishops, robed in eminence purple who preceded the master of ceremonies, Bishop Glorieux, in cope and mitre, attendant priests, and the archbishop and accompanying acolytes. The procession crossed the church to the rear where a temporary cross had been erected on the site of the altar. Here the solemn rites of blessing the cross were held. The procession then re-crossed to the corner of the edifice, where, amid the most impressive services, the cornerstone was laid and

Page 22

*Chapter 3*

*blessed. The mortar which cemented the stone was put in place with a silver trowel which will hereafter be a sacred souvenir of Bishop Glorieux.*[a]

*While the visiting clergy were assembling for the laying of the cornerstone, Bishop Glorieux with the master of ceremonies, the deacon and sub-deacon and two acolytes were blessing the foundation of the church. During this ceremony the large chorus sang "The Heavens are Telling." After the orchestra had finished its third number Archbishop Christie of Portland began his address. The archbishop is a man of most noble and dignified mein and his beautifully modulated voice was heard by the entire throng as he delivered his scholarly address, the text of which was take from Psalms 126-1: 'Except the Lord build the house, they labor in vain who build it.'"*[14]

Laying the cornerstone is, of course, the beginning and not the end of a project of this size. Even after the laying of the cornerstone, delays beyond the control of the men actually working on the building caused problems. In April of 1907 a very

---
[a] That trowel is presently on display in a case at the cathedral parish office.

ST. JOHN'S CATHEDRAL, JANUARY, 1910
Dimensions when completed: Outside, 136x200 feet; inside, width 96 feet, length 170 feet; height 150 feet. Building material, light gray sandstone.

**St. John's Cathedral in January of 1910**
*(Public Domain)*

wet spring caused problems with delivery from a local quarry.

> *Work on the beautiful new St. John's Cathedral has been suspended for the past four days owing to the inability of the contractor, H.H. Adams to secure the stone. The material for the cathedral is a Boise stone, quarried from the Falkstad quarry, back of the penitentiary. This stone has been in great demand for building, but the impassibility of the roads during the entire spring obliged the managers to fall behind with all their orders, and it will be some time before they can get caught up with them."*[15]

It was not only the vagaries of supply and material which caused work on the cathedral to progress very slowly. Because of Bishop Glorieux's extreme distaste for debt he would allow construction to proceed on the cathedral only as there was money to pay for it. Although Tourtellote and Hummel had presented an ambitious Romanesque design with arching ceilings and two soaring towers, and Glorieux had accepted that design, he authorized only work which would completely enclose and roof the basic outline of the building. Even this much scaled down version of the cathedral, given the constraints of "pay as you go," took six years to complete. Finally, on March 23rd, 1912, almost six years after the laying of the cornerstone, the basement area was ready and the first services were held at St. John's Cathedral.

Shortly after the archival photo on the previous page was taken, a roof was laid over the entire structure, the window openings were sealed with heavy duty canvas, and a sub-floor was laid on the main level. No finishing work was done on the above ground portion. For the time being, the subterranean area became the focus of the construction area.

As the work of building the cathedral was going on, painstaking stone by stone, inch by inch, and — at Bishop Glorieux's insistence — dollar by dollar, death came for the bishop. Alphonse Glorieux died, at the age of 73, on August 25th, 1917. His cathedral of sandstone walls, towers, and soaring ceilings was slowly being built. He would never, though, see the completed monument he had begun.

Bishop Glorieux's funeral was attended by a host of church and civic leaders, not just from Idaho, but from Oregon, Washington, Utah, and Canada. The mayor of Boise issued an official proclamation requesting "all public and private business houses to close their doors between the hours of 10 AM and 12 o'clock noon, during the period of the funeral services of our beloved citizen."[16]

The Idaho Commercial Club, the forerunner to the Boise Chamber of Commerce, issued its own proclamation stating:

*Chapter 3*

**R**ESOLVED *That the death of Bishop A.J. Glorieux has caused a vacancy in this community that no surviving citizen of Boise is qualified to fill. In every day life the Bishop was gentle, serene, affable, and kind, and his words and deeds were always weighed and genuine. More than any of his contemporaries, he exemplified the virtue of humility. Moreover he was known to all our people personally and by reputation as a public-spirited citizen, whose character was above reproach. This fact constituted him an ideal trustee and representative in the promotion of civic undertakings where public confidence was indispensable to success. In the long years that Bishop Glorieux was with us we always thought of him as a public asset, wherefore we think of his death as a public loss."*[17]

The man who had begun the project was gone, but the project would continue. Now world events, and not the bishop's frugality, began to play upon the finishing of the monument.

*Stone Wondrously Hewn*

# Chapter 4

## *The Lower Level: The Cathedral's First Sacred Space*

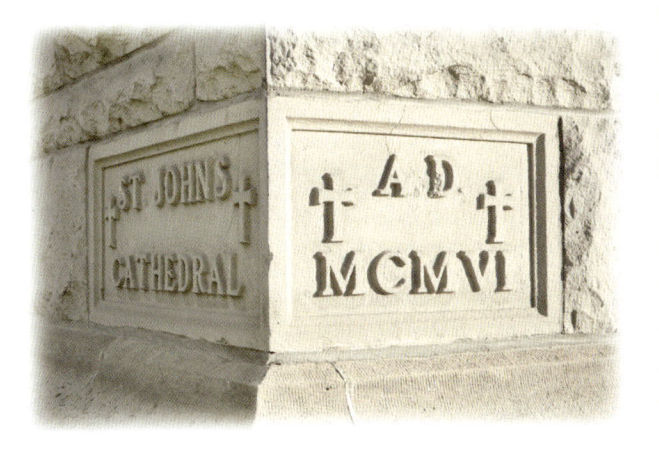

As mentioned, when Bishop Glorieux died his cathedral was still being built, and the basement area of the new building was being used as the cathedral. In fact, it would serve that purpose for nine years. Do not imagine that because it was a basement area, and was never intended to be the permanent manifestation of the cathedral, that there was anything inadequate about the space. It had fifteen foot ceilings and would seat 800 — not very many less than the cathedral now seats.

That subterranean area, many times modified, is still in use today. It is, in fact, the cathedral's oldest "sacred space." Because it served for many years as the cathedral, it has all of the elements—liturgical, architectural, and artistic—that the now "main" cathedral has.

Today, to view the oldest iteration of St. John's Cathedral and to gain a proper sense of the work and reverence which went into it, a visitor has to seek out a discrete entrance below the stairs going up to the main church on the south (Hays Street) side of the cathedral. One enters this area through a long hallway accented with stained glass windows on the left.

As originally constructed, though, the entrance to this basement area was on the front of the cathedral, below and behind the existing main steps leading up to the main entrance. Those main steps have been, several times, re-done and re-graded. If you look carefully at the sides of the steps, you can, on each side, make out the top of the arch which defined the main entry into the cathedral from 1912 until 1921. One entered through those arches into the subterranean cathedral, which at that time covered the entire footprint of the main cathedral. There was no kitchen, dining area, or classrooms as there are now. The original entry archways are now almost completely dominated by vent works for the kitchen, which did not originally come into existence until about 1925.

Entering the chapel, look at the sandstone walls and buttresses surrounding you. Realize that for many years those walls had been covered to give them the uniform flat surface we usually associate with interior walls today. Undoubtedly, earlier generations had considered the rough cut stone unsightly and crude. Uncovered during a 2008 renovation, the blocks were cleaned and left as the interior walls of the chapel. That was certainly a fortuitous decision, for these massive stones give the small chapel an aura of silent warmth and strength.

We know that the earliest Christians, in time of persecution, worshiped underground, and it is not hard in this chapel to imagine oneself in the company of those early believers surrounded by massive stonework, and enveloped in a blanketing silence.

These massive sandstone blocks form the walls not only of the "day chapel," but what is now a combination dining room/community room beneath the main cathedral. The marks of the stone cutters and masons are still clearly visible on the face of many of those stones. Even more intriguing is the fact that a careful examination will reveal sea creatures and shells from eons ago. This is not just a building for the ages, it is a building of the ages. To find these specimens and to realize that they were quarried just a few miles from the cathedral, but hundreds of miles from any ocean, is a reminder of how fleeting our life on this earth is and how little we really appreciate our role in it.

When looking at these sandstone blocks, consider carefully the size and mass of some of the stones. Estimate the weight of them. Think of the crushed fingers, broken bones, and life altering injuries, perhaps deaths, that went into emplacing them. Idaho did not enact any sort of workers protection or industrial compensation law until 1917. Up until that time, a worker who was injured on the job not only suffered a serious, life altering injury with the expenses of it borne solely by him, he very likely lost his job as well. After all, a one-armed hod carrier was of little use to anyone. Because there was no injury reporting system, there were no records kept. We can only speculate about the terrible injuries which would have resulted from moving and emplacing thousands of sandstone blocks, weighing several hundred pounds each. For most of the work of the foundation, only mechanical multipliers or animal power were available. It wasn't until after the cornerstone was laid that power assisted machines came into general use in the United States.

In viewing those walls, we are not just viewing the foundation and basement of the cathedral. We are viewing what in fact was the first—and for a long time, the only—"sacred space" in the cathedral. From 1912 until 1921, this lower level *was* the cathedral. This "proto cathedral" was not by any definition a makeshift, temporary, structure. It originally had seating for 800 people. It extended under almost the entirety of what would become the "footprint" of today's cathedral. Today, it would probably be hard pressed to accommodate 100 worshipers.

This chapel is, interestingly, at once both the oldest and the newest part of St. John's Cathedral. It was the first place in the building where mass was celebrated and served for many years as the cathedral and the only Catholic church in Boise. It was completed and used for almost ten years before the main cathedral was finished.

This lower chapel has been subject to a series of alterations, remodels, expansions, and contractions. Its first

**Ancient seahorse embedded in the walls of St. John's cathedral**
*(Photograph from the author's collection)*

iteration was in 1912, when it became *the* Cathedral of St. John the Evangelist. It would serve in that capacity for almost ten years. It encompassed essentially the entire footprint of the existing cathedral and could seat almost 1000 people.

When the upper level of the cathedral opened in 1921, the lower chapel was effectively cut in half. Space taken from the chapel became a theater and meeting rooms.

In 1958, Bishop Byrne suggested a renovation to the chapel on the lower level which, while it had had its interior dimensions dramatically reduced, never had any changes made to its sanctuary and altar.

**Lower chapel circa 1947**
*(From the archives of St. John's Cathedral)*

As part of this renovation, a new altar was installed in the chapel. This altar was donated by the family of a young man killed in World War II. Forty years earlier, the main altar at St. John's had been dedicated in honor of a young man killed in World War I, and now the church was engaged in the same grim exercise. This new altar was dedicated to Lieutenant Manuel Aldecoa, an Air Force pilot killed on Thanksgiving Day, in November of 1943.

Lieutenant Aldecoa was a native of Boise, one of 5 children born to Basque immigrants, Juan Domingo Aldecoa-Urrusuno, and Maria Pagoaga-Iriarte. He was killed when he and a German ace, Johannes Seifert, who had shot down 56 Allied aircraft, engaged in a mutually fatal battle. Both aircraft were shot down, and both pilots died. Lieutenant Aldecoa was posthumously awarded the Purple Heart, Air Medal, American Campaign Medal, Good Conduct Medal, European-African-Middle Eastern Campaign Medal, World War II Victory Medal, and Honorable Service Lapel Pin.

**Lower chapel circa 1960**
*(From the archives of St. John's Cathedral)*

In 2007–2008 this space underwent its latest remodeling and now certainly has the most "up to date" aspect of any of the church's spaces. If you compare the furnishings and aspects of this chapel with the furnishings and aspects of the main church above it, you will see a very pronounced 20th century, perhaps even 19th century (perhaps 12th century) rendering on the upper level versus a 21st century rendering on the lower level. It is an interesting quick tour of the changes in liturgical art and tastes in a hundred years.

In the 2008 remodeling, a new altar table was installed, and the only part of the altar dedicated to a war hero which remains is the wooden reredos which holds the tabernacle.

In the remodeling, other issues which had created so much controversy forty years earlier arose again, particularly the placement of the tabernacle. As is appropriate for matters such as remodeling of sacred space, the parish appointed a committee to supervise the process. The committee, which included Mr. Charles Hummel, the architect during the 1978 remodeling of the main cathedral, found itself once more confronting the question of the placement of the tabernacle. That question, which had generated so much emotion thirty years earlier, proved to be yet another flash point. In 1978, the question had been the *removal* of the tabernacle from the central position on the altar to a position off to the side. The controversy now arose over *leaving* the tabernacle in a central location in the wall behind the altar. The old altar—against the back wall, and with the priest oriented with his back to the people—was removed, and a new more central and simple altar was installed. What to do with the tabernacle which had been in the middle of the old altar? The decision was made to leave it in the same central place! It would no longer be on the altar, but in the decorative wall which had formed the backdrop to the altar. Now, the decision *not* to move the tabernacle caused the controversy. It is

**Lower chapel altar, with tabernacle in back wall**
*(Photograph from the author's collection)*

an observation on the subtle influence of time that now, a very vocal subset of parishioners had come to accept the new norms and, in St. John's in particular, had grown accustomed to the tabernacle away from the main altar. Now the tabernacle was placed directly behind the altar, in a central, eye-arresting position and the parishioners objected.

The less than clear directions given by church documents on this matter once more found themselves serving not as "all things to all people" but rather as "nothing to anybody." The *Revised General Instruction of the Roman Missal* states that it is more appropriate that "… on an altar on which Mass is celebrated there not be a tabernacle in which the Most Holy Eucharist is reserved."[18] (It isn't in the chapel.) The directives, though, also state "When a tabernacle is located directly behind the altar (as in the chapel), consideration should be given to using distance, lighting, or some other architectural device that separates the tabernacle and reservation area during Mass, but that allows the tabernacle to be fully visible to the entire worship area when the Eucharistic liturgy is not being celebrated."[19] (It either is or it isn't in the chapel, depending on one's interpretation.) These type of vague directions seem almost guaranteed to cause controversy, and controversy indeed ensued. Members of the committee resigned. The parish family got engaged, and the bishop had to personally intervene to authorize the placement of the tabernacle. "The bishop is to determine where the tabernacle will be placed and to give further direction."[20]

This controversy was the perfect embodiment of the premise that, *when it comes to matters of liturgical correctness, whenever you have two Catholics you will have three opinions*. Some would say that this was not just the *consequence* of Vatican II, but the *intent*. If there is one clear movement out of Vatican II, it was to get the people involved in what had previously been a very closed organization. One is always hesitant in a work such as this to report on these controversies, because they are never truly resolved. These questions of "correctness" never end. They may be suppressed, but all it will take is a reminder to bring them to the fore again. The opportunity to say, *"See, I told you so. They didn't do it right,"* seems to be an unremitting characteristic of twenty-first century Catholics.

In the case of the "tabernacle controversy of 2008," perhaps the final redeeming factor in quieting, if not settling, the question was the choice of the artist to decorate its surroundings. Stephanie Wilde, from Boise, was chosen for the task of creating the suitable doors and decorative panels to accent the tabernacle. Ms. Wilde is a self-taught artist of four decades' experience. Her work, elaborate and detailed, examines a wide range of social and political issues. She has a personal attachment to the chapel; she was married there in 1982.

Although her work is on display in a wide range of settings in the United States and Europe, she had never previously been asked to do a strictly liturgical piece. Given that she is not herself a Catholic, her choice as the artist for this very significant enhancement of the chapel was a matter of some controversy. She had her own reservations. She recognized the extremely high place art holds in Catholic practice. She questioned whether she could do justice to both the theme and the setting. Her advocates, though, persisted. They had seen the quality of her work and the depth of her interpretation on matters spiritual and felt very strongly that she would give an exquisite rendering to the front piece of the "holy of holies."

**Lower chapel, tabernacle artwork**
*(Reproduced with permission from Stephanie Wilde)*

As she began the project, a primary objective was not to just impart a sense of sacredness to this particular spot, but to bring that sense of sacredness to all who might worship in the chapel, whether it be at the celebration of the Mass or quiet, solitary contemplation of the Eucharist. Enhancing this sacred spot is actually a tradition which pre-dates Christianity. We are told in Exodus that Moses was given detailed instructions on decorating the Ark of the Covenant. *"For the two ends of this throne of mercy you are to make two golden cherubs."* (Exodus 25:18)

Over a period of two years, Ms. Wilde worked at what she describes as a "painful task" to bring to the viewer an exquisite rendering of angels acting as mediators between God and humans. The artwork itself is ink, acrylic, and gold leaf in a combination of painting and drawing. The finished work is actually four, separate pieces: two tabernacle doors and two side panels.

Depicted on the side panels are the nine orders of angels in ascending order of their importance (angels, principalities, archangels, powers, virtues, dominions, thrones, cherubim, and seraphim). On the tabernacle doors are Gabriel and Michael, the herald and the protector. What to the casual eye is simply elaborate background is, in fact, replete with symbolism.

First, the crosses below Michael and Gabriel are replications of the Celtic Cross on the front of the chapel altar. The eye can travel effortlessly from the Celtic Cross on the front of the altar, where the miraculous transubstantiation takes place, to the doors of the tabernacle where the Body of Christ reposes. The center of the crosses is a flower, a symbol of rebirth and life. Finally, what appears to be just elaborate scrollwork as a background is, in fact, a series of circles, representing eternity, and triangles, the symbol of the trinity.

In that 2008 renovation, the original stations of the cross were taken down, cleaned, refurbished, and remounted. Five of them are likely the first thing which will catch your eye as you enter the chapel.

In the main church on the first floor, the stations are lithographs. In the chapel they are carved wood, beautifully rendered. They begin with number I on the right wall of the chapel (as you face the altar) continue across the back wall, and end with number XIV on the left wall.

**Chapel stations of the cross, five through ten**
*(Photograph from the author's collection)*

# Chapter 5

*Bishop Gorman Takes the Reins in Idaho*

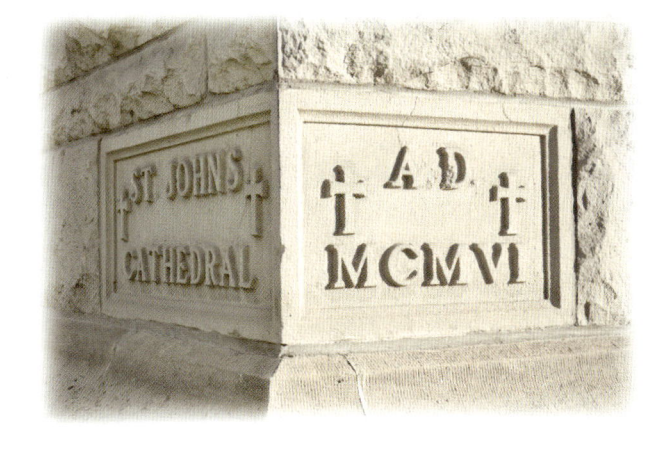

The bureaucracy of the largest church in the world has never been known for its speed in handling transitional events. Alphonse Glorieux died on August 25th, 1917. Appointed to succeed him on February 6th, 1918, was Daniel Mary Gorman. Bishop Gorman would not take up residence in Boise for another three months. Monsignor Remi S. Keyzer of Boise served as the diocesan administrator until Bishop Gorman took office.

With the death of Bishop Glorieux, actual work on the cathedral came to a halt. The

*Stone Wondrously Hewn*

United States had entered World War I just four months before Bishop Glorieux died. Monsignor Keyzer, realizing that he was but an interim administrator, did not feel that he should exercise major decisions regarding a project of this magnitude—particularly not as the United States embarked on its first, but certainly not its last, foreign war. He put the actual building of the cathedral on hold. He did not, though, put planning for its completion on hold. Monsignor Keyzer came up with an innovative plan to support both the United States war effort and the cathedral. He proposed that parishioners should buy war bonds and donate them to the diocese! The parishioners responded willingly. The chairman of committee set up to oversee this effort was one Timothy Regan.

Daniel Mary Gorman took office as the third bishop of Idaho on May 15th of 1918. Bishop Gorman had been born in a

**World War I War Bond Drive, Front Steps of St. John's**
*(Photograph courtesy of Idaho State Historical Archives  Access #1138)*

Page 36

Chapter 5

sod cabin in Iowa in 1861. He attended St. Joseph's College in Dubuque (now Loras College). On completion of his college studies, he was admitted to St. Francis Seminary in Milwaukee. He was ordained a priest in Milwaukee, Wisconsin in 1893 and was appointed to the presidency of St. Joseph's College in 1904. When he took office as president of the college, it had 175 students and 11 professors. When he left to assume the office of bishop in Boise, the college had 534 students and 176 professors.

Bishop Gorman arrived in Boise on May 15th, 1918. At a reception held in the honor of his installation, he made it obvious that the world was shrinking and that events a continent and an ocean away would have their impact on Idaho. The United States was fully engaged now in the First World War. Work on the cathedral would not proceed until that matter was resolved.

> **I do not anticipate any work of this kind just now unless the exigencies of the moment demand it. I do not wish to direct the attention of my people away from the great work of the government at this time. The government must come first in all things. Should local condition demand, for the best interests of the spiritual welfare of the church, some few improvements, these will be made, but nothing must interfere with the war work at present."**[21]

Work on the actual building of the cathedral may have stopped, but work

**Bishop Gorman**
*(Reproduced with permission of the Diocese of Boise)*

on raising funds for it never did. In fact, at the welcoming reception for Bishop Gorman, Father Keyser presented the new bishop with $20,000 which had been raised by the sale of war bonds. Bake and food sales by the Catholic Women's League, theatrical productions by the Knights of Columbus, and in what would prove to be a premonition of changing demographics in the cathedral parish, a dinner which was initially advertised as being served by "the Spanish women" of the parish. Two weeks later that same dinner would be denominated as "prepared by members of the Basque race." The Basques had begun to assert their unique identity at St. Johns!

The First World War, which was delaying the completion of the cathedral, ended on November 11th, 1918. In February of the following year, Bishop Gorman organized a committee to consider the financing and completion of the cathedral. The chairman of that committee was Timothy Regan. The members, in addition to Regan, were Martin Curran, John Gakey, John Daly, Adolph Schrieber, and the architect, Charles F. Hummel.

Timothy Regan had come to Idaho in 1864 and made his fortune in the gold and silver mines of Idaho City and Silver City. Regan, though, made most of his fortune not in actual mining, but as an investor and merchant providing services to the miners. He was also a shrewd observer of the periodic cycles of both gold and silver prices. Watching the swings of these markets, Regan employed the classic strategy of "buy low and sell high." This speculation was the primary source of most of his wealth.

Regan was a faithful Catholic. One of his sons, John M. Regan—a lieutenant in the United States Army—had been killed in battle on August 4, 1918. John was posthumously awarded the Distinguished Service Cross. A frequent charge lodged against Catholics in the United States in the early 20th century was that they were not patriotic citizens. The parish of St. John's did more than its share to forever disabuse the country of that notion. The Idaho Statesman noted that St. John's Cathedral had the largest number of service stars on its banner of all of the Boise churches.

It became the custom during the war for families with a member serving in the armed forces to display a small flag featuring a blue star. If the member died in action, the star was changed to a gold one. St. John's parish had 120 blue star flags to its credit during WWI and three of them made the unfortunate, but honorable, transition to gold. John's was the first. In addition to John Regan, St. John's parish members Robert Fenwick and William Penrod also died in the "war to end all wars." Soon the custom of displaying "service flags" was adopted by businesses and churches. In an article headlined *Churches Make Honor Rolls of Those in the Army*, the Idaho Statesman noted, "The parish of St. John's Cathedral is entitled to the largest service flag, having 56 now with the colors.[a] Although Regan was originally buried on the battlefield in France, in 1921, his body was returned to Boise and interred in the family plot in the Catholic cemetery on Morris Hill.

The finance committee, headed by Lieutenant Regan's father, didn't waste any time in getting the cathedral finished.

---

a    Idaho Statesman, December 4, 1917, Page 4.

**Lietenant Regan's Grave**
*(Photograph from the author's collection)*

Beginning in 1919, and all through 1920 and 1921, contracts were signed one after the other: $13,475.00 for plastering, $30,948.00 for marble work, $6,841.00 for painting, and over $16,000.00 for stained glass windows. Contracts were also let for heating, lighting, and, of course, an organ. The committee was obviously determined to finish the cathedral quickly. Several of the contracts include a provision that the work was to be completed by "Easter of 1920." That target, for a variety of reasons, was not met. It was a year later, May 30, 1921, before the finished cathedral was dedicated.

Despite their urgency to get the cathedral finished, Bishop Gorman and the finance committee drove hard bargains with the contractors. Most of the contracts showed a discount applied after the bids were submitted. One contractor complained in a letter:

> *As you will remember, I did not want to take off the 5% demanded by your committee but finally consented to do so."*

The painting, plastering, and woodwork were done by contractors as local as could be found. The painting was by the Claussen-Nehring Company of Salt Lake City. At that time, interior decorators such as Claussen-Nehring had huge inventories of work rendered in various styles, i.e. "Oriental," "Egyptian," or "Romanesque." The customer would pick a style and the company's artisans would replicate it throughout the space. The Claussen Company, in addition to St. John's Cathedral, did the Owyhee Hotel and Egyptian Theater in downtown Boise, as well as the old Hotel Boise (the Hoff Building). Clausen-Nehring clearly did not skimp on the quality of material used, nor in its application. The painting one sees today in the cathedral is, almost without exception, the original painting. Except where some external force has caused damage, none of the original paint has been re-done.

The cast plaster decorations, scroll work, and figurines were done by Joseph Conradi, a sculptor of some renown who had done work for dozens of churches in the Midwest, as well as the U.S. Supreme Court. Conradi formed a partnership with Nick Blatt of Pocatello, just for the completion of the cathedral. Much of the raised plaster decoration is gilded with gold or antique bronze paint.

The woodwork, pews, confessionals, and Stations of the Cross were awarded to T. F. Phillips Altar Furnishings Company of Dubuque Iowa. Several of the contracts let for the church's decoration were with companies from the Midwest, probably because Bishop Gorman, from his time in Iowa, had seen their work in the Midwest.

The Stations of the Cross are an interesting, and uniquely Catholic, form of iconography. The idea of venerating various points of Christ's final journey, from his appearance before Pontius Pilate, to laying him in his tomb, probably began as early as the third or fourth century. St. Jerome (342–420) discusses pilgrims from around the world visiting Jerusalem and seeking out "the Way of the Cross." In the fifth century, Petronius, the Bishop of Bologna, Italy, authorized the construction of a series of chapels in San Stefano, Italy, which depicted several of the points along the route which people visited in the Holy Land. When the Holy Land came under the control of the Ottoman Turks in the 13th century, travel for Christians to the Holy Land became difficult, and venerating any of the sites of Christ's suffering was forbidden. Thus began the practice of reproducing in Europe the scenes which had become venerated in the Holy Land, allowing Christians an opportunity to retrace in spirit, if not in actuality, Christ's final journey. Throughout Europe, shrines were erected, and by the end of the 17th century such representations were common in churches. It was in the 17th century that the Franciscans, traditional guardians of sites in the Holy Land, began erecting "Stations" in all of their churches.

The number and subject of the stations has varied throughout the years from 7 to 37. In 1731, Pope Clement XII fixed the number at 14, which it is today. The 14 stations depict scenes in the final hours of Christ's life. These scenes are:

1. Jesus before Pilate
2. The carrying of the cross
3. Jesus falls the first time
4. Jesus meets his mother
5. Simon of Cyrene helps carry the cross
6. Veronica wipes the face of Jesus
7. Jesus falls the second time
8. Jesus meets the women of Jerusalem
9. Jesus falls the third time
10. Jesus is stripped of his garments
11. Jesus is nailed to the cross
12. The death of Jesus
13. Jesus is taken down from the cross
14. Jesus is laid in the tomb

These are the scenes which are found around the walls of virtually every Catholic church in the world. (But not all—Stations of the Cross are not a required element in the design of a Catholic church.)

In choosing Stations of the Cross to decorate a church, the actual depiction of the scenes is not mandated. Thus, from church to church, the figures in the scenes, background, and elements of presentation may be very different. The Stations of the Cross may be anything from elaborate, three-dimensional carvings, to paintings, to simple line drawings. Following are two simple, but exquisitely beautiful stations from the Monastery of the Ascension in Jerome, Idaho. These stations were done by Brother Sylvester Sonnen, a monk at the Monastery of the Ascension.

**Stations, Monastery of the Ascension. Top Photo: Seventh Station—Jesus Falls the Second Time. Bottom Photo: Eighth Station—Jesus Meets the Women of Jerusalem**
*(Photographs from the author's collection, reproduced with permission of Brother Sylvester Sonnen)*

These stations are an illustration of the leeway in artistic interpretation given to those creating the scenes. These are simple, wire sculpture on a wooden cross. There is no doubt, though, to anyone familiar with the Stations of the Cross what these outlines are portraying. Two other interesting bits of artistic interpretation in these Stations is that the station number is created with nails, the instruments of Christ's crucifixion, and the figure of Jesus carrying the cross creates the ancient symbol for Christ, Chi-Rho, the first two capital letters of the Greek word for Christ.

The stations at St. John's also invite a very careful look and present the same opportunity for unique consideration. First is the question of the historical accuracy of the scenes, not just at St. John's, but in any presentation of the stations. Of the fourteen stations, only stations 1, 5, 8, 10, 11, 12, 13, and 14 find support in the biblical accounts of Christ's condemnation, execution, and death. The other scenes are tradition and popular belief which have become institutionalized. Historically accurate or not, the Stations of the Cross are one of the more popular and enduring Catholic observances, especially during the forty days of Lent. It would not be at all unusual to walk into an otherwise empty Catholic church and find a solitary figure making a slow progression around the walls, pausing at each station for prayer and meditation.

The second question with regards to the stations at St. John's is a more prosaic one. Did the church get what it paid for? The contract for the stations, signed in 1919, specified that the Stations of the Cross were to be "original oil paintings." The stations hanging on the walls of St. John's, while they are of very high quality, are not "original oil paintings." They are lithographs on copper! Whether there was a verbal change to the specifications, or whether T. F. Phillips Altar Furnishings got away with delivering less than they had promised, we do not know. They are very high quality lithographs, with a protective overlay of varnish—which gives the appearance of oil paint—but lithographs, without a doubt.

The scenes in the stations at St. John's are very common and ancient. These particular scenes are so frequently used and so ancient that they are in the "public domain." The same scenes, with the same placement of figures, can be found in Catholic churches throughout the world, St. Mark's Church in Boise, and Holy Apostles in Meridian being two local examples.

A very careful examination of the stations will reveal some intriguing hidden messages. The artist began displaying some of these messages in the first station, *Jesus is Condemned to Death*. To the right of both Christ and Pilate is a man bearing the standard of the Roman Empire, with the Imperial Eagle and the SPQR inscription (the senate and the people of Rome). This symbol is a clear reminder, as Jesus begins his final journey, that it was the Roman Empire which sentenced Jesus to death. There is a young man, perhaps a court page, in this first station; he is holding a pitcher of water as Pilate famously "washes his hands of the blood of this innocent man." This young man will make an appearance later on, in the seventh station.

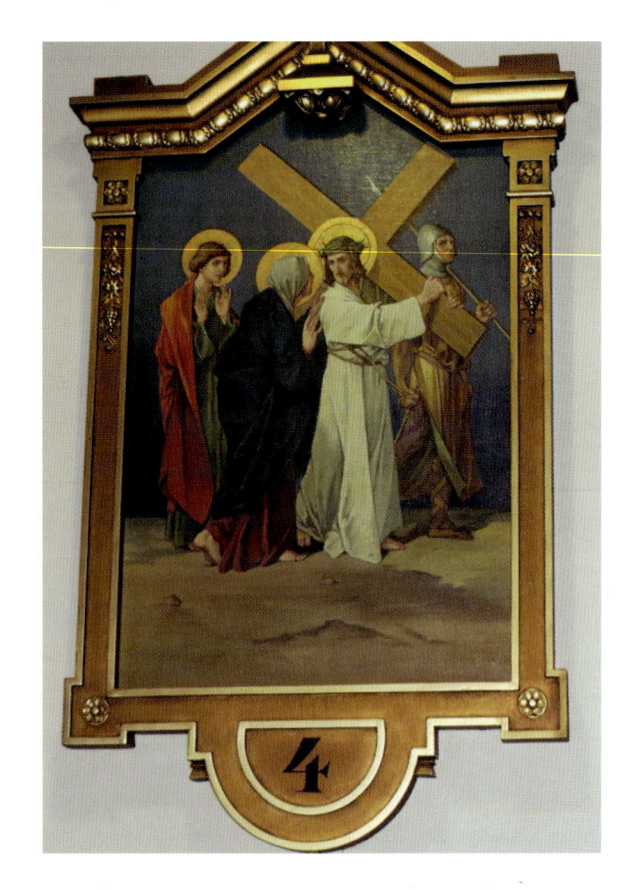

**Fourth Station—Jesus Meets His Mother**
*(Photograph from the author's collection)*

*Chapter 5*

In the fourth station, "*Jesus Meets His Mother*," the patron saint of the cathedral, John the Evangelist, makes his first appearance.

John is the only one of the apostles to appear in any of the stations, and in fact, he appears in three of them: the fourth, twelfth, and thirteenth. Biblical accounts tell us that John was the only one of the apostles who did not abandon Jesus after his arrest. Catholic tradition further holds that John, after the death of Jesus, took Mary, Jesus' mother, under his care. *And from that hour the disciple took her into his home.* (John 19:27) Thus, he is depicted with Mary in the fourth station, and again, at the foot of the cross in the twelfth.

In the fifth station, *Simon of Cyrene Helps Jesus Carry the Cross*, there are two young men in the background. One is carrying a spade, and one a bundle of some sort. Both young men have halos around their heads, which suggests that they are saints. Who are these young men?

The best guess—and a guess is all that can be made—is that the two young men are Simon's sons. Mark, in his gospel, mentions them by name "*. . . Alexander and Rufus. . .*" (Mark 15:13.) Simon, we are told, was a farmer on his way home from the fields when he was conscripted by the Roman soldiers to assist the faltering Christ. His sons, likely, would have been working with their father and on the way home with him.

So how did they become saints and adorned with halos? This is probably nothing more than an indication of how much Christians of the fifth century struggled mightily to biblically justify

**Fifth Station—Simon of Cyrene Helps Carry the Cross**
*(Photograph from the author's collection)*

some of their practices. As mentioned, Mark in his gospel mentions the two young men by name. Paul, who was a contemporary of Mark's, and who in fact traveled with him, in his writings refers to both Alexander and Rufus by name. These were very common names in the first century, and despite the fact that there is nothing to indicate that either Rufus or Alexander whom Paul writes about in his later epistles are the same ones Mark mentioned, tradition in the fifth century dictated such; and thus, artistic license looking backward had assigned saintly status to those two young men in the fifth station. There are depictions of the fifth station without these two young men in them (look at the other set of stations in the cathedral, in the basement chapel). There are depictions in which only one has a halo, and there are depictions such as at the cathedral, where both of them are so adorned. Probably, a book could be written just about these two boys.

No matter whatever speculation might be offered with regards to the two young men in the fifth station, certainly the key figure (other than the fallen Christ) has to be Simon, the Cyrenian who was pressed into service to help carry the cross. Simon is very distinctively dressed: a green cap, a green cowl, a red tunic, and green leggings. (Unfortunately, the Christmas Elf comes immediately to mind.) His distinctive dress, though, will help us to pick him out, not just in the fifth station, but in the ninth station, where he helps the fallen Christ, and in the fourteenth station, where he is in the highly honorable position of being one of the people laying Jesus in the tomb.

Moving on to the seventh station, *Jesus Falls the Second Time*, we come across another intriguing depiction. Behind a Roman soldier in the center of the scene, one catches a glimpse of a young man carrying a sign. He appears to be the same young man who was assisting Pilate in the first station. He certainly is dressed in the same purple robe, and he has the same very distinguishing, and very short, haircut.

On the sign he is holding, we can read a partial inscription in Latin . . . *Nazoreum Judaeroum*. Biblical accounts of Jesus' execution relate that Pilate had ordered

**Seventh Station—Jesus Falls the Second Time**
*(Photograph from the author's collection)*

Chapter 5

In the eighth Station, *Jesus Meets the Women of Jerusalem*, the sign appears again, only now it is being carried by a different young person. It is certainly a young person dressed differently than the one in the preceding station, and with markedly longer hair. In fact, the young person carrying the sign in this station could be a young woman.

Perhaps the sign, which does appear to be somewhat unwieldy, got to be too much for the first young man and he handed it off to a friend. The final comment with

**Eighth Station—Jesus Meets the Women of Jerusalem**
*(Photograph from the author's collection)*

a sign placed above Christ's head, "Jesus of Nazareth, King of the Jews." When the Jews objected to this and suggested instead, "He *claimed* to be King of the Jews," Pilate famously replied, "What I have written, I have written." It seems as if Pilate wanted to be sure that what he had written stayed written, and so he dispatched his page with the task of carrying that sign. The interesting thing about the seventh station is that it takes on a particularly curious aspect when viewed with the very next station.

**Twelfth Station—The Death of Jesus**
*(Photograph from the author's collection)*

*Page 45*

regards to that sign, so carefully prepared, and so carefully carried by at least two different persons, is that it was never used! In the twelfth station, *The Death of Jesus*, the inscription at the top of the cross is the abbreviation all Catholics have become so used to seeing, *INRI* (the first letters of *Ieus Nazoreneum Rex Iudaeorum*)[b]. The sign which was carried by various persons in the seventh and eighth stations is not the sign which was affixed to the cross!

The ninth station, *Jesus Falls the Third Time*, invites a look back at stations three, *Jesus Falls the First Time*, and seven, *Jesus Falls the Second Time*. The original artist, in depicting these scenes, considered carefully the practical ordeal the journey to Golgotha must have been for a condemned, wounded, and punished man. In station three, Jesus' fall is more of a stumble, to one knee. In the seventh station, Jesus now falls to both knees, and in the ninth station, an almost entirely spent Jesus is prostrate on the ground as Simon steps in to lift the cross from his fallen body.

Finally, as has been mentioned, in the final station, it seems as if Simon of Cyrene not only helped Jesus to carry the cross, but helped lay him to rest in the tomb.

We are told that Christ died on a Friday, and was not removed from the cross until late in the day, so by this depiction Simon

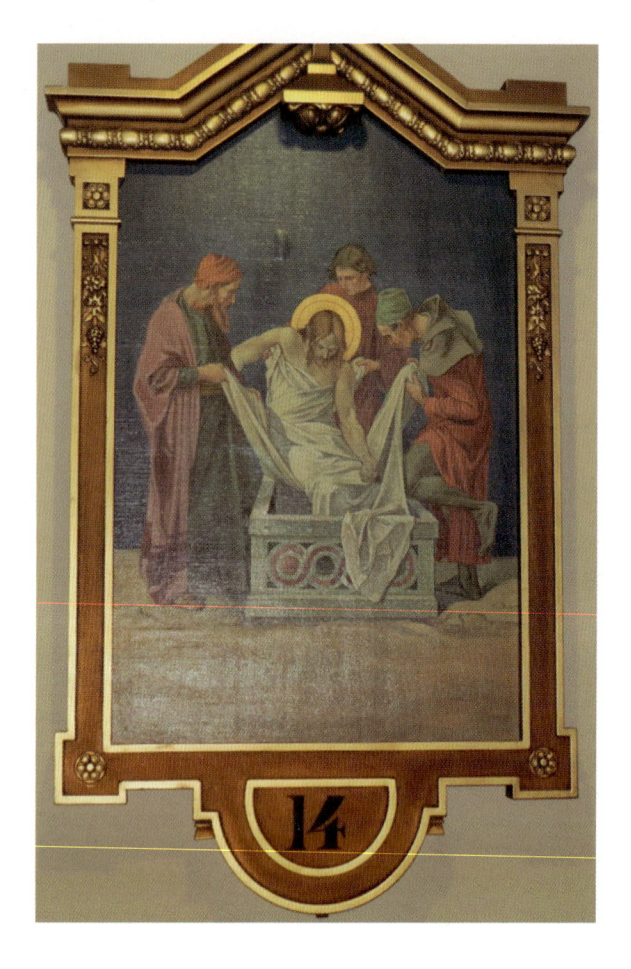

**Fourteenth Station—Jesus is Laid in the Tomb**
*(Photograph from the author's collection)*

must have stayed, or at least returned, to the scene of the crucifixion after fulfilling the duties he was impressed into. Interestingly though, Simon, despite the very close association he had with Jesus in his final hours, is not himself ever adorned with a halo, although his putative sons are.

Bishop Gorman, as he set about to finish the cathedral, in addition to the hard work and very generous contributions

---

b    There is no "J" in either the Hebrew or Latin alphabets.

*Chapter 5*

of his parishioners, had one other factor which facilitated the completion of this project. Gorman did not have the scruples his predecessor had with regards to debt. His was not a "pay as you go regime." His objective was to finish the cathedral and he proceeded to finish and furnish it in the best fashion possible. As has been mentioned, the parishioners of St. John's and others had made generous donations of over $40,000.00. The final price tag though, to complete the work, was almost $246,000.00. The cathedral, which had laid its cornerstone with a firm policy of "pay as you go," opened its doors with a mortgage of over $80,000. That mortgage was slowly and conscientiously paid off, usually with contributions from parishioners in amounts as small as $.50, and occasionally with significant amounts, such as $4000.00. Over the next twenty years, the debt was whittled down until finally, in the financial report for the year 1945, the rector, Monsignor Kenneth Rowe, could report "cathedral debt paid in full January 1, 1946."[22] This ideal state lasted only about two years; in 1948, the cathedral parish went almost $90,000.00 in debt to build the gymnasium for St. Joseph School, which now stands at the southwest corner of 8th and Fort Streets.

Questions of immediate financing and local delays were not the only problems faced in getting the cathedral finished. It was just becoming obvious that the world, in the aftermath of WWI, was a very unstable place. The family of Lieutenant Regan, killed in the first World War, wanted to donate the altar for the new church in honor of their son. In August of 1919, they submitted designs which were approved by the architects. Marble for the altar was ordered from Italy. The year 1920 in Italy is often referred to as the "Year of the Occupation of the Factories." The economic situation in Italy was dire. Both peasants and industrial workers were suffering from the collapse of the *lire*, and the rapid deceleration of factory production, which had boomed during the war. Socialism and concern for worker's rights led to a fivefold increase in unions in Italy. 1920 became the high point — or the low point, depending on one's perspective — of the class struggle in Italy. Factories and works of every sort, including the famous marble quarries in Carrara, were occupied first by the workers, then by government troops, and ultimately by anarchists. The marble intended for St. John's altar sat unquarried and uncut.

Finally, once labor issues in Italy were resolved — to the extent that labor issues in Italy are ever resolved — it became obvious that Boise was just another small spot in an increasingly shrinking world. A telegram received by the building committee in September, 1920, from the Church Art Works Company of Mount Vernon, New York, brought the unwelcome news that the steamship *Trentia*, which had left Italy the month before, had to return to port for repairs, "can do nothing until she arrives." The *Trentia*, among its cargo, had the marble for the altars for St. John's. The marble for the altars finally arrived in New York in April of 1921.

Once the marble was finally delivered, and actual construction of the altar begun, issues didn't end. The Church Art Work Company in New York, the contractors for the actual work on the altar, began petitioning Bishop Gorman for an increase in the amount paid to them. Although the amount due the Church Art Work Company was specified in the original contract, they asked for an additional $3000.00, based primarily on two facts. First, in the initial contract (as in all of the initial contracts), the cathedral had asked for, and gotten, a 5% discount after the final price was arrived at. Second, the above mentioned delays had occasioned extra expenses for the contractor. A sometimes testy exchange of letters ensued from July of 1921 until July of 1922. The Building Committee, something called "The Legal Advisory Committee," the bishop, the architect, and finally, the attorneys for each side, jumped into the fray. When all was said and done, the "four corners of the contract," willingly entered into by both parties, prevailed. No additional fees were allowed.

The marble for the altar may have been delayed, but work continued on the rest of the interior decoration. As early as August of 1919, the managers of the building project were promising that the church would be ready for the Easter service next spring. It was not to be. In fact, two more Easters would come and go before the cathedral was finished.

# Chapter 6

## The Basques Get Their Own Church

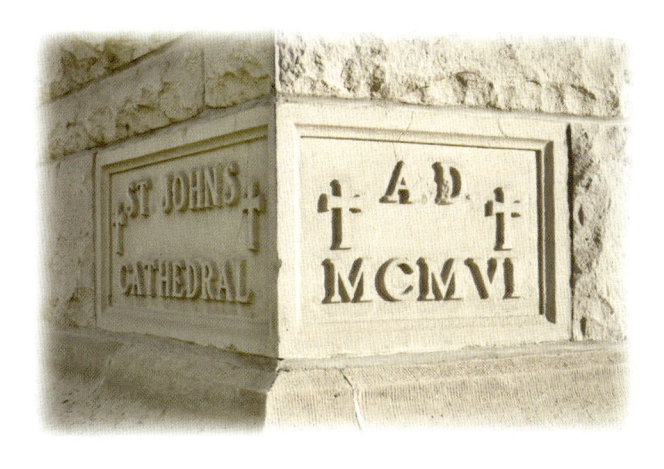

While engaged in the process of finishing the cathedral his predecessor had started, Bishop Gorman didn't fail to pay close attention to the practicalities of administering his parish and diocese. Gorman was a very early proponent of recognizing the cultural and political matters which are so important to any administrative organization. Just as Bishop Gorman took control of the cathedral parish, a very unique segment of St. John's parish was beginning to manifest itself. The Basques, after 50 years of struggle in Idaho, were beginning to claim their niche. The original Basque immigrants to Idaho followed a somewhat convoluted course, not from the Basque Country, but from Argentina, via California and Nevada. They, just as thousands of other treasure seekers, were following the frenzied search for gold which drove so much of the history of the late 19th century.

Basques have always had a significant presence in South America, and indeed in any place in the world which had ever been a part of the Spanish Empire. When gold was discovered in California in 1848, Basques from South America joined the hordes heading to California. They had an immediate advantage over those traveling from the eastern United States. The Pacific coast of South America, particularly the long Chilean coastline, was very favorably situated for someone heading to the west coast of the United States. There was no need to navigate the treacherous Straits of Magellan. Given favorable winds and currents, it was a relatively easy trip to California. It was much easier to sail up the coast of South America and Mexico to California than it was to travel from anywhere east of the Mississippi to California, and in 1848, the population centers of the United States were all decidedly east of the Mississippi.

Proximal advantage notwithstanding, given the pace of communication and travel in 1848, the Basques from South America arrived in California with the distinct disadvantage of being a Hispanic people, just as the "forty-niners" were embarking on a fairly ruthless process of erasing all things Hispanic from California.

The disappointed gold seekers did what immigrants have always done: took whatever work was available to support themselves and their families. Sheepherding was just coming into its own in California, and Basque men found ready employment in the lonely and isolated work of tending sheep in the state's mountain meadows.

Actually, there is no 'old country' tradition of sheepherding in the Basque lands. That was not something they ever did in their homeland, but it was something they took to as a necessary means of survival while establishing themselves in the New World. Although Idaho's Basques have long since moved into positions of prominence in all of the professional and business fields, they still zealously foster an identity with that sheepherding legacy.

In the early 1860's, gold was discovered in Idaho. The territory's population exploded, and a significant portion of California's early settlers headed eastward for supposedly greener pastures. What was true in California was true in Idaho, and in fact is still true today in a "boom" environment. Whether it be gold, silver, oil, or other extracted material, the money is to be made not by a few lucky prospectors, but by those who develop the service and support industries for those prospectors.

In a frontier environment, sheep are the preferred food and material source. They produce the most meat and clothing material in the least amount of time and with the least labor investment. Generally, it would take three times as many cattle as sheep to supply the same amount of both food and clothing material, leather and wool, in a newly developing territory. The Basques, now with established credentials as sheepherders, followed the trail to Idaho in large numbers.

The other significant and identifiable population which had established themselves in the California gold fields was the Chinese. The Chinese found their fortunes in supplying food, primarily vegetables and laundry facilities. The Chinese made the same trek to Idaho at the same time as the Basques.

Neither were well received. The Chinese, because in the late 19th and early 20th century there was an extreme distaste in the United States for all beings Asian. The Basques, because of their unique language, and resistance to assimilation. The Caldwell Tribune didn't hesitate, in 1909, to lump both into one, very undesirable group:

> *The scale of living and the methods of doing business of the Bascos are on par with those of the Chinaman. However, they have some undesirable characteristics that the Chinaman is free from. They are filthy, treacherous and meddlesome. However they work hard and save their money. They are clannish and undesirable but they have a foothold and unless something is done will make life impossible for the white man."*[23]

Aside from their language, perhaps the most significant thing which set the Basques apart from "mainstream" America was their religion. There is a Basque proverb, "*When you say Basque, you say Catholic.*" In the early 20th century, United States Catholicism was a religion very much in the shadows of being a "fringe" religion. This was particularly so in the frontier west.

Bishop Gorman, though he was struggling to finish the cathedral, recognized what a valuable asset to his struggling church Basque people were. Basques may not have been welcome in society as a whole, but they were welcomed with open arms by the Catholic Church. They were numerically small, but financially very important to the cathedral.

Bishop Gorman didn't hesitate to do all he could to recognize them and give them full recognition at St. John's. Gorman's predecessor, Alphonse Glorieux, had ten years earlier recruited a Basque priest from Vitoria-Gasteiz to serve Idaho's Basque population.

When members of the Basque community expressed to Gorman a desire for a church of their own his answer must have been something along the line of "if you build it you can have it." Build it they did, with contributions from the Basque community. John Archabal, perhaps Boise's most successful Basque at the time, and certainly one of its most influential, led the drive not just with major donations on his own part, but with encouragement and urgings to his fellow Basques.

On March 2nd, 1919, the Church of the Good Shepherd, the only church in the United States built specifically for a Basque community, was dedicated at the corner of 5th and Idaho Streets. The church was actually created from two residences at that location, which were remodeled into a church and a rectory. Much altered and diminished, the building is still there and now serves as administrative offices for St. Luke's Regional Health Foundation.

Bishop Gorman was finding it a struggle, financially and otherwise, to get the

**Church of the Good Shepherd, as the Diocesan Chancery in the 1960's**
*(Photograph courtesy of Idaho Catholic Register)*

cathedral finished. That struggle not withstanding, he didn't hesitate to take on more responsibility by opening yet another church in the capitol city. His perspicacity on this issue is somewhat startling. Long before the world gave much recognition to the Basques, and well before the Spanish Civil War brought their plight to the world's attention, Bishop Gorman recognized it. He opened a "Basque church," and had it staffed with a Basque-speaking priest, Father Bernardo Arregui. Father Arregui, though, was at the Church of the Good Shepherd only for two years. In 1921, he was transferred to Twin Falls, to minister to all Basques in Idaho.

It is worth noting that Bishop Gorman considered the Basque parishioners so important that he allowed their church to be built and staffed two full years before his cathedral was finished. He wouldn't have done that had there not been a firm commitment on the part of the Basque community that their church would not add to the financial burden of getting the cathedral finished. Gorman's willingness to accept a significant financial commitment from a people who were struggling to be accepted in the United States was well rewarded. One hundred years later, Basque names comprise a huge part of the cathedral census. As we will see later, Bishop Gorman's forward thinking in this matter would ultimately run afoul of his successor's more practical side.

*Stone Wondrously Hewn*

# Chapter 7

## Gorman Finishes the Cathedral

Finally, on May 30th, 1921, the cathedral was ready to be dedicated.[a] Fifteen years after the cornerstone had been laid, the Cathedral of St. John the Evangelist was ready to open wide its doors. The splendors of its construction became obvious to all. Ironically, Bishop Gorman, who had put so much of his energy in the completion of the edifice, was not able to

---

[a] The cathedral had multiple dedication ceremonies. It was blessed in a private ceremony by Father Francis Bonara on May 23rd, 1921. The first Mass was said the next day, and the formal dedication was held a week later.

attend the dedication ceremonies. He was hospitalized at St. Alphonsus Hospital that day, and had to turn the opening ceremonies over to Father Francis Bonora and Archbishop Alexander Christie of Portland.

In his dedication address, the Reverend Norbert Hoff, president of Mount St. Charles College (now Carroll College in Helena, Montana), made sure to cover all of the requisite bases. The First World War had ended just two years earlier, and in the aftermath of the economic upheavals that war had caused, a new social order was being shaped. Conflicts between labor and capital were the order of the day.

Father Hoff pointed out that the first American officer killed in the war just concluded was Lieutenant William Fitzsimons, a Catholic doctor, and the last American killed in that war was Henry Gunther, a private soldier, and likewise a Catholic. Private Gunther's story is an illustrative one.

Gunther's parents were German immigrants, and at the outbreak of the war he was not overly enthusiastic about fighting Germans. He did not volunteer to serve. In September of 1917, though, he was drafted and dutifully reported. He was soon promoted to sergeant and sent to France. Shortly after arriving in France, Sergeant Gunther made the mistake of writing a letter home in which he complained of the "miserable conditions" at the front. Further, he suggested that any of his young friends at home might do whatever they could to avoid the draft. The letter was read by Army censors, and as a consequence Sergeant Gunther was demoted to private.

Private Gunther was determined to overcome what he saw as the injustice done to him. He resolved to redeem his honor. Just before 11:00 on November 11th, Gunther was part of a patrol which came across a German machine gun emplacement in Lorraine. Against orders, and with fixed bayonet, Gunther charged the Germans. Even though the German soldiers who knew of the impending truce initially tried to wave him back, he persisted and began firing. The Germans returned a short burst of fire, and Gunther fell dead at 10:59 AM, the last American killed in the First World War.

Even as he acknowledged such patriotism, Father Hoff didn't hesitate to castigate the war time profiteering which had enriched so few at the expense of so many. Father Hoff also addressed domestic issues by emphasizing that the church "stood for law and order," while he defended the rights of unions as "historically and morally correct." Collective bargaining, Father Hoff said, would keep man from falling "back into the mule and machine class."

Bishop Glorieux had envisioned the cathedral and planned it. Bishop Gorman had financed it and completed it. Six bishops, thus far, have subsequently claimed it as their cathedral. As we will

## Chapter 7

discuss, though, the cathedral is the work of the people of God, which will never be "finished." Improvements and changes to it, some minor and some major, continue to this very day. Often forgotten in chronicling the building of the cathedral is the fact that while it is located in Boise, it was built by the people of the entire state of Idaho, and in fact major donations were made by people from all over the United States. It was the people of Idaho, from every area of the state, who were the mainstays of the cathedral funding. Every parish in Idaho had an assessment levied against it for the building of the cathedral. The amounts ranged from $250.00 in Grangeville to $1000.00 in Twin Falls, for a total amount of $21,000.00 dollars. (In todays dollars, that would be $255,000.00.)

It is these two men, though, Glorieux and Gorman, who must be given the lion's share of the credit for the monument we are about to visit. In the over one hundred years which have passed since the beginning of the cathedral, dozens, if not hundreds, of people—men and women, priests, and lay persons—have imbued the monument with stories which continue to resonate today. When all is said and done, though, it was Glorieux who had the dream and Gorman who brought it to reality.

The cathedral was finished just in time to receive the body of one of its sons: John Morgan Regan, the son of Timothy Morgan Regan and Rose Charlotte (Blackinger) Regan.

The Regan family, whose son John had been killed in the First World War, had for several years been engaged in efforts to have their son's body returned from France. He had initially been interred on the battlefield in France. In March of 1921, they received welcome news. John Morgan Regan's body would be returned to Boise. Late in May, the body arrived in New York, and in June it left for the final leg of the journey home.

In charge of the ceremonies was Captain Frederic Hummel. Frederic, or "Fritz" as he was known, had been a lifelong friend of Lieutenant Regan. They had been students together at St. Joseph's school. They both served in the war. Frederic's Father was the architect who had designed the new cathedral, and John's family had donated the altar at which his funeral mass was celebrated.

On June 20th, 1921, the first ever military requiem Mass (but certainly not the last) at St. John's Cathedral was conducted for Lieutenant Regan. At the service "Fritz" Hummel reminisced that five years ago that Sunday night, he and John Regan had gone together to the Statesman office to confirm the news that they had both, as members of the Idaho National Guard, been called to active duty on the Mexican border. Now Frederick watched as his friend's body was laid to its final rest in the Catholic cemetery at Morris Hill.

Bishop Gorman, while honoring the sacrifices, often the ultimate sacrifice, which the young men of his diocese had made in the war, was forceful in his denunciation of war as a means of resolving international questions. Almost immediately at the conclusion of the war he began speaking out for the elimination of all war. "The opportunity of helping to stop wars is at hand, and if we do not seize it, as best we can, we shall be contributing causes of the next war." Bishop Gorman's sentiments on this matter, unfortunately, did not comport with the feelings of Idaho's representatives at the national level. The United States was at this time engaged in a heated debate regarding the League of Nations. A majority of Americans, after the horrors of WWI, were in favor of such an international body. Unfortunately, the will of the majority of the American people meant little more in 1920 than it does today. Powerful interests in Congress, including William E. Borah, the senior U.S. senator from Idaho, were opposed to United States membership in the League of Nations. Borah and Senator Henry Cabot Lodge of Massachusetts, pursuing a policy of American exceptionalism, embarked on a campaign of "death by a thousand cuts" for the enabling legislation which would have authorized the United States' entry into the League of Nations. They could see that support for the League was gaining the upper hand with the American public, so they attached to the legislation amendment after amendment, and reservation after reservation, until the measure finally presented to the Senate for approval had "something to offend everyone." When put to a vote, the proposal for the United States to join the League of Nations failed. This would not, unfortunately, be the last time in American history that a group of narrow minded partisan politicians imposed their will on the American people. The next generation of young Americans would find themselves engaged in another world war. *When did World War I become World War I?* Surely, none of those suffering in the mud and horrors of France and Belgium anticipated it as the first of a series.

The Cathedral, for the next several years, found itself involved in the grim business of burying its sons, who one by one—officers, noncommissioned officers, and private soldiers—were returned from their graves on foreign soil to come finally to rest in the high desert of southwest Idaho. The Diocese of Boise had sent over 1400 men to service in the First World War, 7% of the adult Catholic male population.[24] No other identifiable group came anywhere close to that number. Questions about the patriotism and fidelity of Catholics to the United States were laid to rest with these young men.

Catholicism in the United States has always been, and continues today to be, an "immigrant church." In the early part of the 20th century, the immigrants were largely Irish, German, and Italian. Today, they are largely Mexican, and Central and South American. From whatever national origins, were it not for immigrants and their children, the American Catholic Church, instead of being the largest

## Chapter 7

congregation in the United States, would be a very small one.

The Church, while it fully embraced immigrants from all nations, was keenly aware of the rising tide of "Americanism." It wasn't viewed as a necessarily antagonistic trend, but it was one that the church had to recognize and deal with. In 1919, Bishop Gorman had spoken to the Catholic Women's League and stressed the need to address "Americanization" of the foreign born. There was, for many years at the cathedral, an "Americanization" committee. The Catholic Women's League opened a night school, teaching English as a second language. Five years later, when Gorman once more addressed the group, he noted that at this meeting there were thirteen different nationalities present, but they were all citizens.

Gorman, once the cathedral was finished, did not rest on his laurels. He maintained interest and involvement in public affairs. In 1925, he gave the invocation at the opening session of the Idaho Legislature. He arranged for a specially outfitted railroad car dubbed "St. Peter" to serve as a chapel on wheels, bringing Mass to some of the state's remote communities. He had churches built in Twin Falls, Post Falls, Caldwell, Shoshone, and Wallace. He established schools in Idaho Falls, Nampa, and Blackfoot. St. Joseph's School in Boise, and the staffing of it, consumed a large part of his time. All through 1922, 1923, and a good part of 1924, there is an ongoing exchange of letters between Bishop Gorman and various provinces of the Christian Brothers, in an attempt to get them to staff St. Joseph's School. This time period, the early 1920's, was a period of rampant growth of the Catholic school system. The response of the Brothers is always the same "our existent…schools have grown prodigiously in students in the past three or four years."[25]

Unfortunately, his ambitious goals for the diocese began to take a toll, both on the diocesan finances and on his own health. During Gorman's administration, the Catholic Church in Idaho, in addition to contributions from its own members, received almost $100,000.00 from the Catholic Church Extension Society. That pace of expansion could not be maintained.

> *…the time came when an era of self-denial, in order to reduce the accumulation of heavy financial obligation was necessary."*[26]

> *It will be necessary to pray for a happy issue of the case, for, in a letter received only the other day in answer to one I had sent some months ago, the Superior General told his secretary that there were letters enough on hand to fill a good-sized case, all petitions for Brothers, and from everywhere."*[27]

The Christian Brothers never came to Boise, and the Sisters of the Holy Cross continued to ably fill the void until 1985.

It must be noted that orders of religious nuns, of course, were the primary means of staffing Catholic schools until the 1960's, when the decline of commitments to the professed life caused all orders to cut back on their educational obligations. A startling indication of the contributions the Sisters of the Holy Cross made to St. John's/St. Joseph's is that because these were a group of dedicated women, working for virtually nothing, monthly tuition at St. Josephs school in 1933 was $2.00 per month for one student, $3.00 for two, and $4.00 for three.

Bishop Gorman, while advocating for "his" diocesan school, maintained a vigorous travel and visitation schedule throughout the state. "Several years before, Bishop Gorman's doctor had told him that he should spare himself, or his heart would suddenly give out."[28] On May 29th, 1927, while traveling in northern Idaho he became sick and was admitted to St. Joseph's hospital in Lewiston. He died on June 9th, 1927, never having left the hospital.

Daniel Mary Gorman presided over the Catholic Church in Idaho during its period of most expansive growth. When he died, there were 123 Catholic churches (only 51 of them with resident priests, the others were missions or stations served, on a part-time basis, by priests from one of the resident parishes), 18 parochial schools, 6 Catholic hospitals, and 88 priests and other religious serving in the state. The Catholic Church in Idaho would never again have such numbers.

# Chapter 8

## *Bishop Kelly Introduces an Era of Austerity*

The office of bishop for the Diocese of Boise again sat vacant, and remained vacant for over six months. On December 16th, 1927, Edward Joseph Kelly, a priest of the Diocese of Baker, Oregon, was appointed the fourth bishop of the Diocese of Boise. Another three months would go by before he was actually ordained a bishop. On March 8, 1928, Bishop Kelly was formally installed in a ceremony at St. John's Cathedral.

Edward Joseph Kelly was born on February 26th, 1890, on a farm eighteen miles from The Dalles, Oregon. His father was a banker. He himself pursued an education in business, and it wasn't until the relatively late age (for that era) of seventeen that he entered the seminary. He was ordained a priest on June 2nd, 1917. He served in various parishes in Oregon, and in 1919 was appointed to the position of chancellor for the Diocese of Baker. While the apostolic delegate to the United States was visiting Baker City, Bishop McGrath of that diocese took the opportunity to recommend his chancellor for the vacant seat in Boise. McGrath's recommendation was seconded, and Bishop Kelly became the first western priest to be appointed to a western diocese. He spent the first several months of his office traveling throughout the diocese, carefully studying both statewide and local conditions. Banker's son and businessman that he was, he was a bit dismayed at what he found. The parish of St. John's had obligations almost three times the amount of its annual income. The diocese as a whole had no unencumbered funds. There has been serious speculation that Bishop Kelly, when he was appointed to succeed Bishop Gorman, was specifically charged with getting the diocese's financial affairs in order. Certainly, some retrenchment was called for.

Bishop Kelly, in evaluating the needs of his new territory, was perhaps the first episcopal officer to take into consideration the unique configuration of his diocese. Idaho is a large state, covering over 83,000 square miles. More significant, though, is the fact that the area is traversed by several substantial mountain ranges and areas of wilderness. In many instances in Idaho, quite literally "you can't get there from here," at least not in a straight line. As an example, the actual geographic distance between McCall, Idaho and Salmon, Idaho is just over 100 miles. To drive it, though, is a trip of over 270 miles. In snow or ice conditions, that 270 miles can be daunting.

At the time Kelly took office in Idaho, there were 50 parishes, but fifty percent

**Bishop Edward J. Kelly**
*(Reproduced with permission of the Diocese of Boise)*

of the Catholic population was resident in just 10 of them. Clearly, some difficult adjustments were called for.

Bishop Kelly, in one of his first acts, decided that individual parish obligations would be managed by the diocese and not the parishes. Expenditures of over one hundred dollars were prohibited without the specific consent of the diocese. No parish was allowed to construct a new building until a fund of half of the proposed cost of the project was in the bank.

Finally, and most controversial, it was decided to consolidate some of the smaller parishes. One of those selected for consolidation was the Church of the Good Shepherd in Boise.

Although from 1928 to 1933 Bishop Kelly ordered the consolidation or closing of twenty-six churches, it is likely that none generated the controversy which the closing of the Church of the Good Shepherd did. Of all of the consolidations, this was the only church which had been created for a unique and identifiable segment of the population. That unique and identifiable segment, the Basques, saw the closing of "their" church as an assault on some hard fought gains they had just begun making.

Bishop Kelly, though, had not only financial considerations in mind when he made the decision to close the Church of the Good Shepherd. The era of massive immigration to the United States was over. Despite Emma Lazarus' moving words on the base of the Statue of Liberty, the United States in 1928 was not welcoming any "huddled masses." In fact, just four years earlier, Congress had passed the Johnson-Reed Act. Immigration, particularly immigration from Southern Europe, was drastically curbed by this act.

Some of the provisions of this Act will sound outrageous to todays readers, and some will sound chillingly contemporary. A major influencing factor in the passage of the act was a book written by Madison Grant, which had found sweeping popularity in the 1920's. *The Passing of the Great Race* was a eugenic screed, advocating racial purity and claiming that the Nordic races were superior and meant to rule the world. One of the sponsoring senators testified before the Senate that the intent was to "keep American stock up to the highest standard." The act strictly curtailed immigration from Southern Europe, while it gave generous consideration to those from Northern Europe. It severely restricted the immigration of Africans and contained an outright ban on immigration from the Middle East and Asia. It remained the law of the land until a 1965 revision of the immigration laws.

As has been mentioned previously, the American Catholic Church has always been a largely immigrant church. The norm in the late 1800's and early 1900's had been to establish a church in the United States' large urban settings for each of the immigrant groups. There very well might be, in a large U.S. city, a German Catholic church, an Irish Catholic church, a Polish Catholic church, and an Italian Catholic church, all within blocks of each other. It would be unheard of for any one of those ethnic groups to attend a service in any but their own church, even though, in that era, in **all** of the churches the Mass was said in Latin!

Idaho never had the population or ethnic diversity to necessitate this type of consideration. In fact, the Church of the Good Shepherd was the only "ethnic" church in Idaho—and the only church in the United States—ever built for a Basque population. Bishop Kelly, in assuming control of a diocese in dire financial straits, never considered these facts and saw only a small church just eight blocks from the Cathedral. A significant portion of Boise's Basque population had already made the choice of attending the Cathedral rather than the Church of the Good Shepherd. The Church of the Good Shepherd, from its inception, had always been considered a mission of the Cathedral. Newspapers from that era, and the church bulletins themselves, always listed the Church of the Good Shepherd under the heading of "Missions of St. John's," along with churches in Garden Valley, Barber, and Eagle. Given all of this, Kelly remained resolute in his decision. In 1928, he ordered the closing of the Church of the Good Shepherd, and the buildings used as diocesan offices.

The decision was not well received by Boise's Basque community. They had never imagined that "their church" would be suppressed. Several prominent members of the Basque community vowed that they "would never set foot in the Cathedral again," and indeed they carried out that threat. No conscientious Basque, though, is going to forgo a Catholic funeral. As a consequence, while they may have "never set foot" in the Cathedral again, several of them were carried into the Cathedral for their final religious ceremony on this earth.

With the closing of the Church of the Good Shepherd, major contributions to St. John's dropped dramatically. Bishop Kelly was unmoved. The Church of the Good Shepherd never re-opened as a general house of worship. The bishop moved his residence to the property, and a small chapel was maintained. The diocesan offices were moved into the rest of the building, and additional offices were added in 1965 and 1975 as the chancery and diocesan newspaper grew. In 1982, the diocesan offices were moved to a larger building on Federal Way and the building was sold to private interests. It is presently occupied by administrative offices of St. Luke's Regional Health System.

Almost ninety years later, the issue is still a contentious one among Boise's Basques. Generally now, the issue is not *what* was done, but *how* it was done. There was no dialogue or attempt at compromise with those who had built the church. It was

## Chapter 8

a one-sided decision by an unyielding church hierarchy. As a matter of fact, though, there is no disputing that in 1928 *all* decisions made by the Catholic hierarchy were one-sided and dictatorial.

Particularly hurtful was the fact that many years after the closing, when the property was sold to private interests, most of the church's art and furnishings disappeared. The tabernacle is essentially the only item remaining from the only church ever built in the United States by Basques. That tabernacle is prominently displayed in the Boise Basque Museum and Cultural Center. All other fixtures, pews, communion rail, art, and statues are lost. Particularly galling is that the bell, which was donated by several prominent members of the Basque community and which was inscribed with their names, has disappeared.

Kelly was a banker's son and he took a banker's approach to diocesan finances. His new administration started just as the Great Depression was making itself known to the American people. Hard times were looming, and hard choices had to be made. Some of the unused rectories were rented out to commercial interests and some were sold. Those parishes which found themselves in the fortunate and unusual position of anticipating growth were required to have a fund of half of the projected building costs in the bank before construction could begin.

It was Bishop Kelly who instituted the system of deaneries for the geographically sprawling, and challenging, state of Idaho. Kelly originally named five deaneries; that number has since been expanded to six, with some reconfiguration.

Under Bishop Kelly, the diocese instituted a program of having copies of all parish records of baptisms, marriages, deaths, confirmations, and first communions sent to the diocesan offices. This system ensured that in the event of a fire or other cataclysmic loss at one of the churches, these important records would be available for future generations. It is not unusual, as will be demonstrated later, that church records have proved invaluable when civic records have not been available.

The Jesuit mission at Cataldo, which had fallen into a sad state of disrepair, was repaired—and indeed, rescued—under Bishop Kelly's tutelage. $15,000.00 worth of work was done on everything from the roof to the foundation. In 1930, the Society of Jesus, whose priests had built the original mission, deeded the property to the diocese. In 1975, the diocese deeded Cataldo Mission to the state of Idaho, and the church—the oldest building in the state of Idaho—and its grounds became a state park and historical monument.

Perhaps one of Bishop Kelly's most significant contributions to the long-term vitality of the Church in Idaho was the decision to create "home grown" priests. Bishop Glorieux had obtained most of the priests for the diocese from Europe, and

Bishop Gorman had recruited most of his from the eastern United States. Kelly decided it was time for a campaign for native vocations. On June 29, 1929, he issued a directive to parishes throughout the state to periodically announce from the pulpit the process for registering those who might be interested in applying for the priesthood. It didn't take long for these efforts to bear fruit. In 1932, there were 15 young men from Idaho studying for the priesthood. In 1949, Father Nicolas E. Walsh was appointed the first diocesan director of vocations.

Probably Bishop Kelly's most lasting memorial was the work he created in collaboration with Father Cyprian Bradley, O.S.B. Father Bradley and Bishop Kelly, over a period of 15 years, assembled histories and narratives from every parish and mission in Idaho. The end result was *The History of the Diocese of Boise, 1863–1953*, still considered the seminal work to any who are trying to chronicle the history of the Church in Idaho.

Bishop Kelly died on April 21, 1956.

# Chapter 9

## *The Building They Gave Us*

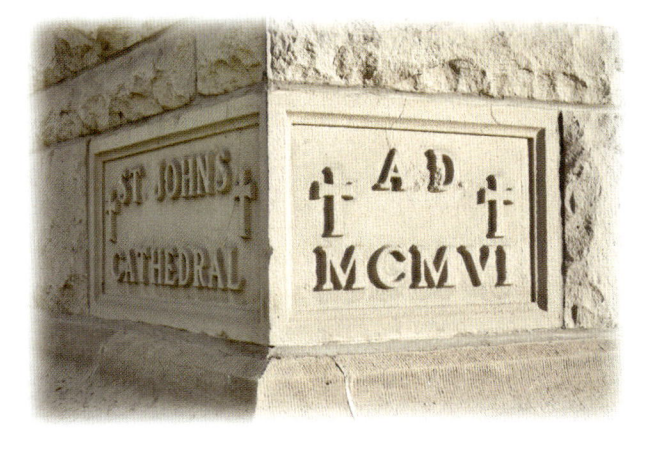

The Cathedral of St. John the Evangelist fronts on 8th Street and faces almost due east. "To the east" is a preferred orientation of Catholic churches.

Nothing is simple with obscure concepts such as "orientation." The basis for the preference is that historically, the early Christians would pray facing the Holy Land (Jerusalem), which was to the east of Rome. Thomas Aquinas, in the 12th century, suggested that our Lord lived His earthly life in the east, and from the east He would come on the final

Judgment Day. This predilection for siting buildings facing "to the east" actually led to criticisms of early Christians as sun worshipers, since it is from the east that the sun rises. Whatever the rationale, accepting "to the east" as preferred, what exactly does that mean as to how a church is sited? The traditional form for a Catholic church is cruciform, and St. John's is very much in this shape.

Given this shape, should the main doorway, situated at the foot of the cross shape, open to the east, or should the altar, toward which the congregation faces and where the mysteries of the Mass are performed, be towards the east? There is a general, but not uniform, consensus that the latter arrangement is the correct one. With that interpretation, St. John's as it was originally built had the priest, as he prayed at the altar, and the people as they faced the altar, both oriented to the west! The debate on orientation, believe it or not, is a lively one even today. For the record, St. John's main doors open to the east, and its altar is on the western end of the building. Actually, prior to the 1978 renovation, while the altar did indeed face east, the priest praying at it was facing the west. After the renovation which so distressed so many "traditional" Catholics, tradition was, for the first time, honored with the priest praying "to the east."

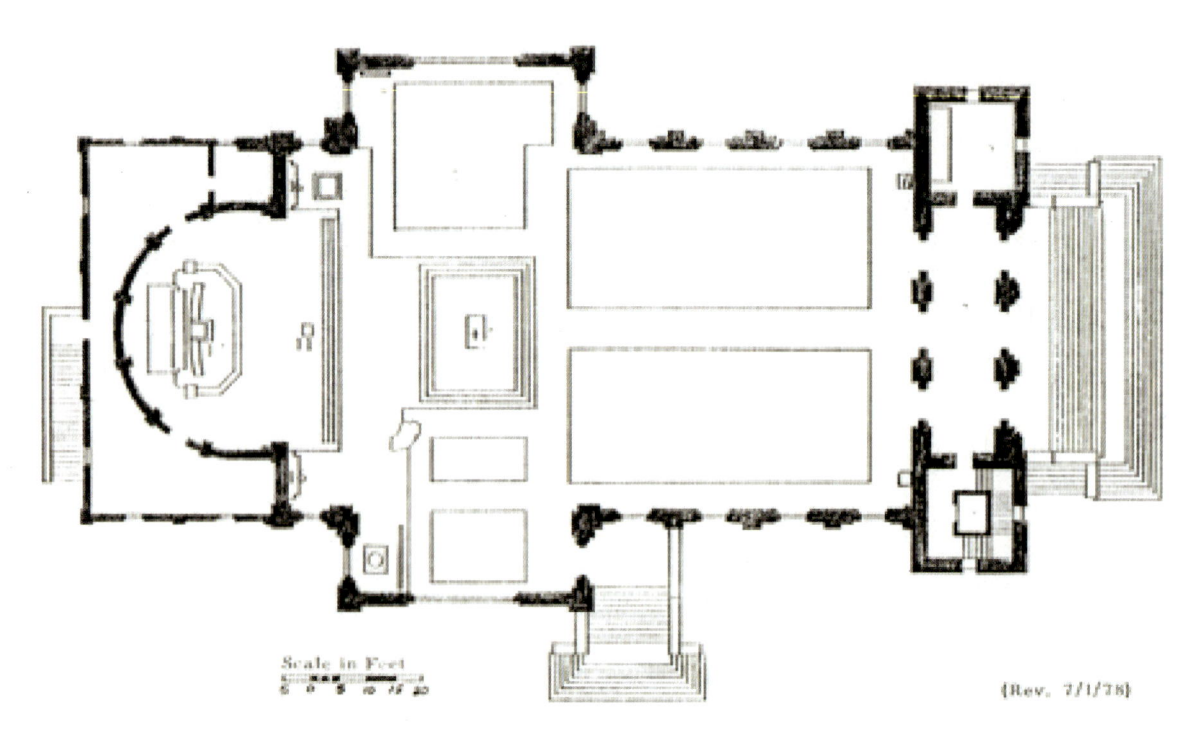

**Outline of the Cathedral of St. John the Evangelist**

*Chapter 9*

**The Cathedral of St. John the Evangelist in Boise**
*(Photograph from the author's collection)*

Whatever the original orientation, whatever the rationale for that orientation, it is certainly an imposing edifice, looming over the edges of downtown Boise. The cathedral is not, as most people assume, a solid sandstone building. It is brick, faced with sandstone. There are early architectural drawings with the cathedral as a full brick structure. Popular lore has it that Bishop Glorieux was originally presented with, and approved, an architect's rendering of a brick church. Before construction had truly begun, though, he discovered that the Episcopalian congregation was building its own cathedral, just four blocks south of St. John's, and it was to be of sandstone. Not to be outdone in grandeur by his Protestant brethren, he changed the design to sandstone.

Bishop Glorieux's personal stationary had his view of the finished cathedral, a brick building with towering spires, which were more Gothic than Romanesque.

The blocks of sandstone were quarried from a still active quarry, in the foothills to the east of the cathedral. Today, the products of that quarry provide mostly decorative accents to home gardens and businesses, but in the early 20th century they provided the building blocks for much of downtown Boise. The State Capitol Building, St. Michael's Cathedral, St. John's Cathedral, Immanuel Lutheran Church, and The Idaho Building being just a few examples. Once cut from the quarry, blocks of sandstone were moved by a tramway system to a shop at the

**St. John's Cathedral as Bishop Glorieux envisioned it**
*(From the archives of St. John's Cathedral)*

foot of the hills, in the approximate area of the Warm Springs golf course. There they were "finished," and cut to sizes which could be lifted by two men. They were then hauled five miles, by railroad cars, to the area of Front and 9th Streets in downtown Boise. From there, they were loaded onto horse-drawn wagons and moved to the construction site. The same quarry and the same system was, at the same time, supplying stone for the State Capitol and for St. Michael's Episcopal Cathedral, just south on 8th Street. The traffic in sandstone up 8th Street must have been constant and impressive in the early 1900's.

St. John's is generally seen as Romanesque in style. It is more properly Romanesque Revival, or Neo-Romanesque. True Romanesque would be a building built in the Romanesque era, which was from the 10th to the 13th centuries. The style is characterized by semi-circular arches over the windows and rounded arches throughout as decorative accents. The walls are generally massive, containing in their bulk the primary supporting elements of the building. All of these features are prominent in both the façade and the interior of St. John's. The defining characteristic of Romanesque design is an impression of massive solidity and strength. This contrasts with Gothic architecture, in which load bearing strength is distributed to a series of columns and pilasters. The walls of Romanesque buildings stand on their own and provide support to overhead arches.

One of the first things that strikes the casual observer looking at the cathedral is that it appears "unfinished." The two large towers on either side of the front seem to be crying out for steeples, or some finishing cap. The church is, in fact, at one hundred and ten years old, still not finished. It was meant to have twin towers going up another sixty feet at each corner of the front. On the day before its dedication and opening, the Idaho Statesman noted that the towers were not finished.

> *At the present time, in their incomplete state, those towers are carried to a height of only 65 feet above the level of the street, but when completed the towers will be 120 feet high, surmounted by steeples 80 feet in height, making a total distance of 200 feet from the ground to the top of the gilded crosses on the steeples."*[29]

Those towers, to this day, are still at "65 feet above the level of the street." Periodic discussions, and in fact, ongoing discussions are had on "finishing the towers." Part of this discussion always has to be, "if the towers were to be finished, what would they look like?"

We have seen a rendering of Bishop Glorieux's idea, and that drawing raises more questions than it answers. The church depicted on Bishop Glorieux's stationery, and in a large framed drawing in the parish office, has towers that are more Gothic than Romanesque. A strict construction of architectural styles

*Chapter 9*

suggest that if the towers were ever finished they would not have a spire rising to a point. True Romanesque towers rise without diminishing in size. They may be capped with a pointed finial, but that is obvious as a cap and not as part of the tower itself. Following this pattern, the towers at St. John's Cathedral would have risen only one more course, of perhaps ten or twelve feet. Arched openings would have been placed just below a capped, perhaps pointed, finial. If finished in this manner, the front of St. John's would be decidedly

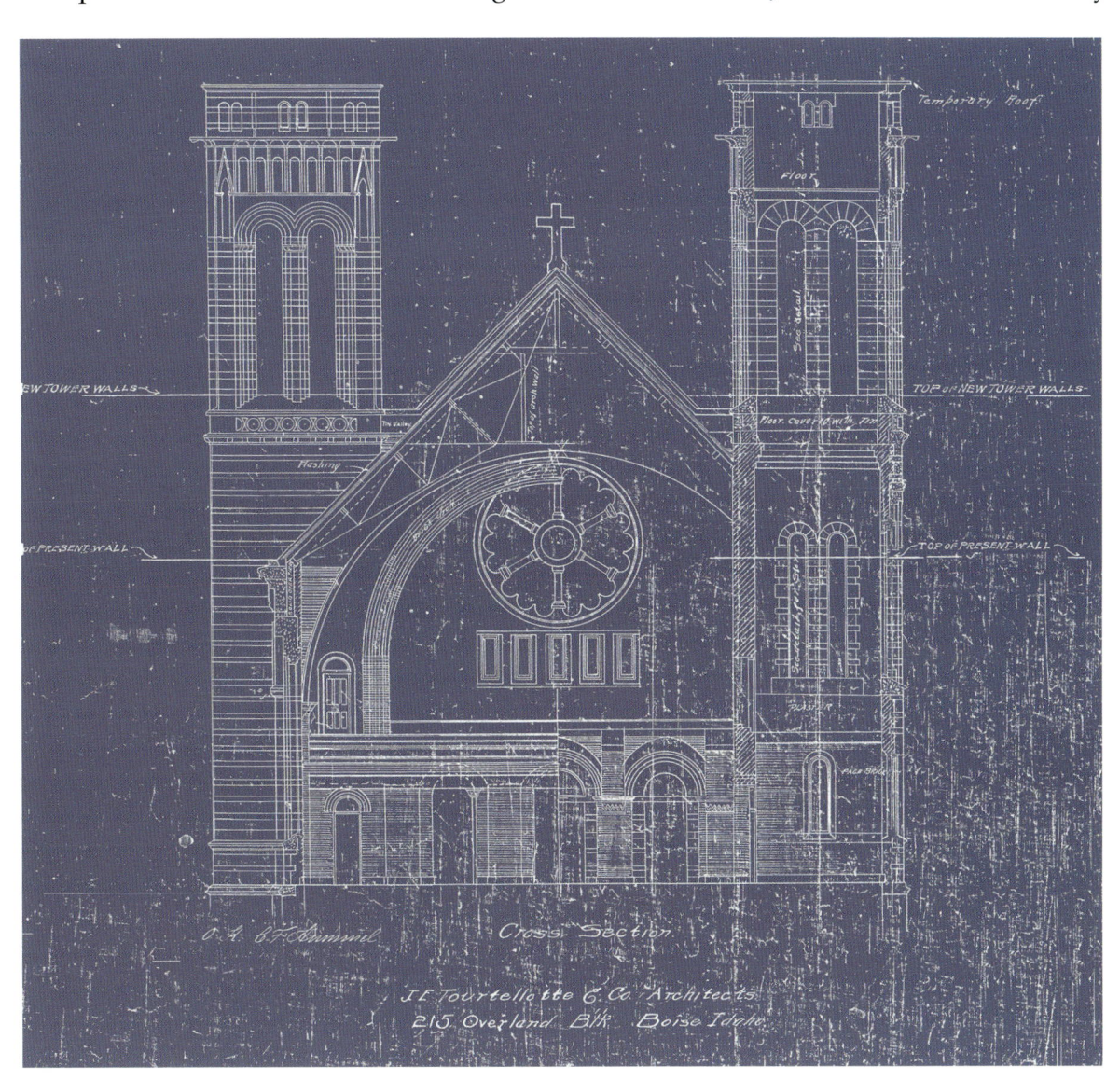

**Drawing by C. F. Hummel, showing the original plan for the façade of the church**
*(From the archives of St. John's Cathedral)*

Neo-Romanesque, and would have two matching towers, rising to the height of the statue of St. John in the center of the current apex. In researching this book, we were able to un-earth a 100+ year old drawing done by C. F. Hummel, which shows the original plan for the façade of the church. There are two drawings on one sheet, one showing the Hays Street elevation, and one showing the 8th Street elevation. This drawing clearly shows the two front towers, which would have risen higher than the existing front apex. In this drawing, a cross stands where the statue of St. John now stands.

Forgetting, for the time being, the missing towers, a major aspect of the façade is the large, circular window in the center. It is a stained glass window, which illuminates the choir loft. It has to be seen from the inside, illuminated by the sun, to be properly appreciated.

This window depicts Saint Cecelia, the patroness of musicians, surrounded by angels playing various musical instruments. It is one of the most beautiful, in what are a whole series, of beautiful windows in the cathedral. Situated, as it is, above the organ and choir loft, the subject, St. Cecilia, is particularly fitting. An intriguing historical fact, though, is uncovered in reading the contract which was signed for the installation of the windows. The original contract for this window shows that it was originally planned to depict St. John, the patron of the cathedral!

The contract with the Kinsella Company is very detailed as to the subject of each of the windows. In the contract, the rose window to go at the back of the choir loft is described as "bust of St. John with busts surrounding same." Anyone who has ever given more than a cursory glance at the beautiful rose window behind the choir loft knows that it is not St. John depicted there, but St. Cecelia. As the patron saint of music, Cecelia is certainly an appropriate figure to have surmounting the choir loft, but one has to wonder. Who changed their mind after the contract was signed? Was it the artist or the bishop who thought, *"Wait a minute, not St. John (who is already depicted in the apse, along with the other evangelists), but St. Cecilia, the patroness of music, and have her surrounded with angels playing musical instruments."* There is no record as to who actually made the change from St. John to St. Cecelia. Very likely, it was Bishop Gorman. A change of that magnitude would not have been made without his assent. Likely all would agree, whoever made it; it was an excellent decision. St. Cecelia's rose window is a wonderful example of stained glass art, and her location in the choir loft is the perfect setting.

# Chapter 10

## *A First Look at the Architecture*

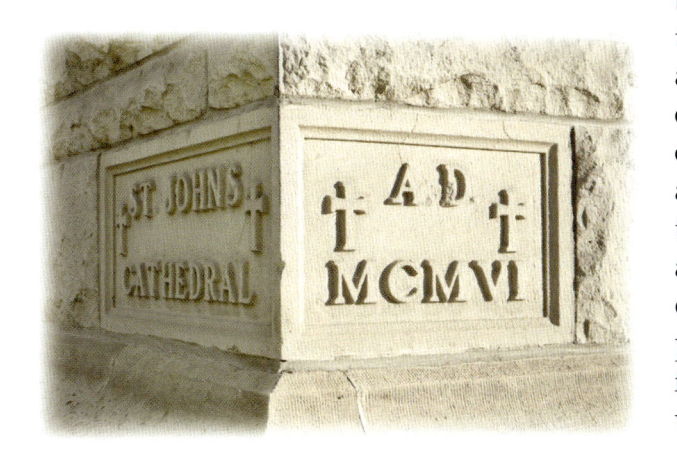

Although it is not obvious at a quick look, the façade of the Cathedral of St. John's offers a theological, religious message before you ever step inside. The front of the church is replete with circles, or at a minimum, half circles. A circle is, of course, unending and eternal and these circles, before we ever enter the church, are a reminder to us all that eternity is the goal. Circles and windows in arches are also a significant, defining element of Romanesque architecture. The most prominent feature on the church's main façade is a large, circular window. This window must be viewed from the inside to be properly appreciated, but don't underestimate its significance on the building's façade. The window shape and the arches on the front of the building are replicated by a carved design on each of the cathedral doors. The cathedral has three "main doors" in its eastern wall. In Romanesque design, churches with three doors are typical and a reminder of the belief in the Holy Trinity: Father, Son, and Holy Spirit.

As you approach and open the doors, you are literally face to face with those eternal circles. The doors to the cathedral are actually of fairly recent design. The original doors installed in 1921 were plain wood. The carved doors were installed in 1973 as part of a major renovation, which also saw the installation of the elevator in the south tower. While new doors were installed, the original hardware was used. The hinges for the doors are not simple hinges, but actually contain ball bearings, to facilitate the opening and closing of the massive doors.

As you enter through the main doors, you are not in the church itself but in a commodious vestibule, or narthex. Narthex—this is one of those delightfully muddled terms which so enrich, or perhaps confuse, Catholic terminology. It is, by any commonly accepted usage, a vestibule; but, like Latin as a language of prayer, narthex as a name persists in the Catholic church.

The word itself is a Latin derivation of a Greek term which described the giant fennel plant. It was the stalk of a narthex which Prometheus used to carry fire to mankind. Prometheus, in bringing fire to man, was not simply bringing another tool. He was bringing the essential source of power in the universe, and the control of it to humans. To all other creatures on the earth, fire is only a feared and destructive force. To humans alone is it a tool to be wielded. The control of fire was the beginning of knowledge. Given this interpretation, narthex, as a term to describe the entrance to a church, is very appropriate. It is in a church that we hope to acquire the knowledge which will serve us *beyond* this life. When first applied to church architecture, narthex referred to a porch on the *west* end of a church. (Remember all early Christian churches were built facing the east.) It was through *this* entrance that the catechumens were required to enter, and they were restricted to this area, behind an elaborate screen until they were baptized and admitted to full membership in the sacred mysteries. The narthex at St. John's is, notably, on the *east* end of the building.

At St. John's Cathedral, the narthex is a place of greeting, welcoming, and assemblage. It is an expansive space of approximately 15 feet by 45 feet. It has to be noted that the present narthex, at best an appurtenance of St. John's Cathedral, is more than *three times* the size of the O'Farrell cabin, where Mass was first said in 1863. By the standards of recently built Catholic churches, St. John's narthex is a small space. The narthex is sparsely decorated, but immediately on stepping into it, if you look down you will realize that this is not just another utilitarian space. The floors are the same rich marble as in the main area of the church. This marble was quarried near Knoxville, Tennessee. Tennessee marble, at that time, was shipped all over the United States and used in everything from churches to the U.S. Capitol.

Look up and you will see arching ceilings and a decorative cornice, where wall and ceiling meet. The molding is embellished with a cast plaster design of zigzags, chevrons, and acanthus leaves. Acanthus leaves are one of the most ancient decorations in architecture, first appearing on Corinthian columns as early as 450–420 BC. If you follow that protruding cornice along the wall to one of the doors and outside, you will find that on the exterior the cornice is plain, without decoration. The design on the inside was originally meant to continue, with carving on the outside stones. Interior plaster casting, though, is relatively cheap, while exterior carving on sandstone would be fairly expensive. The outside carving was never done, for budgetary reasons. The color scheme of the interior decorations, primarily soft reds and apple green, begin here in the narthex and are carried through the rest of the interior. Those red and green borders are still brilliant after 100 years. The highest quality paint was applied at installation, and while it was cleaned in the 1978 renovation, it has never had to be repainted.

The only strictly religious appointments in the narthex at St. John's are portraits on either side of the main door to the church proper: Christ, as the Divine Mercy, on the left, and Our Lady of Guadalupe on the right. Both of the paintings were done by a Polish artist, Janusz Antosz. Now pretty much taken as an integral part of the narthex's decoration, they are an excellent illustration of the premise, previously stated, that the cathedral and its artwork will never be finished. They were the gifts of an anonymous donor in the very early years of the 21st century. When carefully considered, these two paintings are each a reminder of the dynamic and changing character of St. John's Cathedral.

The representation of Christ as the Divine Mercy is a very recent development in Catholic art. The original of this painting was done by Eugene Kazimierowski, based on a dictation given to him of a vision experienced by a polish nun, Sister Faustina (Helen Kowalska), now Saint Mother Faustina. Saint Faustina, who died in 1938, explained the representation:

> *From the opening of the garment at the breast there came forth two large rays, one red and the other pale... the pale ray stands for the Water which makes the soul righteous; the red ray stands for the Blood which is the life of souls."*

As a "downtown" parish, and in a city with a growing population of homeless people, the Divine Mercy picture is a reminder to us before we ever get into the church that Christ reminded us that we are "to be merciful, just as your Father is merciful."

The other representation in the narthex is Our Lady of Guadalupe. This picture, hung at the same time is, unlike the Divine Mercy, one of the more ancient of all of the devotionals in the Catholic Church. The image of our Lady of Guadalupe has been around since 1531. Our Lady of Guadalupe is, of course, the iconic representation of Mexican Catholicism, and Mexican, Central American, and South American parishioners have in recent years made their presence decidedly known in the Cathedral parish.

It comes as a surprise to most American Catholics when they are told that of all of the "approved" Marian apparitions (there are actually nine of them), Guadalupe is the oldest by hundreds of years. The story of our Lady of Guadalupe is essentially as follows.

The Spanish had solidified their conquest of Mexico in 1521, with the destruction of ancient Aztec temples, including one dedicated to the Mother Goddess *Tonantzin* on the hill known as *Tepeyac* outside Mexico City. Ten years later, on December 9th, 1531, an Indian peasant named Juan Diego (his native name is given as Cuahtlatoazin) was on his way to Mass. As he passed Tepeyac, he heard music and a woman's voice calling him to the top of the hill. There he saw a beautiful young Indian woman, dressed as an Aztec princess. She identified herself as the "Mother of God," and asked that a church be built there to honor her. Juan presented himself to Archbishop Zumarraga in Mexico City and relayed the message. The bishop was skeptical and asked for proof of the apparition.

Returning the next day to the hilltop, Juan Diego was startled to find a profusion of roses growing in the dead of winter. (Tepeyac is approximately 8,000 feet in elevation.) He gathered the roses into his cloak and took them to the archbishop. When he opened his cloak to show the roses to the bishop, both of them were startled to see the brilliant image of the lady imprinted on it.

That cloak and its image, the iconic Our Lady of Guadalupe, are now on display in an elaborate basilica on the hill outside Mexico City. Several scientific examinations have been unable to fully explain the pigments and the persistent beauty of the image. After almost 500 years, the image appears unaffected by time and less than ideal conditions of exhibition. The frames holding the image have several times had to be replaced, but the image seems to suffer no degradation from the elements. Pope Pius XII, in 1945, proclaimed Our Lady of Guadalupe "Queen of Mexico and Empress of the Americas." In 1946, he added to her titles that of "Patroness of the Americas," but nowhere in North, Central, or

## Chapter 10

South America does *La Morenita* (the Little Brown Lady) enjoy the adulation accorded her in Mexico.

Off to the right of the narthex is a door which opens into a vesting area for the celebrants of the Mass. This was, in the original design of the church, the baptistery. Here, thousands of not just infants, but adult converts were brought into the Catholic Church. When the church was built, and until post Vatican II changes, baptisms were generally seen as simple family affairs held on some convenient afternoon. Baptisms now are performed in the main church, in a large font to the right rear of the main altar, either during or immediately following a Sunday Mass. In this way, the baptism is seen as a welcoming of the new child to the entire parish family, not just to the immediate biological family.

The original purpose of the now vesting room is manifest by looking at the decorations. The stained glass window on the north wall is the baptism of Christ, by John the Baptist. The window on the east wall is a guardian angel, traditionally assigned to Catholics at baptism, watching over two children as they approach a dangerous cliff. The ceiling is decorated with the same motifs used in the main cathedral, and dutiful cherubs watch over the proceedings from the corners. A careful examination of these cherubs gives a wonderful glimpse into the mind of the artist. There are hundreds of cherubs in the cathedral decorations. They generally have placid, neutral, angelic faces. The cherubs in the former baptistery, though, are clearly crying! They are not just crying, they are howling, as so many infants do when the cold waters of baptism are poured over their head. The sculptor of these cherubs had obviously been witness to a few baptisms, and in a bit of whimsy, he gave these infants a realistic countenance.

The repurposing of this room from baptistery to vesting room was another change brought about by Vatican II. Prior to Vatican II, the priest arrived to begin celebrating the Mass by almost mysteriously appearing from a side door in the sanctuary. It was an exercise in speculation when attending a new church to decide from which of several doors the priest and altar servers would glide in. From the right? Or from the left? Or most intriguing of all, in some churches from a door hidden behind the altar! Vatican II suggested that the priest and other Mass attendants (altar servers, deacons, lectors) should process in, from the back up to the main altar, so that all of the congregation could welcome them and join in the opening rites. The book of the "Word of God" is carried in, elevated for all to see. It may have escaped notice that the book is carried in with great ceremony, but never carried out. This
is not accidental. The Word of God is

processed in, proclaimed to the people, and then goes out with the people, to be further proclaimed.

When at the 1979 renovation this space was converted from a baptistery to a vesting area, it found itself as the area of repose for one of the confessionals which were taken out of the main church. In the original design of the church, there were four confessionals in the Cathedral: one in each of the transepts, and two in the back of the church, where the statues of St. Anthony and the Sacred Heart are today. In the renovation, all of the confessionals were removed from the main floor of the cathedral and new confessionals were constructed in the lower chapel area. In an attempt to retain a historic piece of carpentry from the original construction, the front of one of the confessionals was used to make the closets for the vestments which are in the vesting room. Also in the vesting room, on the counter along the east wall, is a large crucifix on a stand. This crucifix was part of the original altar set of candelabra and crucifix on the old main altar.

On the left hand side of the narthex, there is another door and two sets of stairs, one leading up to the choir loft and the bell tower, and the other down to a basement, which contains a kitchen, dining area, classrooms, and chapel.

# Chapter 11

## A Step Inside

The nave is the term applied to the main seating area of the church, along the center and side aisles. The term comes from the Latin word "*navis*," for ship. The logic of this term is not really obvious from inside the building, but if one should ever have the opportunity to view the cathedral from its attic the term makes absolute sense. Viewed from that perspective, the building resembles, without the slightest stretch of imagination, an upturned wooden ship with a central keel, curved hull, and radiating ribs.

**The nave of St. John's Cathedral, as viewed from above**
*(Photograph from the author's collection)*

When viewed from above, there is an entirely new perspective gained. The building, of sandstone and brick when viewed from the outside, presents an overall affect of strength and solidity. The superstructure above the nave, though, seems to be an impossibly fragile skeleton of steel, wood, and brick. There are no massive beams and buttresses here. A wooden arch is suspended from spidery steel trusses and wooden joists.

From the normal visitors' perspective, the nave is generally considered the area one steps into after crossing the narthex, or vestibule. It extends from the rear interior doors of the cathedral to the transepts, the two arms of the cross in a traditional cruciform church, which St. John's Cathedral is.

Stepping into the nave at St. John's and pausing to consider what is presented

## Chapter 11

can be a daunting experience. One is almost overwhelmed with the beauty of the art work which defines the cathedral. Where, and to which place, are the eyes pulled? The huge, stained glass windows, which in fact make up most of the vertical surfaces in the building? The marble floors? The soaring ceilings, with their rich decoration? The decorative moldings of cherubs, lions, and fanciful gargoyles? The beautiful marble altar in its arresting central location? The stark crucifix above the altar? The long, stained glass windows behind the altar, with the illuminating Holy Spirit window at the center? The senses are almost overwhelmed and, in fact, it will take more than one, quick visit to fully appreciate the beauty which surrounds you. Almost all of these artistic gems will be examined in some detail throughout this book.

The richness of the liturgical art which literally surrounds you is impossible to adequately describe, it takes several thoughtful considerations to fully appreciate. A few beginning reference points, though, are offered.

The first thing(s) you will encounter as you step through the door are the holy water fonts, one on either side of the center door. Every Catholic church has holy water fonts just inside its doors. They range from simple, metal attachments to the wall to ornate stone or marble towers. At St. John's they are tall, solid marble edifices, decorated with Celtic crosses. They are as old as the cathedral. They were installed at the dedication of the church and have been there ever since. At the very entrance of the church, before one is properly into the building, these fonts serve as an introduction to what has been described as the "sensuality" of Catholic practices. One is to dip the fingers into the holy water, and with it anoint the forehead, the breast, and the left and right shoulders (in that order), *"In the name of the Father, and of the Son, and of the Holy Spirit."* In a religion replete with signs and symbols, this is perhaps the most pervasive one. People who have never been inside a Catholic church have seen it hundreds of times, unfortunately quite often without a proper sense of reverence. At football games, baseball games, even boxing matches it is indiscriminately displayed as — a prayer? A supplication? A blessing? A superstitious talisman? As you enter a Catholic church, though, it is the defining separation from you and the outside world. It is a covering of yourself in the sacred. Now you are not just *in* a sacred space, but *enveloped* in sacredness.

To your right, against the rear wall, is that other "icon of Catholicism," a statue — a larger than life white marble rendering of St. Anthony of Padua. Anthony was a 12th Century Portuguese Franciscan.[a] He is perhaps best known as the patron saint of lost articles. Generations of Catholics, and undoubtedly quite a few non-Catholics, have invoked St. Anthony in finding everything from lost car keys to lost children. *"Tony, Tony, look around,*

---

[a] Although he was born in Portugal, Anthony died in Padua, Italy.

*something's lost and must be found."* Anthony was known for his concern for the poor. Thus he is shown with a loaf of bread in his outstretched right hand. This first of several statues in the cathedral is an object lesson on the importance of symbols in the Catholic religion. Anthony, and all of the Franciscans, were known for their love and concern for society's outcasts. In seeing this Franciscan friar offering bread to the poor, we are reminded of our own duties in that regard. Catholics do not worship or idolize statues. They use statues for the same reason one might maintain a picture of a loved grandparent: to remind us of the good qualities that person had, and to prompt us to try to emulate those qualities.

On his left arm, Anthony cradles the child Jesus. Anthony is almost always depicted holding the child Jesus. The reasons why are not entirely clear. Anthony certainly was not a contemporary of Jesus. He lived 1200 years after the death of Christ, and in fact, Church historians tell us that the image of him with the child Jesus did not become popular until the 17th century. One of the legends surrounding his life is that at one time, as Anthony was praying, Jesus, as a child, appeared to him. Often in these statues, the Christ child is depicted standing on the pages of an opened book of scripture. Anthony was an outstanding preacher, and one theory is that he is depicted with the Christ child standing on scripture as an allusion to the opening lines of John's Gospel. "In the beginning was the Word, and the Word was with God, and the Word was God." (John 1:1)

Whatever the origins of the custom, the depiction of Anthony with the child Jesus has given him yet another duty to perform. Anthony is also the patron saint of women wishing to become pregnant!

If you look at the stained glass window next to St. Anthony, you see yet another depiction of children. It is a rendering of the story where Jesus tells the disciples to "let the little children come unto me."

Turning away from Anthony and looking to the left side of the rear of the church is another, larger than life statue, this one of Jesus Christ in the embodiment as the Sacred Heart. This depiction of Jesus, with one arm extended and the other pointing to his breast, where a heart encircled with thorns is superimposed, was popularized in the late 17th century. Margaret Mary Alacoque was a nun who, much to the scorn of her superiors, claimed that Jesus had appeared to her, with his heart exposed, circled with a crown of thorns, and pierced. Sister Margaret Mary was sick at the time and presumed to be dying. The Mother Superior told her that she would believe in the visions if Margaret survived her illness. Of course, survive she did, and devotion to the "Sacred Heart" flourished.

This image of Christ, with a bleeding, wounded heart, is one which invites an answer to a common criticism of Catholic churches. "They are memorials to pain

*Chapter 11*

and suffering." Certainly "the Sacred Heart of Jesus," with its crown of thorns and pierced heart, is a stark portrayal. It is a reminder, though, to a fact which no Christian should dismiss. Jesus did suffer, a crown of thorns was one of the instruments of his pain, and he did die. It was for our sins that all of this occurred. The "Sacred Heart" in the back corner of the cathedral is not the last depiction of pain and suffering we will find in the cathedral.

The pedestals of the two statues are different. The one under the Sacred Heart is slightly more ornate than the one under St. Anthony. After repeatedly making the point that small items are of great significance in liturgical art, we have to make the record clear that there is no significance in these particular differences. The only reason for it would be the particular tastes of the donors who contributed the money for the statues. Persons making these kind of donations would generally be shown a catalogue of models to choose from. They would, at the same time, pick the pedestals they wanted the statue to stand on. The anonymous donor of the Sacred Heart statue simply picked a different pedestal than did the person who donated the St. Anthony statue.

A close examination of these two statues (as well as the statues of Mary and Joseph at the front of the church) reveals that they are not cast plaster, as are most statues today. These four statues are carved marble, and exquisitely carved marble at that. Fine details such as fingernails, the separate pages of a book, and the wounds on Christ's hands are very clear.

On the wall to the left of the statue of the Sacred Heart is another stained glass window depicting one of the well-known stories of Christ's life. Jesus is talking to a rich young man, who has come to him and said that he wants to become a disciple. Jesus tells him that if he truly wants to follow him he must give up all his earthly riches. A careful study of this picture very well imparts the story. Jesus is essentially in the center of his picture; to his left is the rich young man. We know he is rich or of royalty because he is well dressed, in purple and gold robes. Jesus is looking at the young man, but he is pointing to the right. Off to the right, almost unnoticed with a casual glance, are two bowed, cowering figures. These figures, unlike the rich young man, are dressed in very drab, unimpressive robes. Their faces are downcast and abject. They are the poor, perhaps beggars. Jesus is pointing to them and saying, *if you want to follow me, this is what you must become.* There is a decidedly skeptical look on the young man's face and we know "…*when the young man heard these words he went away sad, for he was a man of great wealth.*" (Matthew 19:22)

These two windows, Jesus and the Children, and Jesus and the Rich Young Man, are the first of 24 stained glass windows in the main area of St. John's. They are all exquisitely done pieces of art. True "stained glass" is not just painted glass. It is glass which has been given a particular color by adding certain metallic salts to the manufacturing process.

The windows at St. John's, aside from their compelling overall beauty, are particularly notable because of the amount of lead "cames" used in them. Many stained glass windows are just different colored glasses, fused together to form a scene. At St. John's, because of the liberal use of "cames" used to outline the figures, if all of the color was removed each window would still present an entirely recognizable line drawing of the scene depicted.

Stained glass items have been found as far back as the fourth century, but stained glass as liturgical art probably had its origins in the sixth or seventh century. The early 20th century is considered by many as the apogee of the development of stained glass, and Chicago as one of the most important centers of its production. The John Joseph Kinsella company, which was contracted for the stained glass windows in St. John's, was one of the premier stained glass artisans in the United States, often compared very favorably with Tiffany's. Their windows are found throughout the United States in churches and public buildings. Unfortunately, the John J. Kinsella Company, despite the high quality of their work, did not survive the Great Depression.

The windows were not, by any means, simply mass produced and replicated designs. The subject of each window was chosen by Bishop Gorman and the thought which went into the design of the windows can be seen in the two rear-most windows. All of the windows, including these two, extend almost the full height of the walls they are in and generally utilize their entire area to deliver their message. These two rear most windows, though, are effectively "cut in half" by the choir loft. Despite that, they lose nothing in the message they impart. Very conscious thought and planning went into that. The parable depicted in the scene is completely displayed to the viewer on the main floor. The artist accomplished this with the expedient of reducing in size, very slightly, the figures in the scene. Look carefully at these two windows and compare them with the two windows immediately in front of them. The human figures in these two are slightly smaller than those in all of the other windows. This is not obvious to the casual viewer, but a studied view of them will show this to be very much so. There was a definite realization on the part of the artist that just utilizing the lower half of the total space would not be enough. The scale of the scene had to be reduced as well.

We will examine each of the cathedral windows and its message in some detail as we proceed through the church. Looking at all of them, though, there is one feature they all share. In the lower third of each window, there is a series of plain glazed panels. Quite often, church windows have these panels, and most often they will contain a notation such as "*In Memory of ...*" or "*Donated by the... Family.*" There are no such inscriptions on the windows at St. John's. We know from other records that each of the windows, and most of the statues and artistic enhancement, were in fact paid for and donated by specific families or groups. We know the names of the people who paid for each one of the windows. The absence of their names on the windows, despite a panel obviously designed for such a purpose, was not an oversight, but a conscious decision on the part of Bishop Gorman.

The question of "naming" various features of a Catholic church after their donors is a controversial and questionable one. The position of the church has never been that listing a donor's name on a significant architectural feature (a window, a statue, an altar) imparts any claim of ownership to that feature. Unfortunately, that is not necessarily always the interpretation of the donor, or more problematically, the family of the donor. It is a rare pastor who would not have some horror story of complaints made by a family, many years after the original donor was dead, that "our window" is in need of repair; or worse, when renovations are needed that "our" memorial not be disturbed. In the early twentieth century, the custom of putting names on features of the church began to fall out of favor. It was felt that too often the name of a particular person or family on some part of the church gave an untoward sense of ownership. The church building belonged to all of the people, and no part of it should be claimed by any individual or individuals because they were in a position to donate more than others. Some "older" Catholics can remember pews with a family name on them, and woe betide the oblivious visitor who plunked himself down in a "someone's" pew. In fact, in its very early years St. John's did employ a system of "pew rents." The practice was discontinued in 1928:

> *We wish to state here that the pew rent system has been abolished in the Cathedral Parish..."*[30]

It is intriguing that this change was made while the cathedral was "between bishops." Bishop Gorman had died in June of 1927 and Bishop Kelly did not assume his office in Boise until March 8th, 1928. Father Verhoeven, the rector of St. John's, made the decision in January, 1928, to do away with what was viewed by many as an unseemly commercialization of the sacred. Thank you, Father Verhoeven.

In St. John's Cathedral, there are only two "named" features: the old high altar and the church bell, which has the names of eight parish members inscribed on it. In neither case are the names of the benefactors visible to the general congregation.

The bell in the south tower is an interesting study of not just St. John's history, but Catholic history in the United States. The south-facing side of the bell has an inscription: **McShane Bell Foundry, Henry McShane Co. Baltimore Maryland 1881**. Baltimore was, of course, in the 19th century, the seat of American Catholicism. Maryland had been founded as a Catholic colony. (Could anyone miss the implications of the name "*Maryland*?") A foundry with the name of McShane could not have been anything but a Catholic company, casting bells for Catholic churches, and very likely *only* Catholic churches.

On the north-facing side of the bell, though, are the truly historical inscriptions. First is **S. Joan. AP ET EV. Boise, Idaho, 1881**. This is Latin, abbreviated, for Saint John, Apostle and Evangelist. This, plus "Boise," tells us that the bell, cast in 1881, was specifically cast for our church. Many, many churches in the United States have bells which were recycled and repurposed from other uses. Brass bells, except for falls from a very great height or extremely intense fire—which, unfortunately, often come together in church buildings—are virtually indestructible. Many Catholic churches ring out their hours with bells that started out as train bells, town hall bells, or at best, bells from earlier, not necessarily Catholic, churches. Not so at St. Johns, since the cathedral we enjoy today wasn't finished until 1921, and we know that the bell in our tower came from the first St. John's Cathedral, which stood at the corner of 9th and Bannock, and which had been finished in 1876. As has been noted, that church was destroyed by fire in 1906, but its tower and its bell survived to continue to ring out our services over 100 years later, in a much more imposing structure. It is the oldest church bell in continuous use in Boise. An examination of the inscriptions on the other side of the bell gives a brief overview of early Boise history.

There are eight names inscribed on the bell: **O.P. JOHNSON, ROSANNA C. JOHNSON, KATIE JOHNSON, RICHARD TUCKER, JAMES HANITY, JAMES FLANAGAN, JULIA IVERS,** and **TIM DOWNEY**. These are some of Idaho's earliest and most notable citizens. **O.P. Johnson** was Orvil P. Johnson, who was born in North Carolina, and came to Idaho in 1869 from Tennessee. He was a cattle rancher and an investor in gold mines. Although he was one of the contributors to our bell, it seems as if he left the area shortly after St. John's was first built, and operated a ranch in the Hagerman Valley until, in 1908, he returned to Boise, and lived at 762 9th Street. He died in 1916. **Rosanna Johnson** was his wife. **Katie Johnson** was their daughter.

The next two names are **Richard Tucker** and **James Hanity**. There is nothing in any local historical records which tells us anything of these two men.

**James Flanagan** was a fellow investor in Idaho gold mining. He was involved in a lawsuit with Orvil Johnson in 1890 over the assessed value of one of Idaho's mines. Flanagan's unique historical footnote is that, despite the fact that he was obviously a member of the Cathedral parish and one of the donors of the bell, when he died in 1906, he was buried not in the Catholic cemetery on Morris Hill, but in the "Pioneer" cemetery, between Warm Springs and Jefferson Streets. Flanagan obviously wanted to be buried with his family, and three years before he died, his wife and two children died in a smallpox epidemic. For expediency's sake—and fear of that disease—they were buried in what was interestingly, at the time, the Masonic cemetery. Faithful Catholic Flanagan joined his family in that cemetery.

**Julia Ivers** had been born in Ireland and was a servant for the widow of William Morris, the developer of Morris Hill cemetery. For a servant to contribute to the casting of the bell must have been a substantial sacrifice. Ten years after the bell was cast, Julia Ivers married a James Collins, and disappeared from the records of Boise. **Timothy Downey** (Tim) was another Irish immigrant, who was only about 20 years old when he made his contribution towards the bell. The year before the bell was cast, Downey was actually working in the mines in Leadville, Colorado, and it is speculated that he had come to Idaho and established a business relationship with Johnson and Flanagan.[b] Descending from the bell tower (note that the bell tower is inaccessible to the public), we resume an examination of the interior of the church.

We are still in the extreme back of the church. In fact, we are under the choir loft and can't really see the full range of the walls and ceilings. Look up at the wood work and molding on the underside of the loft. It is a series of arches and molding, painted…interesting, but nothing spectacular. Now, take just one step out from the overhang of the choir loft. Turn around and look up at the lower edge of the loft. A row of gilded cherubs surrounded by leaves and grapes stares down at you. This is your first opportunity to view one of the cathedral's most striking features. An array of plaster cast angels, animals, and fanciful figures watch from every angle.

This decorative plaster work was contracted by Nick Blatt of Pocatello and Joseph Conradi. Conradi was a sculptor of some renown, who did plaster casting for churches all over the United States. He did the decorative work on several of Boise's historic buildings, including the pediment sculptures at Boise High School two blocks to the east of the cathedral. In contracting for the work on the cathedral, he formed a partnership with Mr. Blatt.

Cherubs and heavenly figures share their space in the cathedral with roaring lions and grotesque, perhaps demonic, figures: lions, and dragons, and diabolical faces. Although a lion is, in fact, the symbol of Mark the Evangelist, the lions in St. John's are not the regal animal usually depicted.

---
[b] Credit is given to Charles F. Hummel, who originally researched the information on the provenance of the bell and the names inscribed on it.

They are roaring, fearsome beasts with open, red mouths and prominent fangs, perhaps representing the lions who so famously killed the earliest Christians in the Coliseum.

Likewise, the two central pillars on each side of the nave are supported by red-eyed, bloody-mouthed creatures clawing at and biting each other's tails. People generally describe these decorations as "gargoyles," but in fact, a gargoyle is, by definition, an exterior embellishment found at the base of a rain gutter. "Dragon" is perhaps a better definition of the creatures depicted at the base of the cathedral's two central pillars. By whatever name, these creatures and their unexpected appearance in the otherwise somber surroundings of the cathedral's interior are a reminder that the cathedral, whatever else it may be, is a wonderful exemplar of period art. These type of embellishments have nothing to do with Catholicism or religion.

**Decorations below central pillars**
*(Photograph from the author's collection)*

When describing these particular artistic embellishments, it is perhaps most accurate to characterize them not so much as religious art, but simply as Romanesque. There is plenty of religious art in St. John's, but these are not examples of anything other than the fanciful wanderings of a medieval mind transported to the twentieth century. It is not an accident, though, that these monsters have been assigned the task of supporting the weight of the church's ceiling.

It is not just in three-dimensional decoration that the Romanesque elements of the church design is carried out. Bright colors are used with abandon. Wall and ceiling are joined by an apple green stripe, and lavender defines the base of the windows.

The painted decorations were done by the Claussen-Nehring Company of Salt Lake City. In addition to the Cathedral of St. John's, they were the primary decorators of the Owyhee Hotel and the Egyptian Theater in downtown Boise. Egyptian, Romanesque, Italianate, Oriental: decorators in that era had a catalogue of themed decorations which would be replicated for the customer on demand.

# Chapter 12

## *A Closer Look at the Nave*

Having just entered the main part of the cathedral, we are going to travel up the central aisle and consider some of the church's more striking artistic enhancements—its windows and its ceiling. In doing this, we are going to do a little more than just discuss the scene depicted. "*Nothing in liturgical art is accidental.*" The placement of one figure in relation to a group, the inclusion of a lamp, or a writing instrument, perhaps an animal, or a tool, water, fire: all of these everyday items, when included in a particular scene, have particular

*Page 89*

meaning. It must be kept in mind that early liturgical art, and right up through the Middle Ages, was meant to be viewed by a largely illiterate people. Illiterate perhaps, but not uncomprehending. They had grown up with a rich oral tradition of angels and demons, good rewarded and evil punished, and a God who showed himself in the everyday. Keep that perspective in mind. The art at St. John's Cathedral was created in the 20th century, but it is, almost without exception, art which originated in the 12th–15th centuries.

Before we examine the windows, though, take one more glance from under the choir loft to see two more mundane, almost forgotten, reminders of an earlier era. In the second pew from the back, on each side, there is a well-worn brass clip on the pillars supporting the loft. What is the purpose of these clips? Well, today, not much, except as a reminder of an earlier era.

When the cathedral was completed in 1921, all men wore hats or caps. Coming to church on a Sunday morning, one would be confronted with the problem of what to do with your hat on entering church. To leave it on the pew risked a flattened fedora in the constant sitting, kneeling, standing, sitting, kneeling, characteristic of Catholic liturgy of that era. Catholics of a certain age can remember when every pew, in every church, had across the back of the pew in front a series of these clips. The hat was clipped there at the beginning of Mass and stayed, safe and secure, until the final blessing. Fashions changed, hats went out of style, and the clips had no function other than something for small children to fiddle with. All of the clips were removed, save these two, which were left undisturbed by some renovator who had an obvious sense of history.

## The Windows

There are four of these on each side of the nave. (We are excluding the two

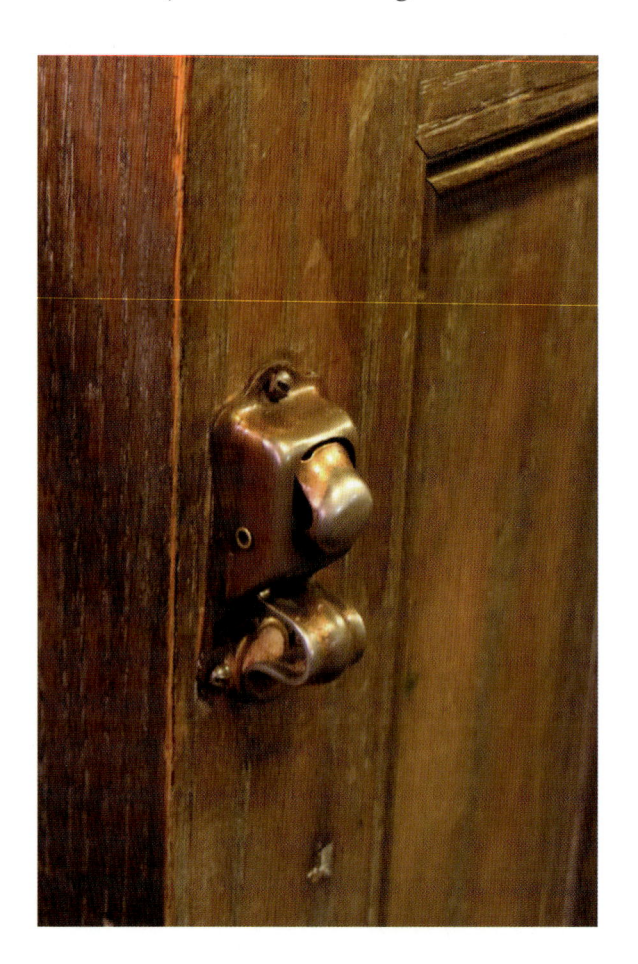

**Hat clip in the second pew from the back**
*(Photograph from the author's collection)*

*Chapter 12*

rearmost windows on each side. These we discussed while we were standing under the choir loft.) To visit these windows with the best sense of their significance, we will walk up the main aisle to the transepts and view them from the front right to the front left. Viewed in *this* order they are a logical progression of Christ's life on earth: the Annunciation, the Holy Family at Nazareth, the finding of the child Jesus in the temple, Jesus and the children, Jesus and the rich young man, Jesus gives the keys to the kingdom to Peter, the agony in the garden, and the Resurrection.

Once more looking to the right wall, we see the window portraying Christ's very first presence on earth. It is the Annunciation. Mary is shown on her knees, a position of both prayer and submission,

> *I am the handmaid of the Lord, said Mary, let what you have said be done to me." (Luke 1:38).*

The angel Gabriel hovers above her, and above him a dove, symbol of the Holy Spirit. When Mary questioned how she could be the mother of the Messiah, since she was a virgin, Gabriel told her

> *The Holy Spirit will come upon you…" (Luke 1:33).*

A blooming lily beside Mary signifies both the purity of Mary and the Christ child, at that moment growing within her.

**The Annunciation**
*(Photograph from the author's collection)*

The next window on the right is the Holy Family. Mary is spinning some wool. Joseph is doing some carpentry work, and the child Jesus is helping by bringing him some lumber. It is certainly not accidental that the artist, in creating this window, has placed the lumber on the child's shoulder in the form of a cross.

**The Holy Family**
*(Photograph from the author's collection)*

Of all of the windows in St. John's Cathedral, this is the one which perhaps gives its most startling impact when viewed not by itself, but in its surroundings. The window is just to the right of the sixth station: Veronica Wipes the Face of Jesus. Consider the portrayals of young Jesus in Nazareth, and the condemned Jesus in Jerusalem. They are disturbingly similar.

Continuing down the right side of the cathedral, we find another scene from Christ's life with his earthly parents, the finding of the child Jesus in the temple. This window depicts the scene described in Luke's gospel:

> *Three days later they found him, in the Temple, sitting among the doctors, listening to them and asking them questions, and all those who heard him were astounded at his intelligence." (Luke 2:49)*

Study carefully some of the elements of this scene. Mary and Joseph, relieved, a little concerned, and displaying looks that can only be described as "parents of a willful teenager" are in the background. Jesus, as an adolescent or young man, is in the most elevated position in the scene. At his feet are two of the "doctors." One of them is bearded, has an open book and a quill, and he is writing down Jesus' words. The other is an older man, by his face, and his closed book lies on the floor, for the time, forgotten. It has always been a tenet of Christian epistemology that Jesus came to give us a new law,

*Chapter 12*

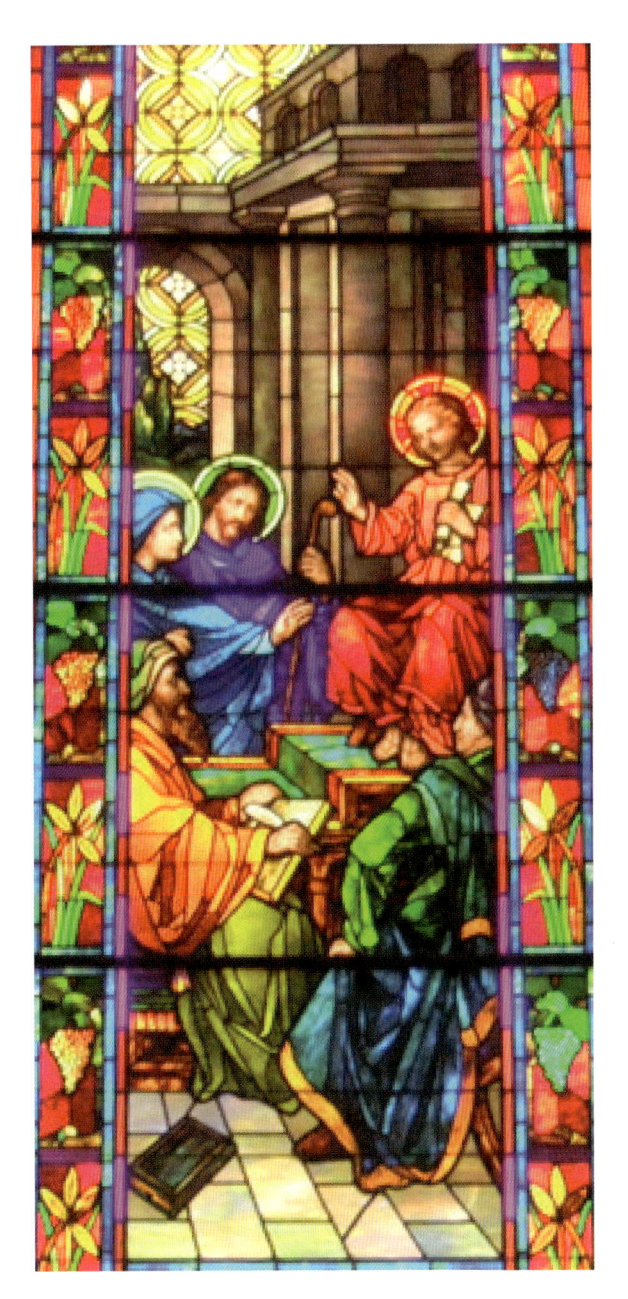

hair. Jesus, a youth, is in the position of authority and is giving instruction. The old law is lying on the floor. The new law is being conscientiously recorded.

The opposite window, on your left, is a depiction of Jesus giving Peter the keys to the kingdom of heaven.

In Catholic belief, this is the commissioning of Peter as the first pope. Lest anyone fail to get the message, there is a representation of St. Peter's Basilica, the seat of authority in the Catholic Church, on the rocks in the background. This is, of course, artistic license of the first order. St. Peter's Basilica was not built until approximately 1500 years after the death of Christ. St. Peter's Basilica, though, is included lest there be any doubt about origin of the "one true church." Certainly, a significant part of the indoctrination of every Catholic in the early 20th century was that it was the only church which could claim unbroken apostolic succession: from Christ, to Peter, to the current pope. Christ, holding the "keys to the kingdom," knows he is about to be executed and is handing on the authority of his church to Peter.

Again, the placing and the postures of the two figures is highly significant. Jesus, of course, is standing, in a position of superiority over Peter. Peter is on one knee, a position of genuflection, a symbol of vassalage, while the one hand on his chest is a sign of acceptance. He is at one time submitting to the authority of Christ, while accepting the authority given to

**The finding of the child Jesus in the temple**
*(Photograph by Michael Brown, reproduced with permission of the Diocese of Boise)*

not to abolish the old, but to give a new. This is what is depicted in this window. The "doctors" are old men, with gray

him. Jesus is preparing to give Peter his authority on earth, and Peter is prepared to receive it. As mentioned, St. Peter's Basilica looming in the background makes the overall message clear. This is the one, true church, founded by Christ.

Continuing forward along the left wall, we find in the next window another portrayal of Christ's final journey, the agony in the garden.

In the window, Christ is imploring an angel, who is offering him the fateful cup. In the foreground, three of the apostles are shown asleep. One of them has a sword, ready to hand, and we know that very shortly he will use it to cut off the ear of one of the servants of the high priest who comes to arrest Jesus.

> "At that, one of the followers of Jesus grasped his sword and drew it; he struck out at the high priest's servant and cut off his ear." (Matthew 26:51–52)

Finally, on the left wall, a window showing Christ's triumphant act over death, the Resurrection. It is Easter morning. Once more, the foreground is taken up with three sleeping figures, only now they are guards who were placed there to keep the disciples from stealing Christ's body. Jesus stands triumphant—in garments of white glory, holding a cross with a pennant attached—at the entrance to the tomb, while an angel kneels in the background.

## The Ceilings

Having viewed the windows along the nave of the cathedral, pause and look up at the ceilings. All of the ceilings at St. John's are decorated in colors and symbols. We will examine and discuss most of those symbols as we complete our tour of the interior, but before

**Peter receives the keys to the kingdom**
*(Photograph from the author's collection)*

discussing individual symbols there must be a discussion about the ceiling itself. The ceiling you see as you look up is not plaster, but canvas. Likely those "canvas ceilings" is one of the first things a new parishioner hears about at St. John's; they are unique, certainly in the city of Boise. Many people have been lead to believe that they are worshiping in a sort of internal tent, stretched under the slate roof. That is not the case. The ceilings of Saint John's are, in fact, conventional lath and plaster, applied to an arched wooden framework hanging from steel joists. Once that ceiling had been installed, though, wooden stretchers were attached, extending from that ceiling perhaps ¼ inch. Decorated canvas and insulating material was then attached to those stretchers. This is what you see when you look up at the ceilings.

This was a common form of decoration in churches and public buildings in the 19th century. The designs desired could be laid out, and in fact painted, without the egregious physical contortions Michelangelo had to endure in the Sistine Chapel. The key element of the ceiling installed, though, had to do with acoustical considerations. The architects realized that the cathedral was a cavernous space, full of hard surfaces. Sound in that space would undoubtedly be harsh and echoing. The canvas, with a sound absorbing insulation bonded to it, would be the perfect solution to the problem. And indeed it was. St. John's Cathedral is viewed by many as perhaps the most perfect place in Boise for a complex musical production. The Boise Symphony and Master Chorale has for many years chosen the cathedral as the site to perform their annual production of Handel's Messiah.

*Stone Wondrously Hewn*

# Chapter 13

## *The Transepts*

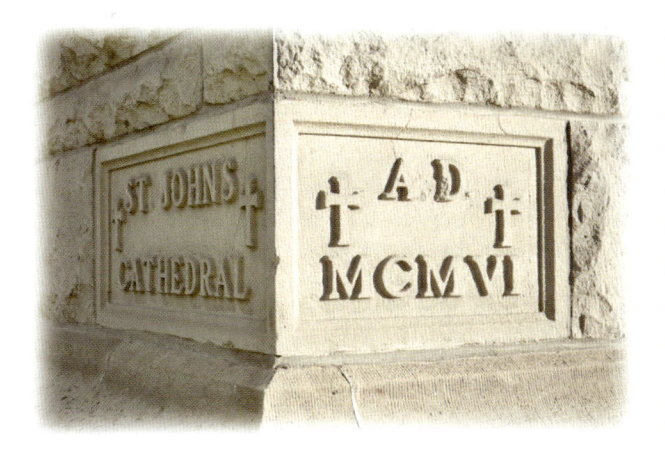

At St. John's, the transept is the area where, if one walked up the main aisle, one would have the first opportunity to turn to the right or the left without entering one of the pews. The transept forms the "arms" of the cross in a cruciform building, which St. John's is. Generally the transept is referred to as either the north transept (at St. John's the right-hand side), or the south transept (the left-hand side), but the transept is actually the entire area, from wall to wall, which crosses the front 1/3 of the church. Transept is an architectural and not a liturgical term.

It is in the transepts of St. John's that one can view two of the largest and most striking stained glass windows in the entire building. The north and south transept walls are each almost completely composed of a set of three stained glass windows, each of which depict a single scene: the visit of the Magi to the newborn infant Jesus in the north, and the Ascension into heaven on the south.

Traditionally, the visit of the Magi is cast as a visit to the manger in Bethlehem, where the child was born. Virtually every manger scene ever constructed, including the one St. John's has prominently displayed in its sanctuary during the Christmas season, has the three "wise men" visiting the infant Jesus in the humble place of his birth. A close examination of the Biblical record, though, suggests that the scene depicted in St. John's north transept is likely more historically accurate. The Magi are visiting the Christ child in very comfortable surroundings.

While both Matthew and Luke discuss Jesus's birth, Matthew is the only one who speaks of the birth of Jesus, of the threat Herod posed, and of the wise men. Matthew's version of the events gives some very good clues that the window in St. John's is a valid representation of the scene.

There is nothing in any of the Biblical accounts which suggests the Magi came to visit the Christ child at the time of, or shortly after, his birth. Matthew simply tells us that the Magi visited Herod in Jerusalem and asked where the newborn King of the Jews was. Herod was obviously distressed at the possible usurpation of his power. He called together his advisors and essentially asked them, *"What is this newborn King of the Jews business? Where is he?"* He was told by his advisors that the Christ child was born in Bethlehem. Herod told the Magi to go to Bethlehem with instructions to report to him when they found the child, with the duplicitous reason given so that he too might go to worship him. There is nothing, though, in the gospel to suggest that the Magi did as Herod asked. The Magi were not subject to Herod's rule or command. There is nothing to indicate that they went to Bethlehem. Instead we are told that after visiting Herod "they went on their way." The "star they had seen in the east, went ahead of them until it stopped over the place where the child was," and on coming to the house, "they saw the child with his mother Mary and they bowed down to worship him." We know that Mary and Joseph were observant and faithful Jews. Within 40 days of Jesus's birth, Mary would have presented herself at the temple in Jerusalem for her ritual purification (Luke 2:21-39). After that, they took up their life in Nazareth. This is the scene we see in the window. Mary, in a rather comfortable setting, with the child Jesus on her lap, Joseph in the background, and three well-dressed men offering their obeisance. On the ground at Mary's feet is a single red rose. Red roses, of course, are virtually a worldwide symbol of love:

*Chapter 13*

the love of God in giving his son to the earth, and the love of Mary in accepting this high honor. A rose, though, because of its thorns, can also be an instrument of pain. Certainly Mary, who would see her son tortured and executed, had to feel the pain of her love. An almost unnoticed, but highly significant, feature of this window is at the very top of the left-hand panel. The horizon in this panel is slightly lighter than in the other panels. A rising sun symbolizes the dawning of a new age, with the birth of the Christ child.

Herod, when he found out he had been outwitted by the Magi, was furious. When he didn't hear back from them about where the child was, he gave orders to kill all the male children in Bethlehem and its environs who were "under two years of age." This is another indirect suggestion that the Magi did not visit the Christ child on the night of his birth or anytime shortly thereafter. If that had been the case, Herod, when he didn't hear back from them, could have allayed his fears by killing all the males less than six months, or under a year. In fact, we do not know for sure where or when the Magi visited the Christ child, but the scene depicted in the north transept certainly has much to support it.

In Catholic tradition, the visit of the Magi is referred to as the Feast of the Epiphany, celebrated six weeks after Christmas. The Feast of the Epiphany is seen as significant because it is viewed as the first manifestation of Christ, and his saving message to the non-Jewish world. Christ was a Jew, born of Jewish parents, in Israel. The Magi came "from the east." Exactly where in "the east" is unknown. At the time of Jesus' birth, most of the area to the east of Israel until the borders of India and China was controlled by a (now, no longer existing) people known as Parthians. The Magi (our word magician derives from them) were astrologers, and powerful people in this area. They alone had the authority, through their divination of the stars, to pick kings for the Parthian empire. Thus, their pronouncements of fealty to the Christ child was a virtual anointing of him as a king. Not just the king of the Jews, but the king of the entire known civilized world at that time. The Christ child in Mary's lap is holding a globe, signifying his dominance over the entire world.

Looking above the Epiphany window to the ceiling decoration, there is one of several "monograms" in the cathedral. This monogram, "IHS" has been variously interpreted as everything from "I Have Suffered" (while there is continued scholarly debate about what language Jesus spoke, there is pretty general agreement that it *wasn't* English), to an abbreviation of the revelation given to Constantine at the Milvian Bridge (In Hoc Signo). IHS is neither of these prosaic interpretations; it is simply, after a long and complex orthography, the anglicized version of the Latin phrase *Iesus Hominem Salvatorum* (Jesus Savior of Mankind). Again, there is no "J" in the Latin alphabet.

*Stone Wondrously Hewn*

The visit of the Magi, while it is the dominant scene in the north transept, is not the only window of note there. To the left of that window, on the north wall, is a depiction of St. Alphonsus Ligouri. Alphonsus Ligouri was an 18th century priest, later bishop, who founded the Redemptorist order. Because of his extensive writings on moral theology, he is considered one of the "Doctors of the Church." St. Alphonsus is the patron saint of theologians and of vocations. The former, because of his writings on church doctrine and spiritual life; the latter, because he forsook a promising career in law to become a priest. As an aside, while the Catholic Church gives much "lip service" to the idea that "vocation" is an all-encompassing term including all walks and callings in life, the Catholic Church, when it speaks of "vocations," is almost always referring to a vocation to the religious life. Thus Alphonsus, when he spurned the law for the priesthood, was fulfilling the higher vocation.

Alphonsus was the patron saint of Alphonsus Glorieux, the bishop of Boise who first planned and began building the cathedral. It is clear, though, that it was not Bishop Glorieux, but his successor, Bishop Gorman, who picked St. Alphonsus as the subject of this window. The contract for the windows, which was signed in 1919, two years after the death of Bishop Glorieux, clearly shows that the subjects of the transept windows were to be "as may be selected by Bishop Gorman." It was Gorman, probably in recognition of the work of his predecessor, who included this not particularly well known saint in a very prominent spot in the Cathedral.

As one looks at the depiction of St. Alphonsus, it will be noted that his head does not seem to be properly sitting on his neck. It is almost as if someone had "Photoshopped" Alphonsus' head onto a body. It is actually an accurate portrayal of Ligouri. In his later years, he suffered from a crippling arthritis of his spine, which caused his head to bend so far forward that his chin created an open wound on his chest.

Nor was physical deformity the only pain he suffered. Alphonsus had the bad timing to form his order at about the same time that "orders" of priests were coming under extreme scrutiny by the Vatican. The Jesuits had been completely suppressed in 1773, and the Redemptorists were having trouble getting their rule approved. Some of his cohorts, in connivance with the King of Naples, changed the rule as he had approved it and presented it to him for his signature. Ligouri, at the time, was very ill and nearly blind. He signed the document, not realizing that he had been betrayed by the very order he had formed. This caused a breach in the Redemptorist order, which troubled him until the day he died, and which was not healed until after his death.

Turning 180 degrees from St. Alphonsus, another Doctor of the Church is memorialized in a stained glass window

*Chapter 13*

on the east wall of the transept, this one a woman: Saint Teresa of Avila.

Teresa is one of four women who have been accorded the title of Doctor of the Church. She shares this honor with another Teresa, of Lisieux, Hildegard of Bingen, and Catherine of Siena. Teresa is depicted in the window holding a book and a quill. This is a reminder to all viewing the window that she was literate, a rather significant accomplishment for a woman of the sixteenth century. In fact, a significant accomplishment for most people in the sixteenth century.

Teresa of Avila was a Spanish nun, a mystic and a reformer of Church practices. She is considered one of the greatest of Spanish religious reformers, "…perhaps the most impressive woman saint of all time."[31] Teresa endured a long period of scorn, repudiation, and outright persecution on the part of church authorities. She and her order were the subject of the unwelcome attentions of the Inquisition. She had a variety of serious health issues, ranging from headaches to malaria. Once she was so ill that she awoke from a four-day coma to discover that her grave had been dug.

Despite the physical and emotional travails of her life, Teresa is remembered as a positive and joyful person. She is famously quoted as once imploring,

> *God save me from gloomy saints."*

When her brother told her that he was about to embark on a spiritual exercise of contemplating the horrors of hell, Teresa's advice was simple and to the point, "Don't." Teresa is the patron saint of headache sufferers and of Spanish writers.

Teresa's death, when it came in 1582, has given her a singular footnote in not just church history but world history. Teresa died either in the very late night of October 4th, 1582, or the very early morning of October 14th, 1582. Why the ten-day confusion?

No one is quite sure if Teresa died before or after midnight, and October 4th, 1582 was the date when the change was made from the Julian calendar to the Gregorian calendar. To accommodate the new calendar and align it more closely with the earth's rotation around the sun, ten days were eliminated. In 1582, people in Europe went to sleep on October 4th, and awoke on October 14th. Those who find their biological clocks upset twice a year by the one-hour change occasioned by Daylight Savings Time should be thankful they were not alive in 1582.

Teresa is a saint perhaps most famous not for anything she ever did, but for the rendering a famous artist gave her. Lorenzo Bernini's *The Ecstasy of St. Teresa* is considered one of the most beautiful, and probably erotic, renderings ever of a woman transposed.

Before leaving the north transept there is one other feature which needs to be

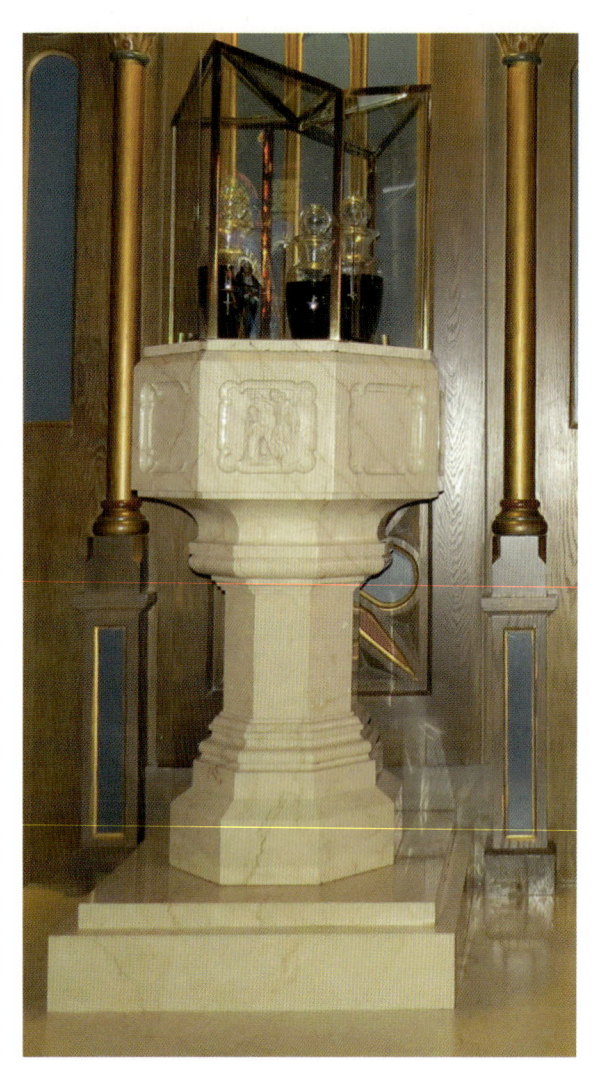

**Ambry**
*(Photograph from the author's collection)*

examined. The ambry is an ornate, glass cabinet, on top of a marble pedestal. Stored in the ambry are the sacred oils, which are used throughout the year in various anointing ceremonies to celebrate the sacraments of Baptism, Confirmation, Ordination, and the Anointing of the Sick. These oils, a combination of olive oil and balsam, are mixed and blessed once a year, and stored in the ambry. The marble pedestal which holds the ambry itself is the original baptismal font of St. John's, donated to the church when it was first built. The ornate wooden backdrop to the ambry was originally the backdrop to the bishop's chair when it sat on the left side of the altar. Prior to the 1979 renovation, these oils were kept in the sacristy, out of public view. The new location, in the main body of the church and utilizing elements from the old interior, is a good example of the efforts at St. John's to maintain as much of the old décor as possible while meeting the mandate to connect the people more with the liturgy. When it was repurposed as the setting for the ambry, three gold plates inscribed with the tree of life, the river of life, and the Holy Spirit were attached to the ambry.

Moving now to the south transept, we have the same pattern: a very large, three-panel window scene from Christ's life dominating the wall, and smaller renderings of other saints at right angles to it.

The visit of the Epiphany on the north wall depicts one of the very earliest events chronicled in Christ's life. The Ascension window on the south wall depicts Christ's final moments on earth.

Here we have the scene as Christ is ascending into heaven. The apostles (accurately, only eleven of them at this point—Judas had committed suicide on the night of the Last Supper) are standing transfixed and somewhat concerned, as the teacher who has guided them for three years, who forty days earlier had suffered a violent and cruel death, now finally leaves them.

Look carefully at the scene. The apostles are decidedly confused as to what is taking place. First, Jesus was crucified, which they really did not anticipate until the very final hours. Next, Jesus rises from the dead on Easter morning—which they certainly had not expected—and then he resumes his life with them. Now before their eyes, with no prior warning, he rises up into heaven. Confused, indeed.

We know that Jesus, many times, spoke in very general terms of returning to his heavenly Father, or to his Father's house. There is no record, though, that on this particular day he had prepared his disciples for what was to take place. In fact, only two of the four gospel writers refer to the event at all. Both Mark and Luke refer simply to the fact that he was "taken up" or "carried up" to heaven, with no discussion of the place, time, or circumstances. Luke, presumptively the author of the Acts of the Apostles, must have realized this lacuna because in the very second paragraph of the Acts he addresses it, although not much more satisfactorily.

> *Now, having met together they asked him. 'Lord has the time come? Are you going to restore the kingdom to Israel?' He replied, 'It is not for you to know times or dates, that the Father has decided by his own authority, but you will receive power when the Holy Spirit comes on you and then you will be my witnesses not only in Jerusalem but throughout Judaea and Samaria and indeed to the ends of the earth.*
>
> *As he said this he was lifted up while they looked on, and a cloud took him from their sight." (Acts 1:6-9)*

Next two angels appear and tell them to "snap out of it."

> *Men of Galilee," they said, "why do you stand here looking into the sky? This same Jesus, who has been taken from you into heaven, will come back in the same way you have seen him go into heaven." (Acts 1:11)*

There are, in fact, two angels depicted at the top of the Ascension window, but lest we jump to the too obvious conclusion that they represent these two angels, we simply have to look back to the north transept to realize that those same two angels are at the top of the Epiphany scene as well. They are simply artistic embellishments to frame the scene.

On the ceiling above this window there is another monogram, this one, the Alpha and Omega. Now the language is Greek, not Latin. Alpha and Omega are, respectively, the first and last letters in the Greek alphabet and their significance in Christian iconography is found in the Book of Revelations not once, but three times, as a reminder to us, from God, of his omnipotence.

> *I am the Alpha and the Omega, says the Lord God, the one who is, and who was and who is to come, the almighty." (Revelations 1:8, 21:6 and 22:13.)*

Continuing our examination of the windows in the south transept, to the left of the Ascension window we find another woman saint, somewhat less well known than Teresa of Avila: St. Rita of Cascia.

Rita was an Italian lady who lived from 1381 to 1457. She certainly suffered more than her share of travails during her life. She was married at age twelve to a rich and somewhat dissolute nobleman. We are told that she was still twelve when she had her first child.

Her husband, Paolo Mancini, was abusive, immoral, unfaithful, and kept very dubious company. He was killed in a vendetta, leaving her with two sons bent on avenging their father's death. Rita could not dissuade them from this path and so she prayed that her sons be taken in death, rather than commit the mortal sin of murder. Perhaps as an example of "be careful what you pray for," taken they were, both dying of dysentery within the year. Rita was now no longer a wife, nor a mother. She entered a convent to spend the rest of her life, and at the same time began to work tirelessly to reconcile the two feuding families before any more senseless deaths occurred. She was successful. The feud was ended, without further bloodshed, and Rita lived out her years in religious life. Rita is, for obvious reasons, the patron saint of abused women and sometimes invoked, along with St. Jude, for lost causes. Her selection for a spot in the cathedral's windows was undoubtedly due to the contributions, both fiscally and otherwise, which the Society of St. Rita made to the cathedral. The Society of St. Rita was founded in 1910. It is an organization of woman dedicated to peace and forgiveness. There was a very active chapter at St. John's when the cathedral was being built.

Rita's portrayal in the south transept is pretty much the standard portrayal one would find of this saint. She is shown in an Augustinian habit and contemplating a cross. Although Rita was an Augustinian nun, historical accuracy would have her not in the classical Augustinian black, but in a brown or beige habit, which was what was worn in her convent, the monastery of St. Mary Magdalene in Cascia, Italy.

Opposite the relatively unknown St. Rita, and somewhat obscured by the tabernacle and it's ornate *baldacchino*, is a saint *very* well known, not just in the Catholic Church, but throughout the world: St. Patrick, the patron saint of Ireland.

Patrick, in fact, was not Irish, but Scottish, and a member of the wealthy ruling Roman class. When he was sixteen, he was captured by pirates and taken to Ireland and put to work as a sheepherder.

*Chapter 13*

After six years he escaped; eventually he took up residence at a monastery in Tours, France, and became a priest. He was visited with frequent dreams suggesting he should return to Ireland and convert the people to Christianity. Patrick did, in fact, return to Ireland and did, in fact, convert the people. It is recorded that he explained the doctrine of the Holy Trinity to the skeptical Druids, the ruling religion in Ireland, by using the example of the shamrock, which was—and is—common throughout Ireland. "Just as three leaves can spring from one stem, three persons can spring from one God." Patrick's greatest claim to fame may be that once, when he invited the people to sit in a field and listen to his preaching, they were afraid to do so because of snakes. Patrick, we are told, thence drove the snakes not just out of that field but out of Ireland entirely. As a matter of fact, while there are poisonous snakes (*Viper berus*) in England, Scotland, and Wales, there are none in Ireland.

During the post Vatican II renovation of the cathedral, there were frequent complaints about "downgrading" various saints or icons. Statues were removed to less prominent locations, altars were eliminated, a stained glass window was added to the apse, but the only image which was really interfered with was Saint Patrick. A frontal view of him is not possible because of the tabernacle, and he can only be fully viewed from an angle. Patrick, with his placid demeanor, does not seem to mind; he is now, after all, the saint closest to the Blessed Sacrament.

A final feature of the south transept, in fact *the* defining feature of the south transept, is the tabernacle. The tabernacle itself is a square vault of burnished brass which sits beneath an ornate *baldacchino*. On renovation of the church in 1978-79 the tabernacle was moved from its spot in the center of the old altar to its present location. The ornate *baldacchino* which had been over the tabernacle on the old altar was moved, as well, to the new location. The pillars which support this *baldacchino* are Breche Violette marble, the most beautiful and expensive marble in the building.

The tabernacle in a Catholic church is, in fact, the "holy of holies." It is where, in Catholic belief, Christ literally resides. Probably the single most defining Catholic doctrine, and the one most troubling to many other Christian religions, is that of the "real presence." Catholics believe that at Mass, at the Consecration, the bread and wine is transubstantiated into the actual body and blood of Christ. It is not representative of Christ, it is not symbolic of Christ, it *is* Christ, in Peter's words, "the Son of the Living God." If that is actually Christ present, in the consecrated Host, it of course must be treated with the greatest of reverence, respect, and care. Consecrated Hosts which are not consumed at Mass are kept secured in the locked tabernacle until they are needed for reception by the sick or those who cannot attend Mass.

In front of the tabernacle, denoting an area of prayer, is a portion of the old "communion rail." This is another piece of beautiful marble, this time a base and top of Verona marble supported by columns of Skyros marble. Prior to the renovation, this rail extended all the way across the front of the church and separated the main body of the church from the sanctuary.

Suspended from the ceiling in front of the tabernacle is an ornate "sanctuary lamp," which is kept perpetually burning. Other candles in the church may be lit and extinguished and re-lit depending on the circumstances and the ceremony. The sanctuary lamp in front of the tabernacle is never allowed to go out whenever the Holy Eucharist is in the tabernacle. The tabernacle, prior to the changes of Vatican II, was almost always located at the very center of the high altar. Catholics who "genuflected," facing the altar before entering a pew, were paying obeisance to the presence of Christ in the tabernacle. That genuflection has become a somewhat confusing exercise now with the tabernacle generally no longer on the altar. Properly done, genuflecting should be done at least facing the tabernacle which now might be off to the left or right, or even, in some churches, somewhere off to the rear.

# Chapter 14

## *The Apse*

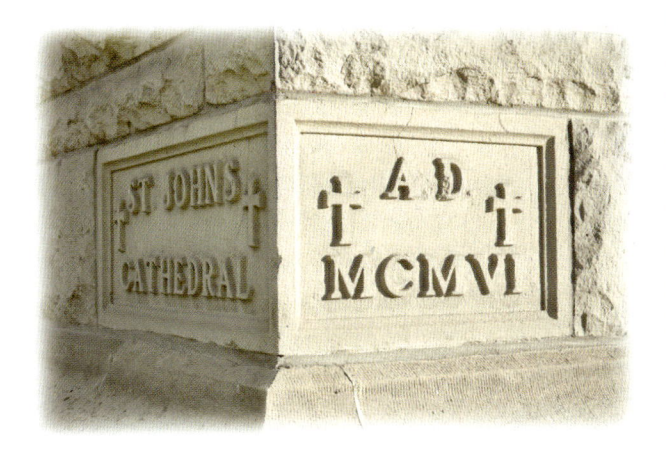

Still in the front of the church and to the rear of the altar is the apse. (Sounds distressingly similar to Cleopatra's *bete noir*.) Apse, not asp, is an architectural term describing a domed vault or arch above a space. Like many of the terms used in Catholic liturgy and architecture, it is of Latin derivation. In Rome a basilica was a public building where legal matters were resolved. The apse was that part of the building, at the front, where the judge sat. In the cathedral it is the location of the bishop's chair (cathedra) and the bishop is, of course, the ultimate judge of all things at issue in the diocese.

In St. John's Cathedral, the apse is the semi-circular area defined by the large arch decorated at the top with the intertwined letters for the Latin name *Maria*. Many people mistakenly refer to the entire area covered by the circular dome above the altar as the apse. If we were trying to fix the position of the altar at St. John's today, with reference to the overall structure of the building, it would best be referred to as "at the crossing" rather than "in the apse." The crossing is the central part of the area where the main aisle and the transepts intersect. The apse, though, is in fact a relatively narrow area covering the space behind the arch with the monogrammed *Maria* on it.

When the church was first built, the apse was immediately above the high altar, and defined the west end of the building. The old high altar was, and in fact still is, beneath the dome of the apse. Now, while the apse at St. John's still defines the west end of the building, and still encloses the old high altar, it is slightly to the rear of the main altar. The arch which sets off the apse is one the two largest "true arches" in the church. (The other is at the other end of the church over the choir loft.) These arches span a space of over 26 feet. The entire nave of the church appears to be a series of arches, but as we shall see, only the first and last of the arches, from either end, are true load bearing arches.

The arches which radiate to the back of the apse are seven in number. The seven arches above the apse are simply an architectural necessity. That is, seven arches were required to properly support the space designed. The decoration of those arches, though, give us a wonderful insight into the spiritual mindset of those who designed the church.

Catholicism is replete with numerical reminders of things spiritual. There are the three heavenly graces (faith, hope, and charity) and the four cardinal virtues (prudence, temperance, fortitude, and justice.) Seven, though, is the number most frequently recurring. There are seven sacraments, seven corporal works of mercy, seven spiritual works of mercy, seven deadly sins and, represented on the arches above St. John's apse, the seven gifts of the Holy Spirit (wisdom, understanding, counsel, knowledge, fortitude, piety, and fear of the Lord). Each arch is surmounted with a cartouche with a descending dove (the Holy Spirit), bringing gifts in the form of hosts. These are the gifts available in the reception of communion. The cartouche, in alternating panels, is surrounded with a garland of grapes, topped alternately with either a cross or a crown.

The singular most defining aspect of the apse is a series of stained glass windows which make up most of the upper west wall of the church. There are seven windows in this area. From left to right they are: St. Matthew, St. Mark, Jesus (in the personification of the Sacred Heart), a dove representing the Holy Spirit, Mary (in the personification of the Immaculate Heart), St. Luke, and St. John. All of these windows, except the central window,

*Chapter 14*

the dove representing the Holy Spirit, were installed at the completion of the church in 1921. The Holy Spirit window is a very recent addition; it was added in the renovation of 1978 and it does not take a detailed examination to arrive at the conclusion that the workmanship is not the same as the others. The church had originally been designed and built with that central window. On installing the original high altar, though, it became obvious that the towering reredos which was the backdrop to the altar would completely block that window. The opening was filled in with sandstone and painted to match the interior walls. In 1978, with the removal of the reredos, the space could finally accommodate a window as had been originally planned, and this was when the Holy Spirit window was installed.

Other than the stained glass windows, a significant feature of the apse is the old "high altar." This altar was installed when the church was completed in 1920–1921. For over fifty years, this altar was the centerpiece not just of the apse, but of the church itself, and the centerpiece of the altar was the tabernacle.

As will be discussed, one of the major elements of the renovation done in 1978 was the placement of the main altar in a more central location and the relocation of the tabernacle from a central spot on the altar to a position of honor to the left of the altar, in the south transept. The "high altar" installed when the church was completed in 1921 had been backed by a towering reredos of brick and marble. Once the decision was made to no longer use the high altar, it was also decided to remove the reredos which backed it, in order to uncover the window which had been essentially hidden for over 50 years. Since that window had never been visible to the congregation it was, until 1978, simply a bricked-up space.

When the altar had been relocated and the towering reredos removed, the space, which for seventy years had been bricked up, could finally accommodate a proper stained glass window. Very serious consideration was given to what should be the subject of that window. This would be, after all, the central window in the cathedral. It would be the window which now, all through the celebration of the Mass, would have the congregation's eyes on it. The changes to St. John's and the exposure of that window had all been prompted by Pope John XXIII's wish to "throw open the windows of the church and let the fresh air of the Spirit blow through." The design suddenly became obvious. The central window of the cathedral's apse now is surmounted by a dove, the symbol of the Holy Spirit radiating the light of faith to the people. In fact, at installation it radiated too much light. That wall has a western exposure and the sunlight coming through that window directly into the faces of the congregation was blinding! Shortly after the window was installed, a light dampening piece of glass was installed over the outside of it and the congregation could once more face the altar without an almost painful exposure to the Holy Spirit.

The other windows in the apse are representations of Jesus, in the personification of the Sacred Heart, to the left of the Holy Spirit, and Mary, as the Immaculate Heart of Mary, to the right. Completing the windows are each of the four evangelists: Matthew, Mark, Luke, and John. Exactly who is who, though, has been subject to some speculation. Traditionally, the evangelists are listed in the order their gospels are arranged in the New Testament—Matthew, Mark, Luke, and John. Thus, if one was viewing them from the congregation's perspective, the extreme left window would be Matthew, next to him Mark, then the Sacred Heart, then Mary, next to Mary, Luke, and on the extreme right, John. This assumption of the placement of the evangelists is not helped by the fact that the designer of the windows did not incorporate into them the symbols traditionally associated with the four writers of the Gospel. From the earliest Christian times, Matthew is identified with a depiction of a man, Mark, a lion, Luke, an ox, and John, an eagle. Almost all representations of these four will incorporate a depiction of their symbol somewhere in the scene. In fact, the statue of St. John at the apex of the front of the Cathedral has an eagle perched on his arm where he is holding a book, presumably his gospel.

The windows in the apse of the cathedral, though, do not have these convenient identifiers. They are simply four men in first century Roman dress. A careful study of some early historical records, though, does give some support to the idea that the four evangelists are, from the congregation's perspective, from left to right, Matthew, Mark, Luke, and John. The basis of this is a rough drawing uncovered in the diocesan archives which was meant to show what was planned for various windows, their costs, and who donated that money. In that drawing, only two of the evangelist windows are identified. They are, on the extreme left, St. Matthew, and on the extreme right St. John. We can fairly assume from this that next to Matthew is Mark and next to John is Luke.

The old high altar is a beautiful piece of Istrian marble flanked on either side with two tall columns of Verona marble, each topped with a funerary urn. This was a common 19th century decoration on memorials to fallen heroes and as has been mentioned, the altar at St. John's was dedicated to a fallen World War I hero. There are two more items of note in the apse. The *cathedra*, or bishop's chair, and the decorations on the walls.

At the top of the steps leading up to the altar, in the very center of the structure, is an ornate, high-backed chair. This is the *cathedra*, from whence every cathedral gets its name.

As has been discussed, any cathedral is, by definition, the seat of the bishop of the diocese. In every cathedral, a prominent

*Chapter 14*

piece of furnishing is the bishop's chair, or *cathedra*, (more properly a throne, an ornate, largely decorative piece of furniture). At St. John's, the *cathedra*, with an elaborate backdrop, had for years been placed against the left wall at the foot of the altar. Remember, the tabernacle had been at the center of the altar and was the focal point of the congregation. Once the tabernacle was moved to the left transept, the visual focal point was no longer the liturgical focal point. To "balance out" the rearrangement, and to accommodate a new baptismal font, the ambo which had been on the right was moved to the left side. An elaborate curving stair case leading up to the ambo disappeared in the move.

Hanging from the center point of the apse is a crucifix—a life-size rendering of Jesus on the cross. Criticism of the focus on Christ's crucifixion, rather than his resurrection, is a constant among non-Catholic believers. One cannot attend any ritual at the cathedral, be it baptism, wedding, funeral, or everyday Mass, without being transfixed by this image. As discomfiting as others find it, that is intentional. While the Catholic Church certainly gives full recognition and celebration to the resurrection of Christ, just look to the window to your left, it has never attempted to minimize or gloss over the horribleness of his death. This is not a transfixion of the macabre. It is a reminder to us of God's love for us, and ultimately, of the value of our souls. This is what he suffered for you!

The side walls of the apse are, in relation to the decorations throughout the church, somewhat restrained. They are covered in large part with what appears to be green and gold mosaic. They are not, in fact, mosaics but very exquisitely painted panels. The one on the left side is slightly brighter, or newer, than the other. When the cathedra, with its huge elaborate backdrop was removed, it was discovered that that wall had not been painted, except in the area above the top of the backdrop. It was now painted to match its opposite. This painting was done with real gold leaf and it is obvious that the one on the right was of lesser quality. The left wall is brighter not just because it is newer, but because it is of a higher quality material.

# Chapter 15

## *The Sanctuary*

In a pre-Vatican II Catholic church, the "sanctuary" of a Catholic church was pretty easily defined. It was the area behind the "communion rail" (altar rail), and topped with a perpetually burning "sanctuary lamp." Now, as mentioned, there is no communion rail, and the sanctuary lamp is off to the left. In the pre-Vatican II Church, ordinarily only the priest and the altar servers (in those days always boys) went into the sanctuary. As far forward as the congregation ever got was to the altar rail, where they kneeled to receive communion, distributed by a priest and an altar boy on the other side.

One of the most dramatic—and for many, traumatic—changes wrought after Vatican II was the elimination of the requirement to kneel at communion, and collaterally, a rail to kneel at. The once revered sanctuary was opened to the masses and became the domain of a variety of lay ministers, men, and women! The sanctuary, though, is still a definable part of a Catholic church and still an especially holy place.

> **The Sanctuary is the place where the altar stands, the Word of God is proclaimed, and the Priest, the Deacon, and other ministers exercise their functions."**[32]

The sanctuary, as the central point of all celebrations in the church, is meant to be richly decorated, yet simple enough so that nothing detracts from the mysteries being celebrated in it. The sanctuary at St. John's fulfills these requirements splendidly.

The primary object at eye level is a simple, yet beautiful, marble altar. This altar is Istrian and Breche Viollete marble from Italy. The top of the altar is a single piece of marble, cut specifically as the *mensa* for this altar when the renovation was done. The *mensa* is incised with five crosses representing the five wounds of Christ (feet, hands, and side.) Sealed in the base of the altar are the relics not just from the old "high" altar, but from the two side altars, all of which were decommissioned in 1978. The relics are remains "of the holy martyrs Prospera and Fulgentsus," as well as "particles of dirt from the tomb of St. John the Evangelist." In 1921, as the altar was being dedicated, the office of the Vatican had prepared a document dated May 6, 1921, authenticating these as the relics for St. John the Evangelist in Boise, and that document is still in the parish archives.[33] This new altar is comprised of the marble from two side altars which were originally installed in the Cathedral in 1921. It was constructed during the 1978 renovation by joining the two former side altars together.

There is a monogram "SJ" in the middle of the front panel of the altar, which is presumed to stand for St. John, and in fact, it now does as the main altar of St. John's Cathedral. It is actually, though, just a convenient use of the fact that the initials of St. John and St. Joseph are the same. When the church was finished in 1921, two side altars had been dedicated to St. Joseph and St. Mary. Each had an elaborate monogram in its front center panel. It was decided to use the front of the St. Joseph altar as the front of the new main altar. The front of the St. Mary's altar was used as the back. The two altars were joined to form one and the SJ monogram became the central item on the new altar. If you view the altar from the other side you will see a similarly intricate "SM" monogram on the back side.

The altar is, of course, the central point of all worship and celebration in a

*Chapter 15*

**Rear of main altar**
*(Photograph by Michael Brown, reproduced with permission of the Diocese of Boise)*

Catholic church. In almost all Protestant congregations, the central point from the perspective of those attending the service is the pulpit from whence the sermon is delivered. The message of that sermon is a primary reason why people go to church on Sunday. Quite often Protestant churches have a reader board outside the church announcing the topic of next Sunday's sermon, sort of a "coming attractions" in case someone was thinking of not going to church next Sunday. Not so in a Catholic church. The sermon (or homily) in a Catholic church is quite often a lamentably forgettable one, and too often, simply an irritating restatement of the gospel which was just read.

In a Catholic church, the core of the service is the Eucharist, the reenactment of Christ's Last Supper. The Eucharist is celebrated not just on Sunday, but every day of the week. The altar is where that celebration takes place, and the altar is where the peoples' attention is (or should be) focused. The altar is not just a piece of furniture or a utilitarian object. The altar—its form, substance, and use—is strictly regulated by canon law.

> *The altar on which is effected the Sacrifice of the Cross made present under sacramental signs, is also the table of the Lord to which the People of God is convoked to participate in the Mass, and it is also the center of the thanksgiving that is accomplished through the Eucharist."*[34]

A Catholic Mass can be celebrated in almost any surroundings and circumstances. Mass today is celebrated on the hood of a Humvee or a rock in the desert, or most recently, and perhaps most famously, on an altar formed of snow and ice on a blocked highway.

In a formal church building, though, the altar is subject to a variety of requirements.

> *The altar should be built separate from the wall, in such a way that it is possible to walk around it easily and that Mass can be celebrated at it facing the people, which is desirable whenever possible. Moreover, the altar should occupy a place where it is truly the center toward which the attention of the whole congregation of the faithful naturally turns. The altar should usually be fixed and dedicated."*[35]

The altar of St. John's Cathedral certainly meets all of the requirements for centrality, permanence, and beauty.

The other major device in the sanctuary is the ambo. The *ambo*, not to be confused with the *ambry*, is the platform from whence the gospel and the epistle are proclaimed and where one of those too often-lamentable sermons is preached. It is commonly called the pulpit. The altar and the ambo are expected to have a "harmonious and close relationship" to one another. The relationship between the ambo and the altar at St. John's couldn't be closer. They are both original material from the church, as it was originally constructed. It was marble from the two side altars which built the new altar, and the ambo, with only slight modifications, was moved from the right-hand side of the old altar to the left-hand side, but still within the sanctuary. Carefully preserved in moving the ambo was the only piece of true mosaic art in the cathedral. A mosaic of St. John the Evangelist graces the front of the platform from whence the Word of God is proclaimed.

# Chapter 16

## *A Plan to Renovate the Cathedral*

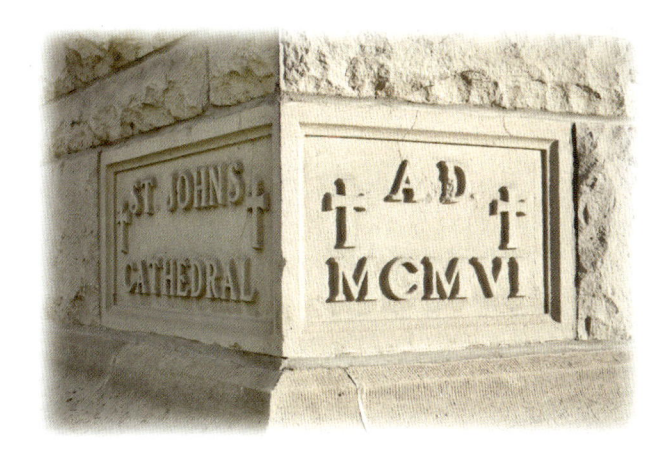

All great buildings are more than just bricks and mortar. They are the history and the emotions of the people who build them, the times which enfold them, and changes which assault them. All of these elements came together at a particularly turbulent time for St. John's Cathedral in the late 1970's.

All of this was prompted by the Second Vatican Council, generally referred to as Vatican II. Vatican II was certainly the watershed event for the Catholic Church in the 20th century. The Council was a more than three-year process under two popes. It began under Pope John XXIII on October 11th, 1962, and concluded under Pope Paul VI on December 8th, 1965. Half a century later its deliberations, decisions, and promulgations are still polemic in the Catholic Church.

What the prelates of Vatican II did, said, decreed, and intended is still being vigorously argued at all levels of the church, from St. Peter's Basilica in Rome to local parish churches. It has been said of Vatican II's documents what has been said of James Joyce's *Ulysses* "More people have talked about it than have ever read it." For our purposes, though, we are going to discuss only one of those pronouncements. The very first of multiple decrees of Vatican II was the Constitution on the Sacred Liturgy, *Sacrosanctum Concilium*. That pronouncement, by design or otherwise, brought about sweeping changes in that central element of Catholic worship, the Mass.

There is a certain misperception, in fact almost universal, among Catholics today that Vatican II directed that the priest's orientation during Mass be *ad populm*—"towards the people." At the risk of fanning the flames of a controversy which was ignited almost as soon as the Council closed and which continues to smolder today, it must be stated that **no document, nor pronouncement of Vatican II nor of any subsequent Vatican authority contained such a mandate**. What *Sacrosanctum Concilium* tried to do was remove the "mystery of the Mass," which had prevailed since the Council of Trent. The norm for celebrating the Mass in 1963 was essentially a norm adopted in the mid-16th century. (The Council of Trent was held between 1545 and 1563.) Thus, certainly in 1963, the institutional memory of every living Catholic was a Mass with prayers said in Latin, by a priest with his back to the people; and responses in Latin, by the altar boys, likewise with their backs to the people. The people in the congregation were, at best, mute spectators, who if they wanted to "follow along" could refer to a Missal with Latin on the left pages, and an English translation on the right pages. The congregation's participation was limited to silently reading the prayers the priest was saying. *Sacrosanctum Concilium* decided to address this situation and did so with the following statement:

> **Liturgical services are not private functions, but celebrations belonging to the Church, which is the 'sacrament of unity,' namely the holy people united and ordered under their bishops"..."To promote active participation, the people should be encouraged to take part by means of acclamations, responses, psalmody, antiphons and songs as well as by actions, gestures, and bearing."**[36]

When examined carefully, that is a tall order which would be difficult to implement with the priest hunched over the altar, with his back to the people, and praying in a dead tongue. To further muddy those murky waters, it would be a rare Catholic church which takes its direction from official documents issued by the Vatican. The controlling authority of every Catholic diocese is the ordinary (bishop) of that diocese. Even bishops don't wade through hundreds of pages of documents couched in archaic Latin to arrive at directions for their flocks. For this, they employ a variety of collegial resources, most often, synods and conferences of similarly situated bishops. It was a series of such meetings in the American Catholic Church, the United States Conference of Catholic Bishops, which led to changes in the General Instruction for the Roman Missal (GIRM), which is the controlling document for things liturgical and ritual. As has been mentioned, the GIRM contains the statement: "The altar should be built separate from the wall, in such a way that it is possible to walk around it easily and that Mass can be celebrated at it facing the people, which is desirable wherever possible."[37] Where and how this statement came about is not significant to this work. What is significant is that once adopted by the bishop of a particular diocese, that becomes a mandate for that diocese. Thus, we come to one of the most significant events in the history of St. John's Cathedral, the 1978–1979 post-Vatican II renovation and rearrangement of the interior, including the altar, the sanctuary, and the nave of the cathedral.

Vatican II ended in December of 1965, and all through the late 1960's and early 1970's dramatic changes—some bad, some awful, and some good—were effected on the interiors of many Catholic churches. Not at St. John's, though. The pastor of St. John's at the time, Monsignor Nicholas Hughes, was faced with the same dilemma as Catholic priests throughout the world. In matters of liturgical environment, just what was it that Vatican II called for? To many, both priest and lay people, it seemed as if "change, for the sake of change" was the order of the day. This did not sit well in a faith which had essentially not changed its liturgical practices for four hundred years. It was not just the clergy which was confused in this matter. The lay people became engaged in the practices of their faith as never before. The positions of "old church," "new church," and truth to the ideals of the faith caused huge tumult throughout the Catholic world. Monsignor Hughes followed a path of caution. Without disturbing the existing high altar or any of the permanent structures in the church, he had an altar facing the people set up in the sanctuary, along with two ambos for preaching the epistles and gospels.

Monsignor Hughes was not prepared to order dramatic, permanent changes to the cathedral until it became clear what was being suggested. (Some might suggest that isn't clear even today, 50 years later.)

In 1974, Father Andrew Schumacher was assigned to replace Monsignor Hughes as the pastor of the Cathedral of St. John. Father Andrew had, for many years, been the campus chaplain at the

**Altar at St. John's, post-Vatican II but pre-renovation: Note the people kneeling at the communion rail.**
*(Reproduced with permission of the Idaho Catholic Register)*

University of Idaho in Moscow, Idaho. He had had the benefit of attending classes at the University of San Francisco for three summers. Those classes were specifically designed to discuss, in detail, the documents of Vatican II and most importantly, their interpretation. When he returned each fall to his church at the University of Idaho, the changes as he explained them were eagerly embraced by his mostly young parishioners.

As with so many other issues, the changes of Vatican II degenerated into an unfortunate "under 40 vs. over 40" debate.

At the University of Idaho, Father Schumacher oversaw the construction of a new church for the campus, the Church of St. Augustine. If St. John's Cathedral is a near perfect embodiment of a Neo Romanesque Church, St. Augustine's

*Chapter 16*

may be the near perfect embodiment of a "post-Vatican II Modern" church.

Father Schumacher may have been the perfect choice to bring these two disparate styles together at the Cathedral of St. John. He was a member of a long-time Idaho family, a family which has given multiple members to Catholic vocations. He had been a priest for 15 years. He was never going to be tagged as "an outside agitator." In all of his previous assignments, he was seen as an affable, capable, and well respected priest. Bishop Sylvester Treinan saw his appointment of Father Schumacher as the rector of the cathedral as the opportunity to effect some changes. As mentioned, there had been some tentative changes made, with the placement of a temporary altar at the front of the sanctuary, facing the people. Those changes, though, in Bishop Treinan's view, were not befitting to the beauty of the cathedral, nor to its position of the "mother church" in Idaho. In the letter he sent to Father Schumacher assigning him to the cathedral, Bishop Treinan specifically asked him to effect the renovation of the cathedral to bring it into conformity with the guidelines of Vatican II.

That simple charge was the beginning of one of the most tumultuous and emotional episodes in the long history of the cathedral. The Cathedral of St. John is fortunate that throughout this turmoil the calm and reasoned Father Schumacher was at the helm. Perhaps even more fortunate was the fact that Charles Hummel, an architect with a long—in fact life-long—history with St. John's was chosen as the chief architect of the project. Hummel, like Father Schumacher, was a native of Idaho, a lifelong resident of Boise, and member of St. John's parish. He had been baptized in the cathedral by Bishop Gorman, who had completed the structure. Perhaps most significantly, his grandfather, Charles Hummel, had been the architect who had designed the cathedral, and his father, Fredrick Hummel, was the architect who oversaw the completion of the interior work when the cathedral was finished in 1921. With Charles Hummel directing the renovation, the parishioners should have been assured that the history embedded in the building would not only be respected, but enhanced.

Despite an amazing degree of openness in the planning process, everyone involved with the project would, over the next several years, find themselves engaged in long and difficult discussions over what was planned. The question of remodeling the cathedral involved not just the parishioners of St. John's, but Catholics throughout Idaho, since the cathedral does, in fact, belong to the entire diocese. Perhaps most interesting was that a variety of non-Catholic public and private interests jumped into the fray. Esthetic and historical fears ran rampant. Totally unfounded rumors of what was planned for the renovation spread through the state. *They are going to destroy our cathedral! They are going to get rid of all the statues and stained glass windows! They are going to make it look like a big auditorium!* Probably all of the principals involved in the plan had expected some controversy; none of them, though, had anticipated the firestorm which erupted, before pencil was ever put to drafting paper. Father Schumacher, today, remembers the renovation project as the most difficult and challenging—but also most rewarding—time of his priesthood, which is now 55 years.

Father Schumacher was appointed to St. John's in June of 1974. He proceeded on the matter in a judicious, even cautious, fashion. It wasn't until 1977 that he began a series of meetings to plan the renovation. Committees were formed, not just in the cathedral, but in the diocese. A series of suggestions and proposals were brought forward, then rejected, modified, or accepted. Open, public meetings were held. Blueprints and drawings were shared.

No institution operates in a vacuum, and St. John's in 1978 was no different from any other institution. The changes brought to almost every aspect of Catholic liturgy following Vatican II had inflamed discourse among Catholics throughout the world, and certainly at St. John's. Changes in form of worship, changes in language of the liturgy, changes in music, even changes in physical posture, were debated and argued over. The discussions over changes to the cathedral—any changes—became a liberal vs. conservative, old Catholic vs. new Catholic, debate. Most interesting was the fact that not just various segments of the church family took positions, drew lines, and circulated petitions, large segments of the secular public got involved as well. At one point, acts of civil disobedience were considered. There was a plan to park vehicles on all the streets surrounding the cathedral so that workers and contractors would not be able to get their equipment in. Families, which 50 years ago had donated art work and sculpture to the cathedral, suddenly demanded the return of their donations.

It would be hard to underestimate the depth of the opposition to any change to the interior of the church. Letters to the Idaho Register were overwhelmingly opposed and were replete with phrases such as "a pack of lies," "a desecration," "horrendous," and of course, "tradition." The Idaho Statesman, a newspaper which no one would ever mistake as an apologist for the Catholic Church, ran one of its early articles on the issue with the caption under a front page picture, "Are Changes Necessary?"

Throughout all of this, Bishop Treinan remained a beacon of calm and reason. Treinan, in response to charges which were at least mean spirited, if not overtly libelous, counseled "patience, kindness, and charity." When all was said and done, it was Bishop Treinan who would make the final decision and he who would bear the final responsibility. He was very clear on that. Finally, necessary or not, changes were ordered, if not by the pope, by the bishop.

## Chapter 16

> "There is no painless way to reach these decisions." (Bishop) Treinen said. "Just remember that it is possible to get wrapped up emotionally in these questions. Anything we do should be done charitably and prayerfully."[38]

A committee, representing every segment of the St. John's parish family, both consecrated and lay, was formed in May of 1977. After 18 meetings over the course of a year, all of them open to whomever wanted to attend, they released a 34-page report and recommendations. A study of this document, preserved in the parish archives, is a study in just how conscientiously the committee approached this delicate task. The key recommendations of the committee were:

1. The erection of a new permanent altar at the crossing of the nave and transept.
2. Arrange seating for the congregation around three sides of the altar.
3. Relocation of the pulpit to a position nearer to the altar.
4. Establishment of a Eucharistic chapel with the tabernacle in the south transept.
5. Moving the cathedra to a central position facing the people.
6. Establish a baptismal font near the sanctuary area.
7. Establish a repository for the holy oil vessels near the baptismal font and sanctuary.

The committee, in its report and recommendation, went to great lengths to stress that in their considerations they had considered not just the new requirements for the celebration of the liturgy, but "the preservation of the established architectural style and of familiar artistic elements."[39]

The seriousness of the task they were undertaking—and their realization of that—can be gathered by the fact that the committee decided to hire as a consultant the firm of E. Rambush Associates from New York. Robert Rambush, a veteran of the Second World War, returned to France in 1947 and for several years studied in a program at the Center for Sacred Art in Paris. The program emphasized that art which is intended to be in a place of worship must relate to the spirituality of the place, must be part of the whole, and must be the visible face of the church. It also must invite the congregation to "open his or her own inner space in a quiet attitude." These were some of the guiding principles which were applied to the renovation of St. John's.

The relocation of the main altar and the movement of the pulpit, it was recognized from the outset, would be controversial to a parish which had, over the past 50 years, become very used to the original design. Actually, the movement of the pulpit took one of the original elements of the original church and placed it in a more prominent position. The pulpit which had been built on the right hand side of the altar had not been used since a forward facing altar and ambo had been placed in the sanctuary as an accommodation to the changes of Vatican II ten years earlier. Its new location restored this original feature of the church to a position of prominence.

Recommendation #4, the establishment of a Eucharistic "chapel" in the south transept was a difficult one for the parish to get its arms around. There was never any serious consideration of a separate chapel with a wall between it and the main body of the church, but that became the rumor. Obviously, if such a chapel was constructed it would have done serious violence to the original design and to one of the cathedral's major artistic enhancements, the Resurrection Window.

The original plan proposed for this area involved "setting it off" from the church body proper with a device of three, large hanging lamps suspended from the arch which defines the south end of the transept. This idea, originally proposed by Mr. Rambush, who had the unfortunate distinction of being from New York, was rejected out of hand by members of the parish as preposterous because "who had ever heard of three sanctuary lamps." The committee now saw an interesting reversal of roles between the "traditionalists" and "progressives" wresting for dominance on the idea of how the church should be redone. It was the "traditionalists" who rejected the idea of three sanctuary lamps. When it was pointed out to them that the Ceremonial Guidance in use at the time suggested that "…more than one light should burn before the altar of the Blessed Sacrament, but always in uneven numbers, i.e. three, five, seven, or more," (Caerem. Episc. (1, xii. 17) their objections took on a decidedly more muted tone. This simple matter, the question of a sanctuary lamp, which every Catholic of that generation took as a defining element of a Catholic church, illustrated the concept that when one speaks of "tradition" one has to be very clear on what tradition itself means. Does it mean "what I remember" or the last forty years, or the last four hundred years? Finally, in September of 1978—after three years of discussions, but with all of the objections by no means disposed of—it was announced that funds would be raised and a renovation would begin.

"There will be no change, just for the sake of change," Treinen said. "Personally, I could get along without doing anything. But the church has spoken to us and I have to be guided by some basic principles given by the church or dictated by sound reasoning. At any rate, only a very small percentage of the building and its furnishings were proposed for rearrangement. St. John's is a parish church and should be made to accommodate present day liturgy. It is not just a past memory. The restoration committee was highly motivated by a desire to follow the guidance of the church and at the same time the committee had an eye to preserving historical integrity."[40]

The "restoration committee" referred to was a group of parishioners, liturgical and

*Chapter 16*

architectural consultants, and the pastor. Over six months later, in April of 1979, Father Schumacher announced that the cathedral would be closed at the end of the last Mass on Easter Sunday. Services from that date would be held, once more, in the basement portion of the church, where they had begun almost seventy years earlier, until all of the renovation and repairs were completed.

# Chapter 17

## The Renovation

Lost in the emotionalism, and indeed sensationalism, which surrounded the renovation of the cathedral was the fact that it was a 70 year old building showing its age. Before considering renovation, repair had to be addressed. Aside from questions of altar placement and priestly orientation, there were serious maintenance problems. Years of heating with coal had left the interior decorations covered in soot. The lighting and electrical systems were outdated. The stained glass windows were sagging and about to suffer serious permanent damage, and the roof needed substantial updating.

The restoration committee, while not unwilling to recommend some fairly dramatic changes, had also not failed to consider that maintenance and safety of the congregation was paramount. When asked to categorize priorities if such became necessary, the committee listed, in order of priority:

1. Repair the steps.
2. Repair the roof.
3. Upgrade the heating system.

Then, and only then, would the remodeling of the altar and seating arrangements take place. Fortunately, the parish and diocesan family responded vigorously to appeals for the work, and all of the recommended projects were undertaken.

From a historical/preservation perspective, one of the most challenging aspects of the interior work was the ceiling. The intricately decorated ceiling over the main area of St. John's is not, as most people assume, painted plaster. It is painted canvas over wooden stretchers which are affixed to a plaster ceiling. This was a technique somewhat common

**Cathedral ceiling**
*(Reproduced with permission of the Diocese of Boise)*

## Chapter 17

for large public buildings in the early 20th century when elaborate interior decorations were much more common. It was, unfortunately, in 1979 an art and a technique which had almost completely disappeared. Damage done to this historical treasure would be very hard to undo. The interior of the church had been cleaned almost 30 years earlier, in preparation for Bishop Kelly's Golden Jubilee. Another cleaning was now necessary. Fortunately, it was found when the grimed ceiling was closely examined that the quality of the original art work, and the paint used, was of the highest quality. The ceilings were cleaned with regular industrial cleaning solutions and no damage at all was done to the design.

The major aspect of the renovation itself, and the one which had generated the most controversy, was the sanctuary and altar. Prior to Vatican II, the sanctuary was easily identified as the area "behind the communion rail." It was an area generally reserved for priests and altar servers. During the service, the congregation never went into it and only rarely at other times. Communion rails, though, were an early victim of Vatican II. The "sanctuary" now is defined somewhat vaguely as "the space in the church for the high altar and the clergy."

The renovation committee had made the decision to move the main altar away from the back wall and out to an area where the congregation would sit, not just in front of it, but around it. The altar of the Cathedral of St. John was the touchstone for all of the concerns the people of the parish had about renovation. There were several reasons for this. One, it was a huge piece of beautiful marble. Two, it was rightly seen as the "holy of holies," the place where for a half a century the holiest of all Catholic services, the Mass, was celebrated in Boise. Three, the altar had a significant history in the lay life of the parish. While the cathedral was being built, it had been donated by the Regan family in honor of their son, Lieutenant John M. Regan, who had been killed in the First World War. To remove that altar would be to remove a memorial to a fallen hero.

The committee arrived at an innovative solution. The altar as a significant part of the church history stayed, but it was "demoted." It would no longer serve as the main altar. Further, its huge *reredos*, the decorative backdrop to the altar itself, would be removed. That *reredos* had, for some time, been obvious to the discerning viewer as an incongruous, rectangular artifice in the rounded Romanesque apse. Further, it was blocking the central window in the west wall of the cathedral.

The decision was made that while the altar would stay the *reredos* would go. Interestingly, on removal it was found not to be a monumental piece of marble, which had been the impression, but brick and straw, faced with marble. While the *reredos* was removed, the memorial to Lieutenant Regan was not disturbed. It can still be seen at the base of the tall column to the right of the old altar.

**Memorial to Lieutenant Regan**
*(Photograph from the author's collection)*

As originally installed, the old altar had five steps leading up to the platform where the priest stood to say Mass. After the renovation and the elimination of that altar as a place of worship, the top two steps were removed and a platform for the bishop's chair installed.

With the old altar disposed of, but not removed, the next task facing Mr. Hummel and the committee was the two side altars. It was a common feature of many Catholic churches that in addition to the high altar there would often be multiple side altars. There are very old churches that may have as many as ten or twelve side altars.[a] Those overseeing the renovation of St. John's cathedral only had two side altars to deal with, but like so many other things in this project they were fraught with history and emotion. They were altars dedicated to two of the Church's most towering saints: St. Mary, the earthly mother of Jesus, and St. Joseph, the foster father of Jesus. Any movement towards "downgrading" these two icons of traditional Catholic belief would be taken only at the risk of extreme distress. These altars, though, were impinging on the space planned for the new sanctuary and altar which was being planned.

Again, an innovative compromise was arrived at. The altars were removed, the statues remain. St. Joseph and St. Mary are in their original locations. The base of these two statues, which originally held the tabernacles of the two altars, contain some of the most intricate carving in the church. Mythical, demonic figures have for some reason been assigned the task of protecting the tabernacles.

**Carving surrounding tabernacle on Mary's altar**
*(Photograph from the author's collection)*

---

[a] In St. Peter's Basilica in Rome, there are forty-four side altars and eleven separate chapels!

*Chapter 17*

**The statues of Mary and Joseph, which remained in place after the removal of the side altars**
*(Photographs from the author's collection)*

While discussing frightful creatures and standing at Mary's statue, look carefully beneath her feet. A large fearsome serpent with an apple in his mouth is coiled there. The stained glass window of Mary to the right of the statue has the same, not so obvious, serpent. Non-Catholic visitors viewing images of Mary are often startled to find beneath her feet a fearsome looking serpent. This is a common Catholic depiction of Mary (do any non-Catholics depict Mary?) and is based on the interpretation of Mary as the "new Eve," and a verse in Genesis:

> *And the Lord God said to the serpent: 'Because thou hast done this thing, thou art cursed among all cattle, and beasts of the earth: upon thy breast shalt thou go, and earth shalt thou eat all the days of thy life. I will put enmities between thee and the woman, and between thy seed and her seed: she shall crush thy head, and thou shalt lie in wait for her heel'"* (Gen. 3:13–15)

The other two marble statues which were in the sanctuary, the Sacred Heart of Jesus and St. Anthony of Padua, were moved to the back of the church. The old altars, though, were not discarded. As has been discussed, the decision was made to use the old side altars to build a new main altar. If one looks at the main altar at St. John's today from the congregation's perspective, one is actually looking at the front of the former St. Joseph's altar, joined to the front of the former St. Mary's altar. It is beautifully done. Again, a wonderful example of the careful preservation of the old while emplacing the new. Other changes were made to the sanctuary. The communion rail was removed. The tabernacle was relocated from the center of the main altar to a position in the south transept. A new tabernacle was acquired at that time.

The relocation of the tabernacle in 1979 was one of the most contentious issues in what was a steady stream of issues in the renovation. If decommissioning an altar dedicated to a war hero caused outrage, there is no describing the emotions generated by the idea of moving "the repository of the real presence" off to a remote corner of the church. Actually, at St. John's there is nothing remote about the location chosen. The tabernacle was moved to a very prominent and obvious location at the left front of the church. The tabernacle in this location is visible from every seat in the church except, perhaps, the most extreme left seats in the very last pew on the left. Again, the renovators had great respect for the history and traditions they were addressing. The tabernacle at St. John's had always been crowned with an ornate *baldacchino*. The *baldacchino* was carefully dismantled, the tabernacle placed on marble remnants from the dismantled *reredos*, and the *baldacchino* placed over it. In front of the tabernacle is a section of the original communion rail which originally traversed the front one-third of the church.

Another major element of the renovation was the placement of the baptismal font to the right of the sanctuary. Previously

## Chapter 17

it had been located in its own room at the right rear of the church, actually not in the church, but in the *narthex* before one entered the church proper. The baptismal font was changed from a more or less traditional font on a pedestal to a pool with running water for baptisms. Catholics do not generally practice baptism by immersion (although that is an acceptable form of baptism) but the idea of a pool with running water was suggested by Mr. Rambush, the consultant to the renovation. He was struck by the prominence of water in the state's topography. Rivers, lakes, and reservoirs predominated and he suggested that the importance of water to the state should be represented in the state's "Mother" church.

The old baptismal font which had welcomed thousands of people in the church was not discarded. It became the base of the ambry in the north transept which holds the holy oils used in anointings and sacraments.

A good idea of the conscientiousness which the renovation committee applied to the process can be found in looking at just one small part of the renovation—the floor of the sanctuary. With the changes to the sanctuary, there was a need to re-do much of the sanctuary floor. The floor of the entire cathedral (with the exception of the areas underneath the pews) is not tile, but marble slabs. The quarry in Tennessee which had supplied the original marble was still there, but it had been closed for many years. A series of very involved, very patient phone calls and letters got the quarry temporarily reopened. Expert marble cutters and setters were hired and St. John's sanctuary was able to maintain its beautiful, original floor.

With all of these moves, a decision had to be made with reference to the bishop's *cathedra*. Prior to the renovation, that chair and an ornate backdrop for it had sat at the left hand side of the apse. Now with the relocation of the ambo, it would be behind, and obscured, by that structure. The decision was made to put the *cathedra* at the top of the platform created with the relocation of the altar. Once more, outrage was the order of the day. *"The bishop's chair is replacing the tabernacle!"* (For that to have been the case, the bishop's chair would have had to have been placed on top of—and in the middle of—the altar itself, certainly a sight which would have been worth seeing.) The elaborate backdrop to the bishop's chair, in the new location, would intrude on the high altar which was being retained. That backdrop was moved to frame the ambry in the north transept.

The criticism of this simple effort at symmetry was unbounded. Most outrageous of all was the charge that the bishop was placing himself in the central space, previously held for the Blessed Sacrament. In the cool light of 40 years later, likely no one would disagree that of the eight Catholic bishops Idaho has had, none was more simple, unpretentious, and unassuming than Sylvester W. Treinan, the fifth bishop and the one faced with the thankless task of upgrading his cathedral. Treinan once commented during this controversy that he would be fine just using a folding chair! In fact, his response to the furor was a perfect demonstration of his humility.

> *Because some people have expressed being scandalized at having the bishop's chair replace the central tabernacle, there shall be no chair for the bishop until such a time as it has been determined that this scandal has ceased."*[41]

The bishop's humble stance may have almost immediately caused critics to consider closely their objections and the "scandal" to cease. There is no record that there was ever any hiatus in the placement of the *cathedra* at the center rear of the altar.

There were many more upgrades and changes to the cathedral in this significant remodeling. They will be visited as we visit the various parts of the church. The intent of this chapter, though, has been to bring to readers some sense of the commitment and the emotions which very dedicated people on all sides of the question brought to the question of the future of their cathedral. *It is not just a church! It is our cathedral.* It is clear now that Father Schumacher and Charles Hummel very much kept that idea in mind. Earlier we referred to renovations done in response to Vatican II as "bad, awful, and good." The renovation of St. John's has, by almost all objective viewers, been elevated to a new category: excellent.

Perhaps the best indicator of the conscientiousness of those charged with effecting it and the value of their work came on the first Sunday in the "new" cathedral. The newly renovated cathedral was dedicated on October 16, 1979. As the Idaho Statesman reported, "'At the 11:30 Mass here last Sunday I explained everything about the renovation. When I finished there was a standing ovation of about 2 minutes,' said Schumacher, pastor of the cathedral."[42]

Recalling the event now, many years later, Monsignor Schumacher shook his head with a winsome smile and said, "The most common comment I got after it was all done, was 'what was all the excitement about?'"

Perhaps the final observation which should be made on this topic is that after all of the renovations were finalized, both the American Institute of Architects and The Idaho Historical League awarded St. John's Cathedral prizes for excellence in historical preservation.

# Chapter 18

*He Who Sings
Prays Twice*

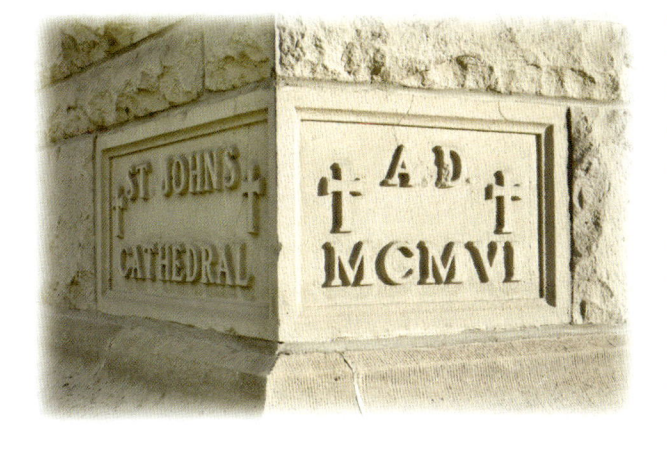

In the construction of St. John's Cathedral, the single most expensive item installed was the organ. At over $17,000.00 the organ from the Tellers-Kent Organ Company of Erie Pennsylvania cost more than all of the stained glass windows combined ($16,775.00). As originally installed, the organ was a 44 rank, 3 manual pipe organ. It was the largest organ in Idaho, and one of the largest in the Northwest.

The organ, as expensive as it was, would have cost even more except for the fact that much of its piping was not new, but recycled from other organs. Aware of the issues that using older piping in a newer console might cause, Bishop Gorman had a five-year guarantee included in the contract. Sure enough, in 1924 he found himself writing a letter to the manufacturer complaining about problems with some of the pipes. Honoring the guarantee, the company sent a worker to Boise to correct it.

In a cathedral as magnificent as St. John's, the musical environment has to be one of its most striking features, and not one casually assigned. A fair comment about the organ and the demands of its magnificence is probably reflected in the fact that while the cathedral—in its 110-year history—has had at least sixteen pastors, it has had only four regular organists[a], including the current one. It is a spectacular musical instrument, and assignment of the responsibility for it is not a task lightly delegated.

It is clear that even the very early designers of St. John's had that in mind. The choir loft and organ, surmounted by a rose window with St. Cecelia, the patron saint of music, dominate the entire rear of the building.

Until the completion of the cathedral in 1921, Father Remi Keyser, the rector at St. John's from 1907 to 1919, was the choir director. Father Keyser was a musician of some note; he actually wrote a musical Mass in Latin (a copy of that Mass is preserved in the parish archives.) The rector who succeeded Keyser, Monsignor Joseph Verhoeven, was also an enthusiastic proponent of a trained choir to compliment the church's grand organ and for a while he assumed the duties of choir director.

However, in 1921 when St. John's acquired its magnificent organ, Monsignor Verhoeven must have recognized his own limitations. It was Monsignor Verhoeven who made sure that a professional musician of the highest order was hired for the cathedral and its organ.

The organ is, by any standard, a magnificent part of the cathedral's history and charm. It was, almost from the outset, perhaps too magnificent for the building. When the organ was started up, and the blower for its pipes begun, the lights in the entire building dimmed! Six years after the cathedral was dedicated, an extensive electrical upgrade was done throughout the building. The cathedral's organ and the cathedral's lighting were finally able to operate in harmony.

Any musical instrument, certainly an instrument as grand as the organ at St. John's Cathedral, is limited by the talents of its musician. The organ at St. John's was honored in its early years to have Fredric Fleming Beale at the

---

a   There have been many more than four who have from time to time played the organ, or substituted often on a fairly regular basis for the full time organist, but in fact there have been only four contracted, regular full time organists.

console. Popular history has it that Beale, a professor of music at the College of Idaho in Caldwell and the organist at the Methodist Church in Caldwell, upon hearing that St. John's Cathedral in Boise had acquired a bigger, more grand organ, "jumped ship" to play for the Catholics. The actual record, though, suggests the situation was a bit more involved than that.

Professor Beale had been playing church organs since the age of seventeen. He had settled in Caldwell, Idaho in 1911 and had been playing at the Methodist Church there ever since, although his primary occupation was that of professor of music at the College of Idaho. His concerts at the First Methodist Church sometimes drew as many as 1000 people to Caldwell. Beale was not a Methodist, but he was not a Catholic, either. Among those who knew him, speculation as to his personal religious beliefs ranges from "free thinker" to Presbyterian. Whatever Beale's religious inclinations, his musical inclinations and talents are unquestioned.

Beale's involvement with the organ at St. John's was not a last minute or spur of the moment arrangement. Fully a year before the organ was ever installed, Beale wrote a six-page letter to Bishop Gorman detailing what he thought would be an appropriate organ. He did not hesitate to recommend that "a larger instrument should be installed."[43] The details of his letter make it very clear that Beale had the specifications of St. John's proposed organ before him when he wrote the letter. He makes reference to them and makes suggestions for different technical enhancements. More significantly, the Taylor Kent Organ company in responding to Beale's suggestions responds to him, not to Bishop Gorman.

Perhaps most significantly, the contract for the organ which was signed on July 29th, 1920, is an agreement of the Tellers-Kent company to "build an organ after and according to the specifications hereto annexed." It was Frederic Fleming Beale who wrote those specifications.

Despite the fact that he lived in Caldwell, was the head of the music department at the College of Idaho, was a Protestant, and as mentioned, enjoyed a significant popularity with his concerts at the Methodist church in Caldwell, Beale wasted no time in securing the position of music director at the Cathedral of St. John. In the Idaho Statesman of May 1, 1921, well before the cathedral was even officially open, Beale is listed as the "music and choir director" for the cathedral. At the official dedication several weeks later, a performance by Mr. Beale and his musical compositions were an important part of the program. Even after the organ was "up and running," it was Beale who insisted that it needed retuning in August of 1921. Apparently Boise's hot and dry summer weather had a negative impact on the instrument. One of the owners of the Tellers-Kent Organ company wrote a letter to Bishop Gorman promising that he would send a man to repair it "…he will be in Boise as soon as the excessive heat lets up. It would hardly be wise to do any tuning to the organ during such hot weather."[44]

Beale's time as the cathedral's first organist and music director was not without controversy. Less than one year after he began, there were a series of letters which indicated that he was finished!

On April 6, 1922, Beale wrote a terse letter to Bishop Gorman. "…I tender you my resignation as organist of the Cathedral, to take effect at once."[45] Exactly what the circumstances were we do not know, but it was apparently an unpleasant situation. Later that very same day, Beale penned another letter to the bishop in which he apologized because, "I left your presence abruptly, and for this rudeness I wish to apologize…I could not do otherwise tho (sic) for I have felt certain matters so deeply that I was not able to control myself. I would have broken down if I had remained a moment longer."[46] Whatever the issues were, a flurry of correspondence ensued. Anyone familiar with parish politics in the 21st century who reads that correspondence will realize that nothing has changed in 100 years. There are letters back and forth with a huge array of emotions coming to the fore, "…if it wasn't for me you wouldn't know anything." There were intimations that the new organist had been out partying the night before and thus showed up late and a little under the weather for the 10:30 Mass. No one could find the key to the cabinet with the choir books. "They managed to get by with the first spasm of the *Kyrie*—but that was all, there was no *Christe* or second *Kyrie* to follow…Father Verhoeven went in on the altar, reached under Father Mroz's vestments and came out with a key." The imagery of one priest marching up onto the altar in the middle of Mass in the staid 1920's and performing a body search of another priest who is celebrating Mass is too fantastic to contemplate. The sad thing about this episode is that the letter writer is obviously taking much glee in this unfortunate situation. "Well—I haven't gotten over laughing about it yet, (and you wouldn't either if you could have heard Nick tell it) and the La Salle girls say it was the funniest thing they ever listened to."[47] She couldn't resist adding a P.S. "I hope Ed goes out on some more parties and comes in late again."

Particularly dire was the warning to Mr. Beale "…we have just heard from Bishop Gorman and I must see you before you go near the cathedral."[48] Are we to imagine that the bishop had an assassin lurking in the choir loft? Dire warnings notwithstanding, it seems as if it all was pretty much a tempest in a teapot. Beale's service at the cathedral was never significantly interrupted; within two months of writing his resignation letter his services resumed and continued for at least ten years.

Through most of the 1920's, Friday evening concerts at St. John's featuring not just Beale, but well known singers, were a regular part of the Boise cultural scene. The cathedral was full for these concerts. Newspaper reports from then mention that at times up to 800 people attended Beale's concerts. It wasn't just Frederic they came to hear. Mrs. Beale was an accomplished soprano, and in fact is listed as the only other person on the program in a 1922 Monday evening recital. While Frederick played the organ "Mrs. F.F. Beale" sang a selection ranging from *Christus Resurrexit* to *Mother My Dear* and *March of the Gnomes*.

In 1926 Beale suffered a "nervous collapse," and although he had to be carried into some of his performances, he continued directing and playing for many years. He maintained not only his full time duties at the cathedral, but gave concerts not just at the cathedral and the College of Idaho, but as far away as Pocatello. Finally, in 1933, Fredric Fleming Beale returned full time to his position as head of the music department at the College of Idaho and one of his students, Reby Feuling, took the position of organist at the cathedral. As late as 1936, there is a Statesman article mentioning that Fredric Fleming Beale was conducting a chorale at Julia Davis Park for Boise's 18th Annual Music Week.

Fredric Fleming Beale actually returned to the Cathedral of St. John at least one more time. On May 22, 1938, Reby Feuling married James Reilly in the Cathedral of St. John and Beale played the organ at the wedding of his former student. Fredric Fleming Beale died on February 16th, 1948.

The organ and the building of St. John's Cathedral seem almost to have been built for each other, and given that Beale was dictating the organ's specifications while the building was being finished, perhaps they were. The volume and timbre of the pipes are complimented by the huge space the organ dominates, and in particular by the excellent acoustic characteristics of the arched, canvas ceilings. The acoustics of the building are perfect for music, although not quite as well suited to voices. Despite repeated upgrades to the cathedral's sound system, people in certain parts of the church have trouble hearing what is being said. No one, though, has ever had any problem enjoying the full beauty of the music from the choir loft. The church was designed for musical frequencies, not for the human voice. The regular Friday evening concerts are a thing of the past, but both the Boise Symphony and the Boise Master Chorale regularly use the cathedral as a venue for public concerts. It probably has the best acoustics anywhere in Boise for musical performances.

The organ has, in addition to ongoing maintenance, undergone several extensive upgrades and remodels. In 1962, it had a 3 manual console added. In 1995, a 4 manual digital console was added, new direct electric chests were added, and all chests were re-leathered and re-sealed.

Music in Catholic liturgy has a long and complex history. Originally, of course, a Catholic Mass was nothing more than a few faithful, gathering in a home to pray and remember the Last Supper. Paul, in the first century after Christ's death, describes the essential element of a Catholic Mass:

> *For I have received of the Lord what I also I handed on to you, that the Lord Jesus, on the night he was handed over, took bread, and after he had given thanks, broke it, and said: 'This is my body that is for you. Do this in remembrance of me.'*
>
> *In the same way also the cup, after saying, 'This cup is the new covenant in my blood. Do this, as often as you drink it in remembrance of me. For as often as you eat this Bread, and drink the cup, you proclaim the death of the Lord until he comes.'*
>
> *Therefore whoever eats the Bread or drinks the cup of the Lord unworthily, will have to answer for body and blood of the Lord."* (1 Cor: 11: 23-27)

The Mass as observed by Catholics was pretty much an unstructured and uncodified remembrance of the Last Supper until about the 6th century. Pope Gregory the Great, in 590, gave specific structure to certain elements of the celebration, and gave the Church its first missals, ritual books, and of course, the first form of music in a Mass, the beautiful chant which still bears his name.

There were no major changes to Gregory's rubrics until the Middle Ages. The history of music in the 17th–20th centuries is suffused with famous names, writing music for Masses for every occasion from joyful to sorrowful. Haydn, Mozart, Beethoven, Verdi, Shubert, Bach, Dvorak—and, yes—Bernstein and Weber all composed music for Masses. (We would be remiss if we failed to mention that Dave Brubeck has composed a *Mass to Hope* and a group called The Electric Prunes a *Mass in F-Minor*.) Obviously, works such as these were meant to be performed by major musical professionals and full orchestras, not a group of people accompanied by a struggling organist.

Although these beautiful works, which continue today, marked major feasts, Gregorian chant prevailed as the music of the Mass until the Protestant Reformation of the 16th century. As more and more churches broke away from Rome and established their own form of worship, one of the first things rejected was Latin, and consequently, Gregorian chant.

While the newly liberated Protestants were lifting their voices in enthusiastic songs of praise, their doleful Catholic neighbors persisted with chants in Latin. As Latin disappeared as a common language, the singing in Catholic Churches became the provenance of a specially trained group of people, the choir. The idea of congregational singing fell out of favor with Catholics. Most observers would say that despite the best efforts of fifty years of liturgical reform, it is still out of favor with Catholics. Catholic liturgy is rich in beauty, symbolism, and language, but

*Chapter 18*

congregational singing is not a great part of that. Some traditions just won't die and a Catholic tradition is that *"priests are for praying, choirs are for singing, and people are for listening to both."*

In the Cathedral of St. John—with a variety of musical groups, styles, and languages, and the imposing organ as the dominant instrument at Easter, Christmas, or a major liturgical event—it is a service which will leave the most callous observer moved to tears. Arresting tympanic instruments introduce stirring trumpets and beautiful chorales. The worst efforts of the congregation cannot diminish the hours of work and practice which the music director and his dedicated choristers have put into a one-hour service.

The organ at St. John's is approaching the 100-year mark. It has undergone several upgrades and renovations, most recently in 1995. It now has 76 ranks, 36 of which are thanks to the wonders of electronic augmentation.

# Chapter 19

## *No Great Building is Ever Finished*

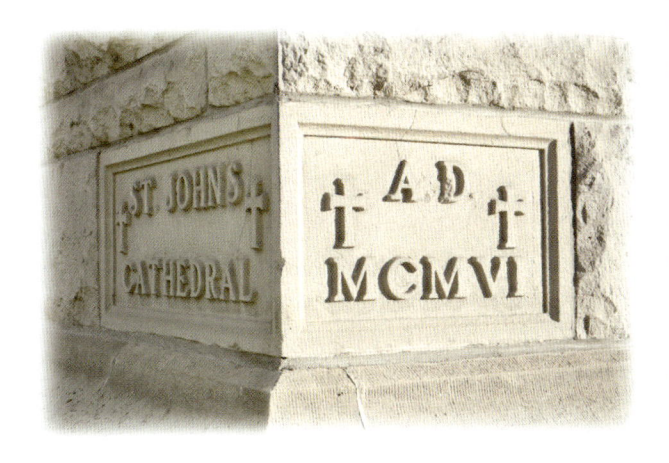

When the dedicatory ceremonies were held in 1921, the cathedral was not finished. The cathedral is not finished today, and the cathedral will never be finished. The building, in its over 100 years, has undergone a series of fairly significant alterations and modifications. Most of those are treated at length in other portions of this book. The purpose of this chapter is to discuss some of the perhaps less noticeable, maybe even forgotten, ones to illustrate that the church as a *building* is only a reflection of the church as a *people*, and people change.

Perhaps the first of these ongoing "upgrades" was shortly after the main cathedral was dedicated. As has been mentioned, until the main floor was completed in 1921 the basement area of the building had been serving as *the* Cathedral.

When the upper level of the cathedral opened in 1921, the lower chapel was effectively cut in half. Space taken from the chapel became a theater and meeting rooms. This was not a makeshift theater. It had a large stage, with multiple curtains, state of the art stage lighting, and dressing rooms. Not just the parish, but the entire city of Boise attended theatricals, musical presentations, and a variety of recitations and events there. Both the Knights of Columbus and the Saint Rita Society held fund raisers in this space, which went a long way towards providing funding for some of the final and enduring enhancements to the cathedral.

In 1952, in honor of Bishop Kelly's 25th anniversary as bishop, the exterior walls were sandblasted to remove 40 years of accumulated grime. In 1973, an elevator was installed in the south tower. Both towers were considered for the elevator, and because there were already stairs which would have to be reconfigured in the south tower it would have actually been cheaper to put the elevator in the north tower. The baptistery, though, was at that time a significant part of that tower. Rather than relocate the baptistery, the decision was made to redo the stairs in the south tower and install the elevator there. Of course, six years later, the baptistery was relocated anyway, to the front of the church. Also in 1973, the beautiful carved doors which dominate the front entrance to the cathedral were added. Up until then, the doors had been rather plain, with no decorations.

The installation of a utilitarian piece of mechanical equipment in 1973 led to the addition of one of the church's most beautiful pieces of art work forty years later. When the equipment room for the elevator was constructed, a window which had faced on Hays street was bricked up. The outline of that window is still visible on the wall of the equipment room. Although the window was bricked up, the frame and glass remained, and for forty years new parishioners puzzled over "the window which wasn't a window" on the southeast corner of the church.

Catholics are blessed with a tradition of reverence for ancient symbols and images. In 2015, a beautiful recreation of a 15th century icon finally filled the empty space in that window. It is the work of a local Catholic artist, Cindi Duft. It is the only piece of religious art in the cathedral which is visible not to those attending church, but to those passing by. That exposure was a decided factor in the selection of that icon and the message it would communicate. The painting is one of Mary as Our Lady (Our Mother) of Perpetual Help.

This representation of Mary, as a serene mother comforting her frightened child,

*Chapter 19*

originated in the 15th century. The original is enshrined in the church of Saint Alphonsus of Ligouri in Rome. Saint Alphonsus, as mentioned earlier, was the founder of the Redemptorist order of priests, and the image is practically the "trademark" of the Redemptorists. In fact, the Redemptorists are the only religious order specifically charged by the Holy See to protect and propagate a Marian image, Our Lady of Perpetual Help.

The story of how a modern reproduction of this ancient image came to be on the corner of 8th and Hays Streets in Boise, Idaho is a wonderful example of a theme repeated throughout this book. A church is not an assemblage of bricks and mortar. A church is a living ongoing monument to the faith of its people. It becomes a reflection of not just the people who attend it weekly, it reflects their lives, their families, and their own particular faith traditions. The icon of Our Lady of Perpetual Help, on the southeast corner of the Cathedral of St. John the Evangelist, is a wonderful congruence of faith, family, and happenstance.

In 2011, Dr. Timothy Johans, a surgeon and member of St. John's parish, had an inspiration as to what would be perfect for that space. His mother had always had a particular devotion to Our Lady of Perpetual Help. She had passed that devotion on to her son. Although Mrs. Johans lived in St. Louis, on a visit to Boise and St. John's she suggested Our Mother of Perpetual Help as a suitable image for that space. The decision was made to donate an artistic rendition of the highest quality for that space. The wheels were set in motion to get Our Lady of Perpetual Help into that alcove as an honor to Mrs. Johans.

That decision itself turned out to be an exercise in faith and perseverance. There was almost a year and a half of research to be sure that an historically accurate representation of the original was being used. Our Lady of Perpetual help has been around for 500 years, and has been reproduced thousands of times, under hundreds of different circumstances. There is actually a very popular current representation of that icon in which Mary is replaced by Archbishop Salvatore Romero of El Salvador, the Christ child is a frightened Salvadoran child, and the hovering angels are helicopter gunships.

Once the particular image was decided on, there began a series of discussions with Cindi Duft. Ms. Duft has done art work for churches, monasteries, and schools all over Idaho, and as far away as New Orleans, Louisiana.

While Ms. Duft had an extensive portfolio of ecclesiastical art covering a wide range of subjects, this project presented particular challenges. Since it was meant for display in a window with an almost total southern exposure, durability and susceptibility to light degradation was a serious concern. Acrylic was her planned medium for the painting, but before even picking the paint she had to give consideration to the surface it would be applied to. Any of the standard platforms for a piece of high quality art—canvas, wood, paper—would eventually suffer some ill effects from the sun and ultraviolet rays. An answer was found by turning from the "pure" art world to the commercial art world. A sign painting shop offered the idea of "alupanel," a polyethylene core sandwiched between thin aluminum sheets. Sign painters have found it ideal for outside signs. Next was the selection of the paint to be used. High quality acrylic paint, specially formulated for outdoor use, was chosen. Only pigments with the highest ratings for lightfastness and permanency were used. Countless layers of paint, mixed with an acrylic medium, went into the final painting. Finally, it was sealed with multiple layers of ultra violet protectant varnish to shield it from the worst effects of sun, moisture, and pollutants. In a final comment to the unfortunate world we now live in, the final varnish applied is removable with mineral spirits. In the event that the icon is ever defaced with graffiti, the graffiti can be removed without harming the paint and topcoat underneath it. From first brush stroke to last, it was an almost three-months-long project for the artist.

While Ms. Duft was making her inquiries as to material and medium, the donor was having multiple discussions with those responsible for the building. While the pastor of St. John's was almost immediately agreeable, there was the diocese to work with as well. St. John's is, of course, the Cathedral for the Diocese of Boise. The final decisions regarding alterations or additions to the cathedral, certainly to its exterior aspects, are made by the bishop of the diocese, not by the pastor of the church. The Catholic Church is the oldest institution known to western mankind, and it did not arrive at that distinction by making snap decisions. The process proceeded slowly.

Even in Boise, Idaho, and even in matters of filling an obviously vacant space, certain deliberations and considerations must take place. After two and a half years of letters, requests, committee meetings, and questions, Dr. Johans had just about given up.

In May of 2014—by Catholic tradition, the month of Mary—he got, within minutes of each other, three significant phone calls. The first was, unfortunately, from his brother, telling him that their mother had just died. Within minutes of hanging up on that call, he got a second call. The bishop had approved the installation of the icon! In Dr. Johans' words, "My mother had gotten up there and immediately resolved the matter."

The third call was from Cindi Duft, the iconographer. She was calling to tell him that she had, after much research and thought, arrived at what she felt were the proper mediums for both platform and paints. With all of the roadblocks out of the way, the decision was made to use the image and the accompanying prayer

*Chapter 19*

which had been used at Mrs. Johans' funeral as a memorial card.

One final, slight change was made. Mrs. Johans' funeral card had printed on it a common version of a prayer of petition to Our Mother of Perpetual Help. The finished icon was to be displayed on an exterior wall of a church on a downtown street corner in Boise, Idaho. It would be viewed, very likely, by more non-Catholics than Catholics. The "traditional" prayer which accompanies the image had its language slightly modified to impress on the observant pedestrian that Mary is a channel of grace, love, and peace to all, not just to Catholics. This is the prayer which accompanies this beautiful icon:

**Our Mother of Perpetual Help**
*(Reproduced with permission of Cindi Duft)*

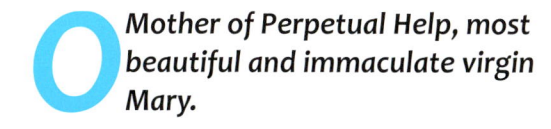

*O Mother of Perpetual Help, most beautiful and immaculate virgin Mary.*

*You know our suffering, our fears, and what evil lurks in this world.*

*We ask that you draw all of us ever closer to your beloved son Jesus, who, in his humanity and divinity, has triumphed over death and won our salvation.*

*O most compassionate mother, you hear the prayers of any who call on you.*

*Please be with us in our trials, and protect us under your mantle of peace.*

*Teach us how to trust without fear and be ever faithful to the Father's will, like you.*

*In Jesus' holy and precious name.*

*Amen"*

This prayer, on the icon on the outside wall of St. John's Cathedral, is yet one more adaptation of a prayer originally written over five hundred years ago. It has been modified multiple times. This latest iteration was written with the hope that passersby would see it and see in Our Mother of Perpetual Help a message of consolation and hope to all, not just to Catholics. Mary, as the Mother of God, is the mother of all. Hopefully Our Mother of Perpetual Help will be an instrument of quiet evangelization for some non-believers.

The icon was dedicated to Dolores Teresa Johans, and blessed on February 9th, 2015. It fills a space which had sat empty for forty years, and it does it so well that any who did not know the history would assume it has always been there. There are plans to illuminate the alcove so that the placid countenance of our Mother of Perpetual Help, comforting a frightened child, will be visible to all passersby at all hours.

Passing that icon and entering into the lower level of the cathedral, you will pass a series of stained glass windows on your left. These windows are another very recent addition to St. John's; in fact, they were dedicated just a few months before the icon of our Lady of Perpetual Help. The story of these windows is a wonderful example of the thought, work, and effort which goes into the ongoing job of creating a beautiful monument to God.

For years, this hallway had been a long, institutionalized corridor which connected the cafeteria/parish hall with the chapel and the outside exit. The exterior wall was a series of plain, frosted glass windows. There had been many discussions, over many years, about putting stained glass into those spaces. Money, as it is in so many matters, was an issue. Finally, in 2015, funds were available. Now there began a series of conversations on what would be the scenes in these windows, and where would qualified artisans be found. There are actually quite a few stained glass artisans working today. To find one with the skills and the resources to undertake a job of this magnitude, though, was the challenge. The Cathedral of St. John's on its upper level has, since 1921, had some of the most magnificent stained glass windows in the state of Idaho. No one was prepared to pair those windows with any sort of "good enough" windows on the lower level. The search ended, surprisingly, close to home and in the unlikely location of Fargo, North Dakota.

Classic Glass Limited of Fargo, North Dakota, had—over the last 25 years—made a name for itself not just regionally, but nationally. They had done all the windows for the recently finished St. Mark's Catholic Community in Boise and came highly recommended. Classic Glass also had the advantage that they not only had skilled artisans and technicians in stained glass, they had particularly skilled painters as well. This last was very important to the committee seeking a company to do the windows. Most people, when looking at a stained glass window, do not realize that much of the scene is not stained glass, but painted glass which has been fired to fix the colors. Depending on the scene and studio doing the work, a stained glass window may be 30–50% painted glass. Certainly faces, hair, skin tones, and subtle fabric colors appearing in a stained glass window are painted on and then fired. This operation itself requires a very high degree of skill. At the extremely high temperatures necessary for firing glass and fixing the scene, if the artist doing the painting is not very sure of pigments and

## Chapter 19

chemical composition of the paints used, there is no guarantee that the color they are seeking is the color which will come out of the oven.

As if those technical difficulties were not enough, the committee selecting the windows added just a little more friction to the problem. They wanted the windows to very closely resemble the windows on the main floor of the cathedral, not just in relatively simple details such as color shades, frames, and borders, but in the more fine matters regarding facial composition. Since two of the windows on the lower level depict the same scene as windows on the main floor—the agony in the garden and the resurrection—and all of them depict characters very much present in the windows of the main floor—Jesus, the apostles, Mary—it was decided that the faces on the new windows should, as much as possible, resemble the faces on the old windows. Now there was a challenge for all concerned, not least of all the artists painting the new windows. Photographs were actually taken and sent to Fargo. *Here, this is what Jesus looks like. Here is a picture of Peter, make him look like this.* Despite the certain fact that no one on this earth knows what Jesus, Peter, nor any of the earliest Christians looked like, the artists at Classic responded nobly to the challenge. Take a good look at Jesus' face on the first floor, and compare it to Jesus' face on the lower level. They were created by artists in Chicago in 1921 on the first floor, and by artists in Fargo in 2015, and they are, to a very discerning eye, twins. This process of arriving at not just the most technically correct, but artistically correct, windows consumed almost four years of committee members' time from idea to completion.

That last point, that some of the windows on the lower level duplicate scenes on the main floor, has actually led to some criticism. Given the chance to put in new windows why didn't we put in something we don't already have? The subject of these windows was ultimately chosen by Father Henry Carmona, the pastor of St. John's at the time. Father Carmona was very clear that he wanted the windows on this hallway, which connects school space with sacred space, to give a single, compelling message to the children: the passion and suffering which Christ underwent for each one of us. The windows certainly do that. They represent the final scenes of Christ's earthly life. The five windows depict:

1. The entry into Jerusalem
2. The last supper
3. The agony in the garden
4. The crucifixion
5. The resurrection

Just as the windows in the main cathedral are not just randomly placed, neither are these on the lower level. As you walk down the hallway to the chapel, you pass these windows in the order that the events occurred. You end that brief journey when you enter the chapel and become part of that defining sacrament of Catholic worship, the Mass, which is a triumphal re-enactment of the last supper and the resurrection: *Christ has died. Christ is risen. Christ will come again.*

These windows, a huge enhancement to the cathedral's esthetic appeal, as almost all of the cathedral's art, merit a very careful look to fully appreciate them. As has been mentioned, they are stellar examples of stained glass art. A few items which a casual glance might not reveal:

1. The human figures have facial features which are based on the facial features of those figures on the main floor of the cathedral.
2. In every one of the windows along this wall, some portion of the picture goes "beyond the frame." Look, for example, at St. Peter's sword and robe. This is an important artistic technique, because people just tend to forget about the edges of a picture, thinking they are not as important as the middle. Presumably there is more to a piece of art than what is shown on the canvas, (or in this case, glass) that needs to be conveyed. This is particularly important in liturgical art, because almost always, the scene depicted is one meant to move us to a higher plane. Other events and other messages are to follow. In the agony in the garden scene we know, or should know, that very soon after the events depicted, Peter is going to draw that sword and injure one of those who had come to arrest Jesus. Christ will use that incident to give us a lesson in forgiveness and healing, and to

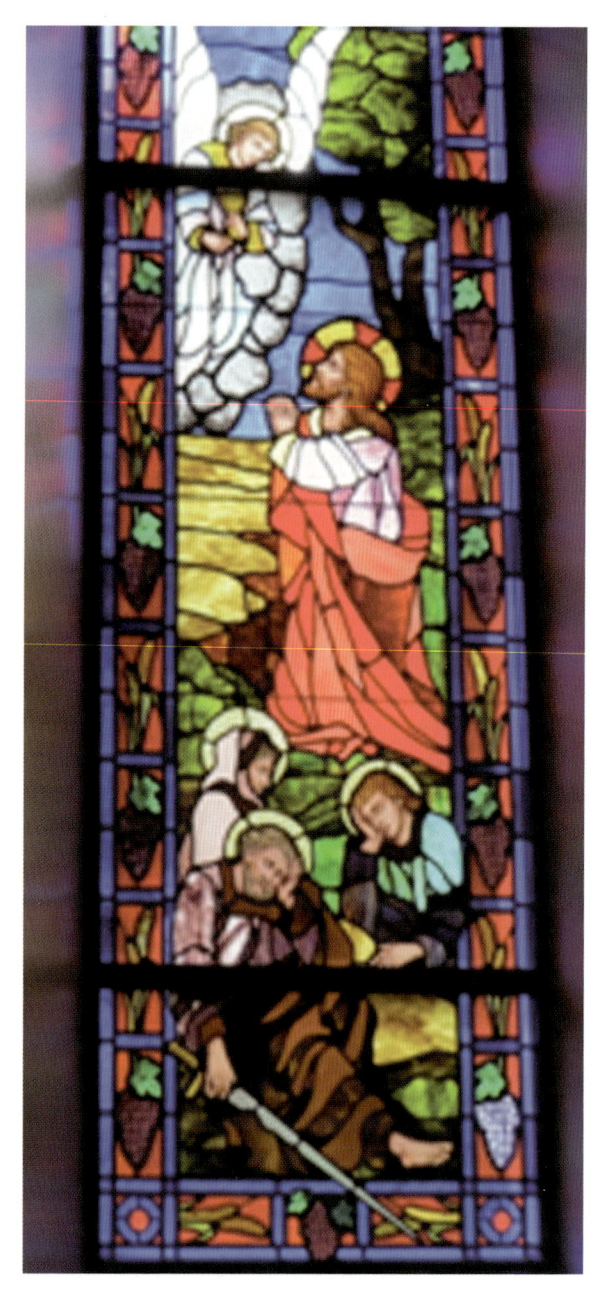

**The Agony in the Garden, basement level**
*(Photograph from the author's collection)*

remind us that, "They who live by the sword, will die by the sword." Look at all of the windows now — beyond the frame.
3. Note that the borders of these windows, wheat and vines (bread and wine), are patterned after the borders of the windows along the nave on the main floor.
4. Look very carefully at what at first glance appears to be a red circle imposed on a cross at each corner of each window. Those are actually beautifully sculpted, three dimensional roses.

In the 2008 remodeling of the lower chapel, a separate adoration chapel was added to the left of the main chapel, and a proper shrine to Our Lady of Guadalupe was constructed just inside the entrance to the chapel. In each of these locations, another stained glass window was added in 2015: Christ offering the first Eucharist in the adoration chapel, and Saint Juan Diego receiving the miraculous *tilma* from Our Lady of Guadalupe to the left of the statue of Our Lady of Guadalupe.

If you look to the left as you cross what might be considered a very small narthex leading into the chapel itself, you will see a near life size statue depicting Our Lady of Guadalupe. This statue, and the stained glass window to the left of it, were added in the 2008 renovation. They are a striking example of the changes the Cathedral of St. John's has undergone in the past 100+ years, and another illustration of the thought that the "Church" is the people of God, and the people of God are constantly changing.

When the lower chapel was completed in 1912, if there were any families of Mexican origin in the parish they probably kept a very low profile. In 1912, the Mexican revolution was in one of its more fulminate stages. The Texas/Mexican border was the locus of a lot of contentious activity between Pancho Villa and the United States Army. There was a state of near war between the United States and Mexico, and both sides regularly violated the border. In fact, several members of the cathedral parish in the Idaho National Guard were federalized for service on the Mexican border, including C.F. Hummel, the cathedral's architect, and his good friend John Regan, who would ultimately die in the First World War.

One hundred years later, families from Mexico and Central America have become not just a large, but a vital, element of parish life. Every Sunday, a Mass is said in Spanish, and throughout the year celebrations of feast days, holidays, and special celebrations which originated in Mexico are important observations. *Dia de los Muertas*, *Quinceaneras*, and *Las Posadas* have added a vibrancy to parish life which all cultures can enjoy. With their very strong commitment to family and faith, these newcomers have reminded many of us of the values our immigrant parents and grandparents were too often forced to surrender in order to become "American." Given a mother country that is just across a river, and not an ocean, these newcomers are demonstrating to the community that there is room in the new country for some of the values of the old.

The representation of our Lady of Guadalupe in the chapel at St. John's sits in an alcove just to the left as you enter the chapel. The shrine, containing the statue of our Lady of Guadalupe, continues a pattern much in evidence in the main cathedral. That is, a statue almost mirrored by a stained glass window of the same scene. (On the main level of the cathedral, both the statues of St. Mary and St. Joseph are right next to stained glass windows depicting— St. Mary and St. Joseph.) To the left of the statue of Our Lady of Guadalupe is a stained glass window of that same scene, only in the window, Saint Juan Diego is shown.

The final works of the Classic Glass Company were the stained glass transoms above the doors of the adoration chapel, and the "Holy Family" scene behind the statue of St. Joseph to the left of the seating area.

The "Holy Family" stained glass (it is not a window) has generated lively questions as to why it would be called the Holy Family window when none of the Holy Family is in it, although Joseph is near it. This is one of those esoteric religious shrines which takes some interpretation. First, at the top of the scene is depicted a Middle Eastern town of the first century. We are told that the town is Nazareth, the town where Joseph, Mary, and Jesus spent most of their lives. The real key to the name of the image, though, is not in the scene but in its border. It is a combination of lilies, roses, and vines. The traditional symbol for Joseph is a lily, and he is almost always depicted holding one—in fact, he is holding one in the statue in front of the Holy Family scene. The traditional symbol for Mary is a rose, and one of her titles is "Mystical Rose." Finally, Christ described himself as; "I am the vine, you are the branches." The Holy Family scene explained!

**Our Lady of Guadalupe**
*(Photograph from the author's collection)*

*Chapter 19*

Even though these very recent, very involved, and very expensive improvements to the cathedral were just finished, plans continue in the constant evolvement of a great building.

There are two holy water fonts in the lower chapel—simple bowls on unadorned tables. Imagine now, as a backdrop to these fonts, paintings depicting, perhaps, Jesus and the Samaritan woman at the well or John baptizing Jesus. Plans are in the works. It may take months, or it may take years, but what is done will become a lasting part of the cathedral's enduring legacy.

No great building is ever finished.

**Holy water font in the chapel**
*(Photograph from the author's collection)*

# Chapter 20

## *History is Not Dates; History is People*

Establishing a diocese and building a church are demanding undertakings, but the day to day duties of administering a church, particularly a church as bound by episcopal authority as the Catholic Church in the mid-20th century, were even more so. Anyone who is familiar with the issues, dynamics—and yes, politics—of a large church bureaucracy will, in reading this chapter, discover some very familiar scenarios. In examining records from the totality of St. John's existence, we find a host of situations which make it clear that

*Stone Wondrously Hewn*

"the more things change, the more they remain the same." A church and its administration is a human organization, replete with human failings.

At 110 years, the Cathedral of St. John's, of course, has no parishioners left who can speak of the very early days. At the cathedral though, as at any Catholic church, there are detailed records covering every aspect of life, literally from birth to death. Every Catholic church keeps detailed records of baptisms, first communions, confirmations, marriages, and burials. Catholic Church records have been kept in the United States since the 1600's, while civil recording of births, deaths, and marriages was not uniformly required until the twentieth century. Many times, in the history of the United States, records maintained by Catholic churches have been used to reconstruct civil records lost through fire, flood, or other natural disasters. In reviewing the records of the cathedral, we can uncover a wide variety of human events. Some of these situations are tragic, some uplifting, some are emotionally wrenching, and some are simply risible in the extreme.

A look at the early records of St. John's, now well over one hundred years old, is an interesting look at history progressing. All of the very early records are written in beautiful cursive script, in black India ink. Many of these early records are entirely written in Latin. Even the parties' names are "Latinized," i.e., John becomes *Johanus*, Alfred become *Alfredi*, and Roberta becomes *Roberti*. It is interesting to note that while Father Van der Hayden faithfully created all of his records totally in Latin, Bishop Glorieux did not.

In the very earliest records, the names are almost without exception Irish: McMahon, Doherty, Dolan, Ryan, Burke, etc. These would have been the children of those who fled the famines of the 1840's in Ireland. At the end of the Civil War, like so much of the American populace, they moved west. Many of them sought their fortunes in the gold veins of the Boise Basin.

Around 1894, German names begin to appear: Schrieber, Lofgrens, Eifler, Diederichs, Hoffman, etc. These were people fleeing the political turmoil of the late 1800's which engulfed what eventually became the new country of Germany. Germany as a country did not exist until 1871. Prior to that, and in particular in the twenty years immediately prior, hundreds of landlords, princes, and dukes presided over a feudal system which was one of the most oppressive in Europe. German peasants faced a lifetime of unrelenting labor, punctuated only by periodic drafting as cannon fodder for the privileged classes. Added to this, the same potato blight which had visited Ireland wreaked its ravages on the German countryside. America was a shining beacon of hope to a country wracked with poverty and war. From the mid 1800's until 1900, almost two million people immigrated to the United States from Germany. Almost all of them settled in the upper Midwest,

*Chapter 20*

but their numbers were so large that they began to represent a major part of the American expansion westward into the Oregon Territory.

Shortly after the marked increase of German names, what are probably westward moving "Americans"—Phelps and Dickinson, Johnson, Kimball, and Clark—begin to show up on the register. In March of 1896, we see the first of what will turn out to be a major population in the cathedral parish: Agustine Ascuenga marries Maria Urguisa. The Basques have begun what will be a formidable presence in Idaho, in Boise, and at the Cathedral of St. John the Evangelist! All of the records, no matter of what nationality, when examined carefully give further insight into the people and the time.

One of the first things that strikes in reviewing early marriage records is that fully forty percent of the marriages recorded between the end of the 19th century and the beginning of the 20th are marriages with a dispensation because of *disparitatus cultus* (different religions)—one of the parties, most often the woman, is not a Catholic. The Catholic Church in the late 1800's was philosophically and vehemently opposed to marriage between a Catholic and a non-Catholic. Be that as it may, Catholics, in particular Catholic women, were a minority in the west. There was little to be done about the fact that when it came to marriages for Catholics, there were just not that many potential partners to go around. It is clear from the records that a very pragmatic approach was taken by the cathedral's priests and not just with reference to religious differences. One of the more interesting records is one in which it is obvious that the marriage is a marriage "by proxy." The bride is not present, but there is a "stand in" for her! The same flowery Latin which tells us that there is one dispensation for *disparitatus cultus* refers to a second dispensation for *gravis causae* (a grave cause), which in this case is further listed as *gravida* (pregnancy). All we can do is speculate about the actual circumstances, but it is entirely possible that at the moment of the wedding the bride was "confined" in the process of giving birth! It goes without saying that such a marriage would not be countenanced by the Church today.

The records, as mentioned—created by obviously very pragmatic priests—offer intriguing insights into the question of culpability and discretion. One dispensation is necessary because the couple "*Were married by Governor Stephens seven years ago, one of the parties having a living husband then.*" ( Hmmm…wonder which party?) It seems as if that husband must now be dead, because whatever other dispensations the Church may have been willing to grant, bigamy would certainly not be one of them.

The death register also gives an intriguing look at the changing times. In the late 1800's and early 1900's, before widespread immunization and aggressive public health initiatives took hold, childhood deaths were common. "Croup"

and "influenza" seemed to be general phrases which undoubtedly covered a multitude of sins, but there were also entries which are nothing more than a "?" (14 years old) or "drank kerosene" (11 months old).

For the adult population as well, it was a perilous time. "Shot through the head," "shot," "accident in Greyhound mine," "scalded by steam," and "crushed by rolling log" are some of the more eye-catching entries. It is clear that post mortem pathology was not a very precise science in 1907. One cause of death is given as "cramps," and it must be noted that the deceased was a male.

As mentioned, all of the original entries are in beautiful script written with uniform black India ink. In the 1920's through the 1950's we can see the dominance of the fountain pen taking place. The entries are still in liquid ink, but a variety of colors, different shades of blue and black, begin to show up. 1961 shows the first entry clearly made with a ballpoint pen. Ballpoint pens were, of course, in common use well before then, but there seems to have been an unwritten rule against using them in the church ledgers. Today virtually all entries are made in ball point pen. Undoubtedly, before too long the entries will be digital.

Priests assigned to the parish in the early years (the 1920-30's) were under the almost absolute authority of the pastor. At that time, only the pastor had a car. When Father McGowan was assigned to St. John's, he was told that the pastor would "allow the use of car for Barber, and Eagle, sick calls and the Academy when he thinks necessary." The same memo allowed that "the principal of the school (who at that time was one of the parish priests) may have a car but "the principal of the school will have no recompense for the use of his car." A later memo made it clear that the pastor "is allowed $250.00 a year for the use of his car provided he allows it to be used by the Missionaries when needed." Obviously terms such as "when he thinks necessary" and "when needed" left final authority in these matters with the pastor.[49]

Early in 1933, there was an exchange of letters between Father Dougherty, the pastor of St. John's Cathedral, and Bishop Kelly regarding the future of the boy's high school at St. Joseph's. The bone of contention is the future of that school. We'll never know what some of the early conversations involved, but in January of 1933 Bishop Kelly initiated a formal exchange of letters with the pastor. In a letter dated January 26th to Father Dougherty the bishop asks bluntly, "That there be no misunderstanding of your attitude…we will ask that you put in writing your answer to the following questions…". (One cannot help but note the use of the imperial "we.") There were four questions; the first was:

"Is it your opinion as Pastor that the St. Joseph's High School should be discontinued. Why?"[50] The other questions were equally to the point, and

*Chapter 20*

it is clear that the bishop is trying to get "on the record" the pastor's role in this, and perhaps more importantly the role of the "parish committee." Some blame fixing is about to come down the pike and everyone is covering their bases.

This was obviously an era when a letter mailed in Boise on January 26th could be received on the same day, or perhaps the bishop felt the matter pressing enough that he had it hand delivered. In any case, Father Dougherty's answer is dated the same date! Father Daugherty is just as direct with his answers. Yes, he answers, "the high school is not essential to the parish." To one of the bishop's queries—which took an entire paragraph to pose—his answer is a one-word, succinct, "Yes."[51] There are several more letters in the exchange, and the end result is that on April 17 of that year, the bishop notifies Father Dougherty that "…beginning September 1933 the High School department of St. Teresa's academy will be co-educational, St. Joseph's High School will close this June not to reopen in the Fall."…"I would ask of the parents likewise to this new, and I believe most beneficial undertaking, their loyal cooperation."[52] Case closed.

The actual dynamics involved in this situation will likely never be known. All of the original players are long since departed. It cannot escape observation, though, that the very next year Father Dougherty—just three years into his term as rector—was replaced.

There were matters of concern well beyond the question of whether the cathedral should have a boy's high school or not. Public health issues totally foreign to our world today were of real concern. "…in September and other times Father O'Toole urged Father to have his chest x-rayed, as his continuous coughing and emaciated appearance suggested T.B.….For three or four months parishioners have not liked to have him around the children as they suspected he was a T.B., and moreover he was not very carefull *(sic)* Finally a month ago Father O'Toole insisted that a doctor give a thorough examination, and the x-ray picture showed his lungs were effected *(sic)* and his sputum was filled with active germs."[53] There are a lot of overblown concerns in the 21st century about diseases, infectious and otherwise, but in the 20th century tuberculosis was a very real and very dangerous condition, especially towards children.

In the 1940's and 50's, we can infer the growth of government after the second world war by the letters which occur with regular frequency in the cathedral files. There are letters seeking the services of a priest from the cathedral to serve as chaplains for the United States Army, the Civilian Conservation Corps, and the Idaho State Penitentiary. After a series of exchanges with the YMCA regarding the use of their facilities for practices for the Catholic school teams, a decision is made to tear down the old gym, which had originally been the first church on the 8th Street site.

It is hard to believe in today's world that in the 1940's advice was sought **by** Rome **from** Boise, on matters of significant theological consideration. Father Verhoeven, in 1946, in response to a request from the Vatican, wrote a letter to Bishop Kelly. "In my humble opinion I regard the corporeal Assumption of the Blessed Virgin Mary as a dogma of the Faith which can be proposed and defined. It is my humble opinion that the clergy desires this and that the people would desire it explicitly, if they realized that such a definition would bring greater external honor and glory to God and his blessed mother."[54] Four years later, Pope Pius XII declared the Assumption of Mary as a dogma, and the diocese of Boise can justifiably take some credit for having this dogma proclaimed.

In 1947 Father Rowe, the rector at the cathedral, is offered the title of *monsignor* and his letter acknowledging this also acknowledges that he has to pay a "tax" to acquire the honor. Also in looking at records from 1947, we are reminded of how much the state has changed in the past 70 years. Father Carey, a priest at St. John's, gets a letter that he is being reassigned to St. Anthony's Church in Wendell, and as "chaplain of St. Valentine's Hospital, in Wendell." The church in Wendell today is a mission of the church in Gooding, and there is no hospital of any description in Wendell.

Matters of regalia and titles were much more important in the 40's and 50's than they are now. A series of letters contain much discussion about the proper place for a monsignor in a liturgical procession, who might wear a cope or a surplice, and where and when a biretta is proper attire during the celebration of a Mass.

Catholics, of course, belong to a highly structured church with its own rules of conduct, and up until 1964 one of the most strict had to do with fasting before receiving Holy Communion. Before changes allowed by Pope Paul VI, Catholics were required to fast from all food and drink from midnight of the night before they were to receive Communion. A petition from the parish archives illustrates just how structured the church was and just how bound the faithful felt by its rules.

In June of 1947, one of the parishioners had a petition sent to Rome. It is an elaborate document, written entirely in Latin and directed personally to Pope Pius XII. The subject of this document? The lady is in ill health, and she wishes to be excused from the necessity for fasting from midnight. It takes six months, but an answer is returned from Rome, in the same flowery Latin: permission is granted. Finding documents such as this, one is reminded of how Church discipline has changed in the past 50 years. Today, a much more benign fasting requirement—one hour—is found burdensome by many.

More prosaic matters were also discussed. The east side of the cathedral has water leaking from the gutters and leaching the

## Chapter 20

mortar from the stone work. In response to this, a contract is let in 1951 for copper gutters, flashings, and a new roof. A sound system is installed at the same time.

Things do not always run smoothly between the various branches of the Church. Nowhere is that more true than in matters involving priests and teaching nuns. Women who have devoted their lives to teaching children the essentials of the Catholic faith are not easily intimidated and not swayed by episcopal titles. That has very recently been evidenced in a controversy involving American nuns and the Vatican. It took the personal intervention of a new pope to defuse the situation.

In 1958, such a situation arose at the cathedral school. There is a letter from the motherhouse of the Sisters of the Holy Cross in Notre Dame, Indiana. Sister M. Leonilla, the "Supervisor of Schools" for the Holy Cross Order, writes Bishop Byrne to relate that:

> *Last week it seems that Monsignor Rowe asked rather emphatically that one of the sisters at St. Joseph School take down the religious charts she had been using."*

Sister Leonilla's letter is a detailed and polite one, but her point is very clear.

> *In Los Angeles, Sacramento, Washington, Fresno, and Utah "The Archbishop… outlines the content (underlining is hers) and leaves the teaching method to the Sisters. We would appreciate having the same freedom in Idaho. The teacher in question is one of my best young teachers who has been teaching in the San Francisco Archdiocese."*[55]

If there is any lesson a life-long Catholic has learned, it is "don't mess with the sisters." Bishop Byrne wastes no time in writing Sister Leonilla back:

> *I am confident that there must have been a misunderstanding."*

The bishop orders a meeting between his chancellor, Monsignor Rowe, and the sisters. The charts, and the Holy Cross Sisters, stayed.[a]

Not all of the conflicts the church is asked to resolve are ecclesiastical. In 1966, the chancellor of the Diocese of San Diego wrote to the bishop of Idaho asking that he help a couple escape an inconvenient section of California law. It seems as if the young man is not 21 years of age, cannot obtain a marriage license in California without his parents' consent, and the parents will not give it. Since the age for obtaining a marriage license in Idaho is only 18, he asks that they be allowed to come to Boise to be married. Father Weigand, the chancellor of the Boise Diocese, is happy to facilitate that process.

---

[a] The Sisters of the Holy Cross stayed at St. Joseph School until 1985, when declining numbers in their order forced their withdrawal.

How happy the putative in-laws might have been is not recorded.

Ever since the late 1960's and early 1970's, and the precipitous departure of teaching sisters and brothers from the Catholic school system, the education of the faithful has been a major effort of the Church. One would be hard pressed to find an older Catholic who would not be of the opinion that "no one did it as well as the sisters." Monsignor Hughes, the pastor of St. John's in the early 70's, was apparently of this school, and didn't hesitate, in 1972, to express his contempt for the process which was being used to replicate the sisters' service.

> *In 1969 a survey was made relative to the effectiveness of the C.C.D. program[b] in the Diocese. The results were far from flattering. I am wondering if a similar survey were done today, what the results would be."... "Lets not fool ourselves into thinking that the more money we spend on a project the better job we are doing."... "It is a mystery to me what two Nuns, two secretaries and three priests are doing besides spending money. What return is the Diocese getting from all the travel involved? If we spend so much time at conventions, meetings, etc. when is there time to do the work of the Church?"*

---

b    The Confraternity of Christian Doctrine (CCD) was a program of religious education begun by the Catholic Church in the mid 1960's and staffed primarily with lay volunteers.

Monsignor Hughes concludes his curmudgeonly letter with a delightful,

> *I can only write and call the shots as I see them."[56]*

At St. John's itself, one can often find correspondence referring to the important "back up" role church records can play. On November 17, 1975, a letter was written to St. John's stating simply, "I am in need of proof of my marriage in order to file with the Veteran's Administration. Ada County has been unable to supply the necessary information and I am hoping you will be able to do so. We were married in Boise, Idaho on May 4, 1934. My husband's name was…and my maiden name was…." Just three days after this letter was written, the church was able to write back and confirm that the couple were indeed married on May 4, 1934, in Boise, Idaho in St. John's Cathedral by the Reverend John T. Toomey. The Veteran's Administration had the proof it needed to see that a widow had her just due come to her.

In reviewing old church records, one will uncover puzzling stories, uplifting stories, tragic stories, and sometimes absolutely heart wrenching stories. One such story buried deep in the archives of St. John's Cathedral spans two continents, an ocean, two world wars, and now, one hundred years. It involves an abandoned son who not only went to great lengths to care for the father who had abandoned him but who never stopped searching for the siblings he had never met.

## Chapter 20

Because of the nature of the story, in my recitation I have obliterated last names, but changed none of the facts. The letter reproduced below — except for the last names — is an absolute copy of the letter in the archives. The circumstances of Father Salvatore's surroundings, which I have constructed as the introduction to the actual letter, is an imagining on my part. Obviously, we have no way of knowing what Father Salvatore's surroundings were on September 28, 1947.

We do, though, know a lot about Father Salvatore's background, history, and thought processes in the later years of his life. With this information, I have chosen to tell his story to emphasize that he was a thoughtful, concerned man living with the human side of great events. Father Salvatore's story is an excellent reminder to all historians, certainly to this one, that history is not dates and events — history is people.

### Father Salvatore's Story

Father Salvatore settled down on the terrace of his little home in Campobasso, Italy. It was late September, 1947. As he contemplated the valley below and thought of the battles which had so recently been waged there, he couldn't help thinking of the earlier war far removed, which had stolen four years of his young life.

As a young priest he had been conscripted into the Italian army and with the rest of Cadorno's army had spent almost four years advancing and retreating, back and forth, across the Isonzo River. What folly! What carnage — 60,000 young men killed and 150,000 wounded and not one inch of ground gained! As a chaplain, he was spared the worst of the insane and fruitless frontal assaults on the well-entrenched Austrians. As a chaplain, though, he was exposed to the worst of the wounded, mangled, and terrified young soldiers. Ill-equipped, ill-trained, and ill-treated thousands of Italian peasants were sacrificed to the stupidity and callow uncaring of generals using Napoleonic tactics against machine guns, barbed wire, and indirect artillery.

He shook his head again. Now, perhaps with less stupidity but with just as much carnage, World War II had just been finished. He mused, *When did someone decide that "the Great War," the "war to end all wars," was just the beginning of a series, and would best be named World War I? Was World War III looming in another twenty years?*

It was a still, warm Sunday afternoon, with just a hint of autumn, and an even more slight promise of the winter which was coming. He took in the view of the mountains running down to the river below, the neatly terraced vineyards, and orderly vegetable gardens. He considered his own small, but comfortable house and vineyards which brought him a certain measure of comfort and security in his old age. Certainly, more comfort and security than he might have if his meager pension as a retired country priest was all he had to depend on. He had his father—his hardworking, American/Italian (or was it Italian/American?) father—to thank for this modicum of comfort. Ah…yes, his father. It was his father, who though long dead, had brought him out here this afternoon, to use the declining light of an autumn afternoon to write a long overdue letter. He took a sip of the wine he had brought out, sat the glass on the table, and settled back to compose himself before he set about the letter.

He dated it and carefully addressed it:

Sept. 28, 1947

Most Rev. Edward Kelly, D.D.
804 N. 9th St.
Boise, U.S.A.

*Your excellency, The undersigned respectfully begs permission to explain the following. My father, Antonio \*\*\*\*\*[c] during his stay in Schoschone[d], Idaho, U.S. had bad relations with a woman by the name of Madalena \*\*\*\*\*. She bore him three children who were registered both ecclesiastically and civilly under his name. At Baptism they received the names of Carmelo, Pietro and Leonello \*\*\*\*\*. In 1911 Madalena \*\*\*\*\* died leaving my father with the care of the children's education. This he undertook with great diligence.*

---

[c] I have chosen not to record last names from this letter.
[d] Poor Father Salvatore struggled 50 years later to commit to paper a story given to him by his dying father and spelled phonetically an American Indian name he had heard but never seen.

*I was ordained a priest in 1913. In that same year my father fell gravely ill. He was in hospital where he paid by the month but was treated very badly. Moreover he suffered from an incurable disease, namely, progressive paralysis. Two cousins who lived near there informed me of this fact and I prepared to have him return to Italy to give him the care needed for his condition.*

*My father admitted his fault to me and told me the condition of the three children. He had built three houses for them with gardens and vineyards and he had loaned money from various friends which would care for them in the orphanage until such time as they would be able personally to administer the sum assigned to each. Before returning to Italy he named Mr. Gennaro Di \*\*\*\*\* as their procurator or guardian. From that time on I have written various times to America to get information about the children but I have never received an answer.*

*In October 1914 my father died and I redoubled my efforts to get to the bottom of the case because it displeased me no end to think that the children might be suffering want whereas my father had provided well for their care and future. In fact, I must tell Your Excellency that during the twenty five years (and this is a bitter admission) which my deceased father lived with the concubine he entirely forget about his own family in Italy.*

*Not having received any satisfactory answer I decided to go to America. Just then, however, in 1915 the First World War broke out and I was called to the service of my country. After four years of military life I returned to*

## Chapter 20

*my family and resumed writing letters – this time to various religious houses – but without result. Last year I wrote again and in June, 1946 a certain Father Luigi ***** P.S.M. told me the place where my brothers live but unfortunately he did not name the street and number. It displeased me very much to hear that none of my brothers lives in the place of his birth, namely Schoschone, Idaho. This shows that the will of my deceased father has not been respected. My brothers have been defrauded of their inheritance and have had to suffer much, find a place in other cities and live separately.*

*By good fortune I have an Annuario Pontificio and I see that your excellency has charge of Boise, Idaho where my brother Pietro ***** lives. I rejoice over this as I hope that your Excellency will be able to find my brother and quiet my sacerdotal conscience.*

*No doubt your Excellency could have inquiries made in the Parish registers of the city and find my brother. Or if he belongs to some non-Catholic sect perhaps in the civil registers or telephone book.*

*I hope that the Pastor uses every prudence lest my brother think I'm looking for help or that I want an account of the property my father left in America. Nothing of the kind! I have no need. I am a Pastor and I receive a Pastors salary. I have personal income besides and I own family real estate. I am interested only in knowing that he is well, and has sufficient means to live.*

*On account of my age and condition of health I cannot travel to America to know him personally. He, who is younger than me should come to Italy. If this is not possible he should kindly send me his photograph together with that of his family and I will also send my photo.*

*I beg him to tell me news of my other brothers. The bonds of blood, no matter how they arise cannot be destroyed.*

*In the hope that Your Excellency will give benign ear to my plea I thank Your Excellency in advance for whatever you can do for me.*

*Begging a Blessing I remain*

*Respectfully yours in Christ*

*(Rev.) Salvatore *****

In researching thousands of pages of archived records, I have not found a more poignant, heart-rending, nor powerful letter. There are angry letters, there are pleading letters, there is the occasional comedic letter, but nowhere, except in Father Salvatore's letter, is there a more epic chronicle of the consequences world events have on the lives of simple people. In this one letter we have a complete chronicling of the 20th century. Major wars, lives disrupted, social upheaval, and families dispersed. Emigration and return to the homeland, children lost, and brothers seeking reconciliation.

The truly unfortunate postscript to this story is that several months later Father Salvatore received an answer to his eloquent plea:

*In regard to Pietro \*\*\*\*\* I have made a thorough search of our files, and parish list and other sources, however his name does not appear. Also, I have asked Father \*\*\*\*\* about this man and he does not have him on his list.*

*I contacted the Postmaster, the City Directory, the Boise Water Corporation and the Idaho Power Company who have quite a thorough record of the families in Boise, and none of these have such a name on their records.*

*Also, I have made several inquiries from Italian families here in Boise but none have heard of Mr. \*\*\*\*\*. The local Banks were also contacted and there is no one by that name who has an account with them.*

*With all best wishes, I am*

*Obediently yours in Christ*

K.F. Rowe

Father Salvatore, despite his very conscientious efforts, eloquent pleas for help, and obvious sincerity, would never find his brothers. He would never have his questions about their welfare answered. Father Salvatore is long since dead. Are there some great nephews or nieces still in Boise, or perhaps, Shoshone?

History is not dates and events. History is not great battles; history is people!

Aside from such sweeping events as chronicled in Father Salvatore's letter, much which occupies the time of church administrators can only be characterized as frivolous and trivial. It seems as if there is no matter too mundane for people to bring to the attention of the pastor of the cathedral, and quite often, to the bishop himself. There are, in the files, letters complaining about women wearing sleeveless and "suntan dresses" in church and letters about people who have leadership roles in the parish who are not living up to someone's view of a "faithful Catholic." Divorced people receiving the sacraments come in for scathing criticism, as does the pastor because he allows the outrage to take place. Another letter complains that "the church is too cold" (apparently not for the women wearing "sleeveless and suntan" dresses). The bishop himself is advised in a typewritten letter of the outrageous situation prevailing in that there "are no doughnuts after Mass."

# Chapter 21

## *The Future is Mestizo*

*Mestizo:* Of mixed race. (Oxford Spanish Desk Dictionary, Fourth Edition.)

On many Sunday afternoons at 2:00, the sidewalk in front of St. John's Cathedral is transformed from an arterial on the edge of Idaho's capitol city to a plaza in front of a Mexican church. The 1:00 Mass each Sunday is a Mass celebrated in Spanish and the unique color and cultural nuances of that celebration do not end when the final blessing is given. In fact, in very large measure that is when it begins. It is a time for migrants, second generation—

and indeed fourth and fifth generation—families to get together, visit, raise funds for their common causes, and most of all celebrate their culture and language.

The congregation at the 1:00 Spanish Mass is an amazing amalgam of recent demographic changes which are seen throughout the United States. While the vast majority of the attendees at the Spanish Mass are of Mexican lineage, Uruguay, Honduras, and El Salvador are also represented. From time to time almost every country in Central and South America has had a presence. One could almost compile a report card on political turmoil in Central and South America by studying this group.

Virtually every Catholic Church in the United States has, over the past forty years, seen a huge influx of parishioners from Mexico and Central America. Idaho, and Idaho's cathedral, has been a particular beneficiary of that influx. An acute shortage of priests in Idaho (47 priests for 52 parishes) would be even more acute were it not for priests from Mexico, Central America, Columbia, and other "third world" countries serving in the state. To some, this has been a sudden, and not always welcome, transition. An objective assessment, though, cannot fail to demonstrate that it has "been a long time coming" and it has enriched and benefited the Catholic Church in Idaho.

Thirty-five years ago, the Idaho Statesman ran a series of articles entitled *Idaho Hispanics—A People in Transition*. A look at some of the points raised in those articles is illustrative and will serve as a stark reminder that the times have changed. Sandwiched between articles on the economic impact of migrants, and the difficulties migrants endured, was one entitled *Language Divides Anglo, Hispanic Catholics*.

In that article, Father Mauricio Medina, the first priest specifically assigned to Idaho's Spanish speaking Catholics, commented on the problems he faced early on. Father Medina came to Nampa, which at that time had the largest Mexican American population in the state, to set up a new parish for Spanish speaking parishioners. There were almost 2,500 Mexican Americans in a town of 25,000 at that time, and they had found an awkward, and sometimes unwelcome, reception at the one Catholic church in Nampa.

As Father Medina pointed out, the history of the church in Mexico over the past 100 years had been one of wild swings from a church which was virtually a department of a repressive government, to a church which was outlawed by the government, to a church of "benign neglect" which struggled to survive in a huge landmass controlled by a favored few. The United States was an attractive beacon of hope for those who struggled under this system and who sought a better life for their families. They were not, though, in Medina's words "…tied closely to the structured church, the arrangements, and strict Mass attendance."[57]

## Chapter 21

For a variety of reasons, language being the prime one, many Mexican Catholics, once they had settled in Idaho, engaged in the practice of their faith in their own homes or small faith sharing groups, not in the institutional church. Today, Mass is regularly said in Spanish at 30 Catholic churches in Idaho and almost every priest in the state is at least conversational in Spanish.

It was Sylvester Treinan, the bishop of Idaho from 1962 to 1988, who began emphasizing not just ministry, but active outreach, to the Spanish speaking members of the diocese. Once the church began offering Mass in Spanish, and bilingual priests, it discovered it had tapped into a huge and enthusiastic reservoir of committed Catholics.

The Diocese of Boise now has an Office of Cultural Ministries, which serves not just Hispanics, but Native Americans, immigrants, and refugees from around the world. Often forgotten in discussing these issues is the fact that the Office of Cultural Ministries, in addressing issues for Idaho's *minority* population, provides a valuable service to the *majority* population as well. In an increasingly small world, the Office of Cultural Ministries offers tools and education to those seeking to build cross cultural understanding. We are all children of God and the Office of Cultural Ministries' mandate is to bring the family together.

The inclusion of Spanish speaking people in the institutional church has been a slow, and sometimes painful, process. Interestingly the cathedral, the "mother church" of Catholics in Idaho, was one of the very last of Idaho's churches to enthusiastically embrace the process. The reason for that is largely simple demographics. Initially, Hispanic migration to Idaho was in the form of farm laborers and their families. Boise, the state capitol of Idaho, has no agricultural basis to its economy. Government, business, and education are the mainstays of Boise's economy. There were no jobs beckoning farm workers, migrant or otherwise, to Boise. Canyon County to the west, and the Magic Valley to the east, were where the farm jobs were, and those were the areas where migrants settled. It was, until fairly recently, a presumption that the likelihood of a member of the cathedral parish being of any sort of Latin background was just not very high. That presumption, beginning in the 1990's, was found to be an erroneous one. There was, in fact, a large reservoir of "hidden" Latinos in Boise.

Boise had undergone an explosive surge of growth in the waning years of the 20th century and the early years of the 21st century. With that growth, two large segments of the workforce grew concomitantly: construction and the service industry (maids, housekeepers, waiters, kitchen help). These were jobs which had always beckoned to new arrivals. Boise suddenly found that it had its own large Hispanic community. A recent survey of attendees at the 1:00 Spanish Mass found that over 60% live in the Boise-Garden City area while the other 40% come from areas as far away as Caldwell, Nampa, and Star. This last point illustrates another interesting fact. Half of all Hispanic Catholics in the United States report that they drive by their territorial parish to attend Mass somewhere else. No one wants to worship in a church where they do not feel welcome.

The question of "parishes" and of parish membership is a confusing one for many people, including many Catholics. A Catholic parish is a well-defined geographic area, and all Catholics within that area are presumed to be members of the parish. Being a member of the parish, though, should not be confused with being registered and worshiping in that parish. Catholics are not obliged to worship only in the parish church in which they reside, but "…may for convenience or taste attend services in any Catholic church."[58]

In 2003, Father Henry Carmona was appointed as the pastor at St. John's. At his appointment, a specific charge to Father Henry was that he embark on a program of recruitment of Hispanic members to the cathedral parish. Father Henry, a native of Columbia and fluent in Spanish, sought out Boise's "hidden Hispanics."

Since the late 1990's, Sacred Heart Church in Boise's "Bench" neighborhood had been offering Masses in Spanish on an unfortunate and unorganized "hit and miss" basis. Bishop Driscoll, with his orders to Father Carmona in 2002, was trying to make it all hit and no misses. St. Mary's Church, Boise's second oldest Catholic church, was offering not one, but two Spanish Masses on the weekend, and filling them both. Clearly it was time for the cathedral to address the need.

The response of the area's Hispanics was immediate and enthusiastic. "We thought you'd never ask!" They joined the parish life of St. John's with vigor. They brought to St. Johns's not just a new language and new music but an introduction to a deep and very personal spirituality.

The dominant Eurocentric Catholicism which has prevailed in the United States for the past 250 years is a well-structured, very hierarchal, and decidedly "top down" organization. Hispanic Catholicism is much less hierarchal and much more personal. It is not a Sunday celebration. It infuses every aspect of the believer's life. Signs, symbols, and deeply held beliefs of the supernatural as part of each day's events permeate the culture. God is not "there," God is everywhere, and in everyone.

Exposure to these concepts has been an enriching experience to those in the "Anglo" community who are open to them. It could be the vibrant and enthusiastic music at a Spanish Mass. It could be the predawn darkness of December 12th (Our Lady of Guadalupe) or a winter evening accompanying Mary and Joseph as they seek lodging (*Los Posados*). Perhaps it is sharing with the community a remembrance of a deceased loved one (*Dia de los Muertos*). No matter what the religious observance, Latinos bring to it their own unique "take" on things, and in particular the very personal nature of human interaction with the spiritual.

Change of any sort is difficult for the human animal. Change in matters of cultural and racial identity is particularly fraught with problems. Change, though, is inevitable. Some simple numbers will put this into perspective. While Hispanics make up 34% of American Catholics overall, which is in itself a significant number, they make up 60% of Catholics under age 18! Clearly the future of the Catholic Church in the United States is going to be skewed very heavily Hispanic. The future is *Mestizo*!

# Chapter 22

*Quo Vadis?*

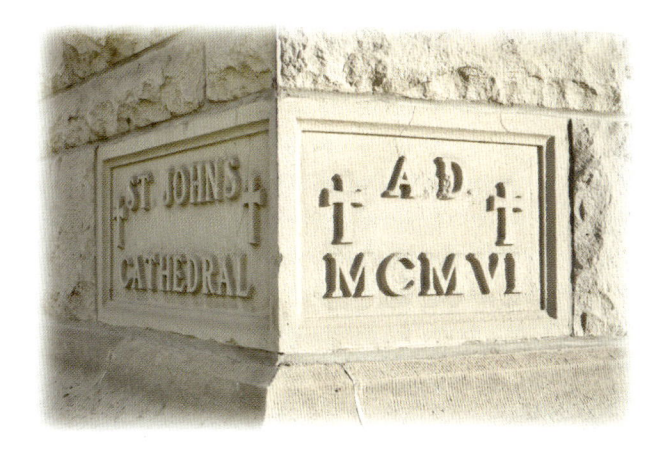

We have completed an exhaustive look at the past 110 years of the Cathedral of St. John the Evangelist. What of its future? Aside from the obvious points made in the previous chapter, that it will be increasingly Hispanic, what will the church look like in the next 100 years? As Edmund Burke said, "You can never plan the future by the past." None of us has any idea what the future will hold for the Cathedral of St. John the Evangelist. The future of religion generally, and the Catholic Church in particular, is an extremely popular theme of analysis and introspection of late. At the height of the post Vatican II furor in the early 1970's, there were actually predictions that by the year 2000 there would be no Catholic Church. Obviously, that dire prediction has not come true.

St. John the Evangelist has survived two world wars, several smaller wars, a depression, recession, a crisis in vocations, scandal, and a huge array of day to day crises. It will survive for the foreseeable future, and a few things are obvious at least for the short term.

We can say with some confidence that:

- The Cathedral of St. John the Evangelist will continue to serve as a stellar architectural/artistic monument for all of the people of Boise.
- It will be protected, preserved, and enhanced by those entrusted with its care.
- It will continue to offer its religious messages and theme of hope.
- The lay people, who have always done so well in protecting and preserving their church and the faith it imparts, will be called upon to do more.

As to what particular issues or crises it might be called to address, we can only speculate.

# Appendix A

## Glossary

## A

**Altar**
The central element in a Catholic church. It is where the main celebrant of a Mass or other liturgical ceremonies stands.

**Ambo**
A raised stand for reading the Gospel and the Epistle.

**Ambry**
A cabinet or niche where the sacred oils used in various anointing ceremonies are kept.

**Apse**
*Latin: Abis.* An arched vault usually defining a central space in a building.

**Archbishop**
A bishop of a province or area who has some limited authority over dioceses in that area.

**Archdiocese**
The geographical area which an archbishop presides over.

**Architrave**
Painted decorative band below the frieze.

## B

**Basilica**
In Catholic usage, a church which has been given this special designation because of its architectural or historic significance.

**Baldacchino**
*Italian.* A permanent, ornamental canopy above a central point of an altar.

**Biretta**
A small, decorative cap with three ridges worn by Catholic clergy.

**Bishop**
The highest ecclesiastical authority in a particular geographical area. Generally a

bishop is the highest authority most lay Catholics are answerable to.

# C

**Cartouche**
A drawing or carving, usually in the shape of an oval or shield, which is often used to cap a decoration.

**Catechumens**
Candidates for membership in the Catholic Church. Catechumens undergo a period of instruction and formation before they are admitted to full communion in the Church.

**Canon Law**
The officially enacted rules of the Catholic Church which govern those practices binding on Catholics, both lay and ordained.

**Cathedra**
Literally, chair. The bishop's chair in a cathedral.

**Cathedral**
A church in a particular diocese which is the bishop's "home church."

**Chalice**
A cup or goblet which holds the consecrated wine during the celebration of the Eucharist. According to the General Instruction of the Roman Missal, "Sacred vessels should be made from precious metal. If they are made from metal that rusts, or from metal less precious than gold, they should generally be gilded on the inside."

"As regards chalices and other vessels that are intended to serve as receptacles for the Blood of the Lord, they are to have a bowl of material that does not absorb liquids." (GIRM Numbers 328 and 330)

**Church**
The term *Church* refers to the living temple, God's people.

The term *church* also has been used to describe "the building in which the Christian community gathers . . ."

**Cope**
A shawl-like ornamented garment worn by a priest at certain ceremonies.

**Cornice**
An ornamental molding where walls and ceiling meet.

**Cruciform**
In the shape of a cross. If viewed from above, a cruciform building would be in the shape of a cross. The main body of a cross is generally referred to as the nave and the arms of the cross the transepts.

# D

**Diocese**
The geographical area where a bishop exercises authority. A diocese is itself contained in an archdiocese.

### Doctor [of the Church]
A title bestowed by the Church in recognition of the contributions a person has made to the understanding of scripture and Christian doctrine. There are 35 Doctors of the Church, ranging from the Patristic Era (300 to 750 BC) to the Modern Era ( 1700 to 1900).

## E

### Ecclesiastical
A term used to describe matters which pertain only to the Church, particularly ritual and internal matters. (*Latin: ecclesia, Greek: ekklesia*; a properly summoned group)

### Epiphany
A sudden or striking realization. In Christian belief, the Epiphany refers to the visit of the three kings to the Christ child, and thus refers to Christ's revelation to the non-Jewish world.

### Episcopate
The office of a bishop.

### Eucharist
The highest form of Catholic worship. The process of consecrating bread and wine, thereby transforming it into the body and blood of Christ. In Catholic theology, the Eucharist is not a representational nor symbolic transformation, but an actual change of the hosts and the wine into the Body and Blood of Christ. The Mass is not complete without the liturgy of the Eucharist.

## F

### Font
In Catholic usage, a receptacle for holy water. It may be an ornate, free standing sculpture, or a simple receptacle attached to a wall.

### Frieze
A painted decorative band below the cornice.

## G

### GIRM
*The General Instruction of the Roman Missal, Third Edition.* The work which contains the norms and instructions for the celebration of the Mass, and the appointments and forms for Catholic Churches in the United States. The *GIRM* is the definitive document to answer questions regarding appropriate liturgy and procedures. This work is published by the United States Conference of Catholic Bishops.

## H–L

### Holy Day [of Obligation]
Certain days of the year when Catholics are obliged to attend Mass. Holy days—with the exception of Sunday, which is always a Holy Day—vary from country to country. In the Vatican there are ten Holy Days in addition to Sundays. In Hong Kong there is only one. In the United States the Holy Days, other than Sunday, are six: the Solemnity of Mary,

the Ascension of Jesus, the Assumption of Mary, All Saints Day, the Feast of the Immaculate Conception, and Christmas. Easter, of course, is always on a Sunday.

**Hosts**
The wafers of unleavened bread which at the Eucharist become the body of Christ.

**Liturgy**
Public worship

**Liturgical**
Pertaining to the rubrics and form of public worship.

# M

**Mass**
The entire public worship at which the Eucharist is celebrated.

**Mensa**
"Top." The flat stone which is the top of altar.

**Monsignor**
An honorific given to Catholic priests to signify titular distinction. It was formerly given as a recognition of distinctive service. The title has recently largely fallen out of use.

# N

**Narthex**
The entry area or vestibule immediately preceding the main body of the church. The name is derived from the Greek word for the stalk of a giant fennel plant. In mythology it was such a stalk which Prometheus used to carry fire to mankind.

**Nave**
The main seating area of the church, generally defined by the central and side aisle. The term is derived from the Latin *navis* for ship, which the form of a church very generally conforms to.

**NCCB**
National Conference of Catholic Bishops. A collegial body of bishops which determines the official position of the United States Catholic Church on a wide variety of matters, ranging from liturgical norms to policies of social justice.

# O

**Ordinary**
Another term for the bishop or other person who has immediate authority over a diocese or archdiocese.

# P–R

**Parish**
The community attached to a particular church. In the United States a parish is no longer a geographical designation. Persons who have attached themselves to a particular church are seen as members of the parish, no matter where they might actually live.

*Appendix A*

### Reredos
*Middle English: areredos*, back or behind. The decorative screen or backdrop behind an altar. Reredos range from a plain background to ornate carved niches with a variety of decorations in them.

## S

### Sanctuary
*Latin: Sanctus*, sacred or holy. In Catholic churches today, generally the area around the altar or the area where the altar is located.

### Surplice
A loose, white, flowing garment worn over the shoulders and extending to below the waist.

## T-Z

### Tabernacle
In a Catholic church, a specially secured and secure area where the consecrated hosts—the Body of Christ—are kept until they are needed for the sick, or for consumption at a Mass.

### Theology
*Greek: theo+logy/God+study*. A Church's formalized beliefs regarding God and humankind's relationship to Him.

### Transept
A transept is a cross section of any building, which lies at 90-degree angles across the main body of the building. In a church, the transept is an area set crosswise to the nave. It would be the "arms" of a cross in a cruciform building in Romanesque architecture.

### Transubstantiation
The doctrine that bread and wine, without changing their outward appearances, have been transformed into the Body and Blood of Christ.

# Appendix B

## Bishops of the Diocese of Boise

### Louis Aloysius Lootens

*3 March 1868–27 February 1876*
Resigned. Bishop Lootens was the vicar apostolic for the territory of Idaho, under the authority of Archbishop Blanchet. There was no diocese in Idaho until 1893. With Bishop Lootens' resignation, the vicariate of Idaho came under the direct administration of the Diocese of Oregon until 1885.

### Alphonse Joseph Glorieux

*27 February 1885–25 August 1917*
Died in office.

### Daniel Mary Gorman

*8 February 1918–9 June 1927*
Died in office.

### Edward Joseph Kelly

*19 December 1927–21 April 1956*
Died in office.

### James Joseph Byrne

*16 June 1956–19 May 1962*
Appointed bishop of Dubuque, Iowa.

**Sylvester William Treinen**

*19 May 1962–17 August 1988*
Retired.

**Tod David Brown**

*17 December 1988–30 June 1998*
Appointed bishop of Orange, California.

**Michael Patrick Driscoll**

*18 January 1999–4 November 2014*
Retired.

**Peter Forsyth Christensen**

*4 November 2014–*

## The Bishop's Coat of Arms

Prominent in the Cathedral, on the back of the bishop's *cathedra* is the coat of arms of the current bishop of Boise. The bishop's coat of arms is a heraldic symbol which is meant to impart the authority of the bishop over the diocese. It is rich in meaning. Following is an explanation of the coat of arms for Bishop Peter Christensen.

The bishop's coat of arms is the left-hand side of the total image. (The right-hand side is the diocesan coat of arms.)

The coat of arms of the diocese is a variation of the coat of arms of Pope Leo XIII, who erected the Diocese of Boise on August 25, 1893. They are composed of a silver (white) field on which are seen a green terrace that has a green pine tree growing forth from it. The name "Boise" (Les Bois) suggests a tree, and the Latin name of the diocese, Xylopolitanus, meaning "wood city" or "wooded place," further indicates this.

Across the center of this field is a red, embattled fess (horizontal bar) to represent the fortifications that traditionally surrounded all cities, especially the frontier cities like Boise. The beginnings of the city of Boise were, in fact, the establishment of a U.S. Army fort in the location.

In the upper left (chief dexter) of Pope Leo's arms is a comet that is taken from his family's arms, the Pecci family. In this design for the Diocese of Boise, that comet has been replaced with a small, red ornamental cross that has a comet-like tail. For his personal arms, seen in the sinister impalement (right side) of the shield, Bishop Christensen's coat of arms pays homage to St. Peter, the first bishop of Rome, St. Francis de Sales, and of course his baptismal name.

The external elements of the shield are composed of the green pilgrim's hat with its six tassels on each side, in three rows. These are the heraldic insignia of a bishop. For his motto, Bishop Christensen selected a text from Mt. 16:16, *"Tu es Christus Filius Dei Vivi."* (You are the Christ, Son of the Living God.)

The barque on the coat of arms was based on a design by Bishop Christensen, who has a background in the graphic arts. Bishop Christensen's crest was designed by James-Charles Noonan, Jr., a well-known church historian and ecclesial heraldist from Gwynedd Valley, Pennsylvania. Linda Nicholson, a craft painter of the Society of Heraldic Arts in England, painted the arms designed by Noonan.

There is also tribute to the Blessed Virgin Mary evidenced in blue on the base of the shield. Besides Mary, blue also represents philosophy, symbolic of a bishop's teaching role. Above a depiction of a wave in silver is the barque (boat) of Peter in gold. Gold represents the first of the heavenly attributes, as well as divine wisdom and the Petrine office. The mast of the boat is in the form of a cross in gold, representing the heroic sacrifice of Christ. This image is particularly significant, since Bishop Christensen was ordained to the episcopacy on September 14, 2007, the feast of the Exaltation of the Holy Cross. The sail of the boat is silver, its fullness representing the fullness of truth that the apostle Peter carried to Rome. The star on the sail is the Star of Mary, with red rays representing the graces that flow from her. Its position near the base of the mast recalls Mary's steadfast presence at the foot of the cross.

On the top, in gold rectangle, is a circlet representing a halo of holiness to which all in the church are called. It consists of eight thorns (black for human sinfulness) tipped in red, the color of Christ's redeeming blood. Here is a reference to the sorrows that pierced the heart of St. Francis de Sales, a saint with whom Bishop Christensen shares a deep spiritual kinship.

Behind the coat of arms is the episcopal cross, with one transverse arm. The crozier on the cross represents St. Peter and the sword, St. Paul. The ruby is reminiscent of the martyrdom each saint suffered in witness to Christ.[a]

---

[a] Reproduced from the Diocese of Boise website.

**Bishop Christensen's coat of arms**
*(Reproduced with permission from the Diocese of Boise)*

*Appendix B*

Following are the coats of arms of each of the other seven bishops who have served the Diocese of Boise. The only thing which changes on each coat of arms is the right hand side of the shield. Most interesting, perhaps, is the first bishop's (Glorieux's) coat of arms. There was no Diocese of Boise when Bishop Glorieux was appointed, so there is no "diocesan" symbol on the left; the entire coat of arms is Glorieux's as the vicar apostolic of Boise.

**Bishop Glorieux's coat of arms**
*(Reproduced with permission from the Diocese of Boise)*

**Bishop Gorman's coat of arms**
*(Reproduced with permission from the Diocese of Boise)*

*Appendix B*

**Bishop Kelly's coat of arms**
*(Reproduced with permission from the Diocese of Boise)*

**Bishop Byrne's coat of arms**
*(Reproduced with permission from the Diocese of Boise)*

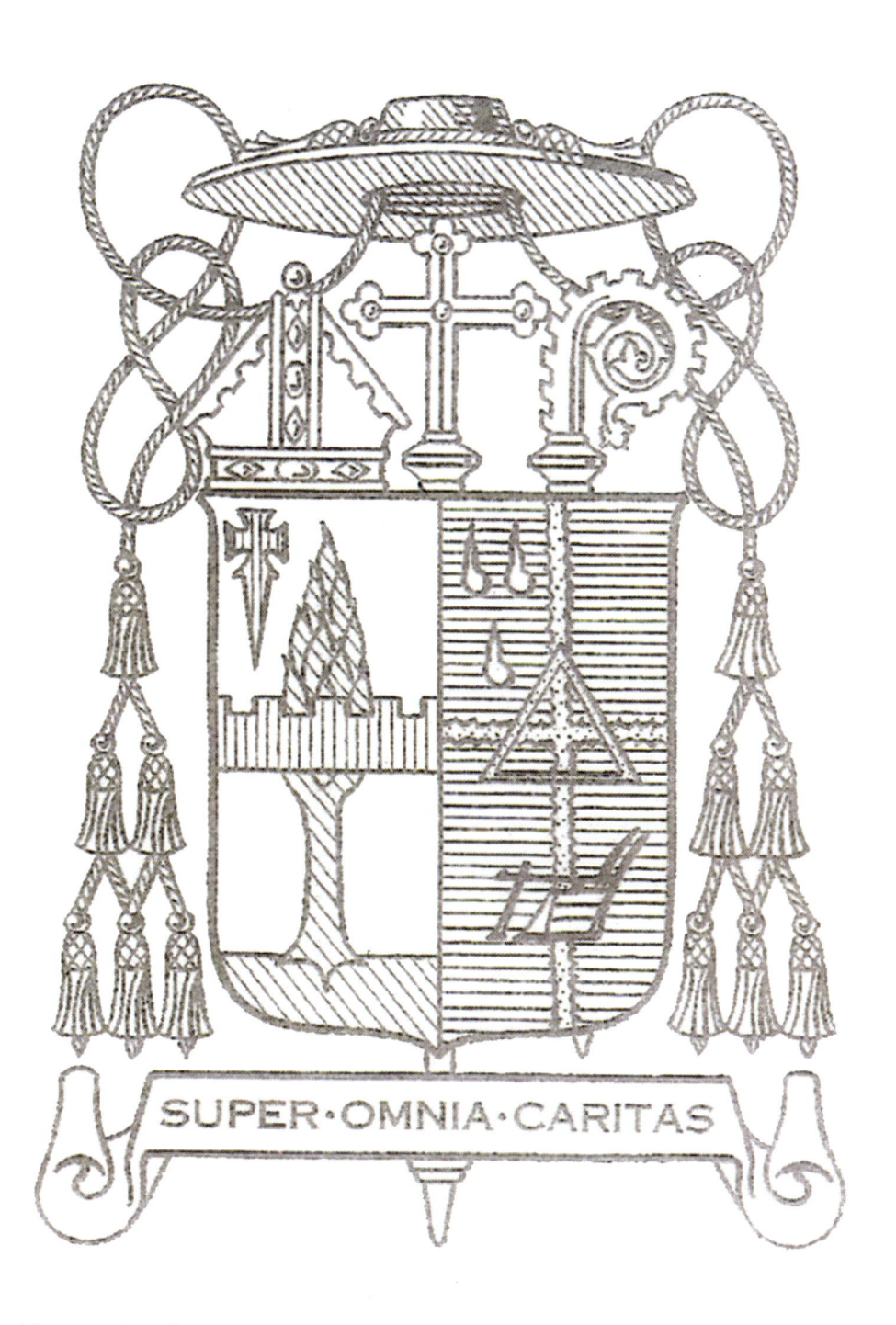

*Appendix B*

**Bishop Treinen's coat of arms**
*(Reproduced with permission from the Diocese of Boise)*

**Bishop Brown's coat of arms**
*(Reproduced with permission from the Diocese of Boise)*

*Appendix B*

**Bishop Driscoll's coat of arms**
*(Reproduced with permission from the Diocese of Boise)*

*Stone Wondrously Hewn*

# Appendix C

## Pastors/Rectors of St. John's Cathedral

The honorific assigned to the priests appointed to lead St. John's Cathedral is sometimes given as pastor, sometimes as rector, and oftentimes the titles are used interchangeably.

**1907–1919**
Reverend Remi S. Keyser, *Pastor*

**1919–1921**
Reverend Nicholas F. Wirtzberger, *Rector*

**1921–1922**
Reverend Roger O'Callaghan, *Rector*

**1922–1930**
Reverend Joseph Verhoeven, *Rector*

**1930–1931**
Reverend M.J. McGowan

**1931–1934**
Reverend Linus Dougherty, *Pastor/Rector*

**1934–1942**
Right Reverend Joseph F. O'Toole, *Pastor/Rector*

**1942–1944**
Right Reverend Michael Mroz, *Rector*

**1944–1964**
Right Reverend Kenneth Rowe, *Rector*

**1964–1974**
Right Reverend Nicholas Hughes, *Rector*

**1974–1984**
Right Reverend Andrew Schumacher, *Pastor*

**1984–1998**
Reverend Donald Riffle, *Rector*

**1998–2003**
Reverend Joseph McDonald, *Rector*

**2003–2014**
Reverend Henry Carmona, *Rector*

**2014–**
Reverend Gerald Funke, *Rector*

# Appendix D

## Myths/Mysteries of St. John's Cathedral

1. The cathedral is constructed entirely of sandstone blocks.

   *The cathedral is largely a sandstone edifice; however, the building is actually a brick/sandstone composite. The foundation and subterranean walls are sandstone. The exterior walls above grade are brick, faced with sandstone. This is true of virtually all of the sandstone buildings in Boise.*

2. The main "high altar" at St. John's was originally meant for the Cathedral of the Madeline (Magdalene) in Salt Lake City. The train which was delivering both altars unloaded the one meant for Boise in Salt Lake City, and the one meant for Salt Lake City in Boise.

   *This is a completely unsubstantiated and persistent myth. If any train mixed up the two altars and delivered the wrong one to the wrong church it was a train running on a very much delayed schedule. The Cathedral of the Madeline was finished in 1909 over ten years before St. John's Cathedral even got properly started.*

   *The Cathedral of the Madeline was substantially remodeled in 1919, and as part of that renovation the old altar was removed and sold, not to St. John's, but to the Diocese of Lake Charles Louisiana where it is still in use.*

   *This story apparently has its basis in an offhand comment one of St. John's docents made many years ago, that the five red marble disks in the front of St. John's altar "may have" been sent, by mistake, originally to Salt Lake City! This comment, regarding some very small decorative accents on St. John's altar, has transmogrified into an enduring myth of "wrong altar, wrong church," which will not die.*

*The myth has been fed by the presence of two funerary urns atop tall marble columns flanking St. John's old "high altar." These urns, common decorations in memorials to fallen heroes in the early 20th century, supposedly represent the jars of "precious spikenard" which Mary Magdalene brought to the tomb to anoint Jesus' body on the first Easter.*

*The urns are, instead, the Regan family's memorial to their son, Lieutenant John Regan, who was killed in the First World War. A plaque honoring Lieutenant Regan can be found at the base of one of the columns holding the urns.*

3. What are the relics in the altar at St. John's Cathedral?

*When the cathedral was renovated in 1978–79, the relics from the old high altar, as well as those from the two side altars, were placed in the new altar in the center of the transept. At that time, the relics and their documentation were studied and it was determined that the three relics were "relics of the holy martyrs Prospera and Fulgentius" as well as "particles of dirt from the tomb of St. John the Evangelist."*

4. Why were the towers of St. John's never finished?

*Money, or rather the lack of it, was the plain and simple reason. In May of 1921 the cost of building the cathedral had already put the diocese in debt some $80,000.00. Finishing the two towers was estimated to cost another $35,000.00. The cathedral had been under construction for over ten years and the decision was made to "finish" it without the towers.*

5. Why was the name of the church, which had been in existence in Boise since 1870 as St. Patrick's, changed to St. John the Evangelist when it was rebuilt at 9th and Bannock?

*An exhaustive search of the records in both Boise and Portland (Boise was, and is, part of the archdiocese of Portland) has not provided any clue. It is particularly puzzling since the record is clear that major contributors to the building were Irish soldiers from Fort Boise. Further, the commander of the Fort at that time was Major Patrick Collins, an Irish immigrant. Major Collins actually detailed soldiers to assist with the building, an activity which certainly would not be countenanced in this era of sensitivity regarding "separation of church and state."*

*Appendix D*

6. Why is the parish school attached to St. John's not named St. John's?

*The first Catholic school in Idaho was St. Mary's school, founded in Idaho City in 1868 and operated independent of any church by the Holy Name Sisters. In 1869 that school was taken over by the parish of St. Joseph in Idaho City and renamed St. Joseph's by Father Archambault.*

*In 1877 Father Archambault was transferred to Boise, which was beginning to supplant Idaho City as the largest city in Idaho. He brought his school with him and operated it out of the parish hall at 9th and Bannock streets. Three years later, Father Archambault was transferred once again, now to Portland, Oregon. He couldn't, this time, bring his school with him and the school closed for twenty years.*

*In 1900 Bishop Glorieux re-opened the school at the corner of 9th and Bannock streets in the community hall of the then Catholic church. Although that church was named St. John's, they had named the hall St. Patrick's Hall in honor of Boise's first Catholic church. The school was generally referred to as St. Patrick's Hall School.*

*The building was moved to the new location of the cathedral at 9th and Fort streets in 1905. Around that time the awkward "St. Patrick's Hall School" name was dropped and it was once again referred to as St. Joseph's school. St. Joseph's school – sometimes a grammar school, sometimes a high school, and under different names – has operated continuously for over 115 years, longer than the cathedral which claims it.*

# Appendix E

## Key Facts About St. John's Cathedral

1. Below ground work on the cathedral began in 1905.

2. The cornerstone was laid on November 10, 1906.

3. The basement area was completed and used for services in 1912.

4. The main cathedral was completed and dedicated on May 30, 1921.

5. The original construction cost, including all furnishings and decorations, was less than $250,000.00.

6. The cost of the renovation and repairs done in 1978 was $365,000.00.

7. The two towers on the front rise to a height of 65 feet above street level. (They were originally planned to be twice as high.)

8. The cathedral is cruciform in shape, 170 feet long, 65 feet wide in the nave and 95 feet wide across the transept.

9. The main floor will seat approximately 800 people.

10. The building is a brick/sandstone composite. All of the foundations are solid sandstone; the exterior walls are brick, faced with sandstone on the outside and lath and plaster on the inside.

11. The ceiling one sees from the interior is actually painted canvas. Above that is a conventional lath and plaster ceiling, but stretchers have been attached to that and

decorated canvas is what one is seeing looking up.

12. The floor of the main aisle is Knoxville marble from Tennessee. The floor of the altar area is Siena marble from Italy.

13. The bell in the tower of St. John's Cathedral is older than the building. The bell was originally installed in 1882 in St. John's at 9th and Bannock. It weighs 1400 pounds and is the largest bell in the city of Boise.

# Appendix F

## Timeline for St. John's Cathedral

**1863**

First Mass said in Boise at the home of John O'Farrell.

**1870**

First Catholic church in Boise, St. Patrick's, is dedicated on the block bounded by 4th, 5th, State and Jefferson streets.

**1871**

St. Patrick's Church burns down just two weeks after opening.

**1872**

Block situated at 9th, 10th, Jefferson, and Bannock streets is purchased.

**1876**

New church, St. John's, is finished at 9th and Bannock streets, with Midnight Mass for Christmas of 1876 being the first Mass.

**1879**

First school formed at St. John's to prepare children for Confirmation.

**1882**

St. John's buys eight acres on Morris Hill to be used as Catholic cemetery.

**1885**

Alphonse J. Glorieux arrives in Idaho to assume the episcopacy. He makes St. John's his cathedral.

## 1889

- St. Patrick's Hall is built on Bannock Street to the west of the church.
- Holy Cross Sisters open a grade school in St. Patrick's Hall.
- Holy Cross Sisters open an academy at 4th and State streets.

## 1893

The Diocese of Boise is established.

## 1900

St. Patrick's Hall is remodeled as a school, for boys only, named St. Joseph's.

## 1902

Bishop Glorieux purchases the block bounded by Fort, Hays, 8th, and 9th streets.

## 1904

- Rectory is begun at 9th and Hays streets.
- Meetings begin to consider construction of a new cathedral at the new location.
- Knights of Columbus Council is formed at the Cathedral.

## 1905

- Excavations begin for new cathedral foundations.
- Temporary church begun at corner of Fort and 8th Streets.

## 1906

- Cathedral cornerstone is laid November 10, 1906.
- St. Joseph's school is moved to the new site at 8th and Fort Streets.

## 1910

Bishop Glorieux celebrates his Silver Jubilee.

## 1911

- Catholic Women's League is formed at the Cathedral.
- First Basque priest, Fr. Bernardo Arregui, is assigned to the Cathedral

## 1912

- Upper walls completed and roof is placed.
- Basement interior is completed and used for services.
- Old church becomes school.

## 1913

Diocesan Priests Eucharistic Conference is held.

## 1916

Boise Catholic Monthly begins publication.

## 1917

- Bishop Glorieux dies.
- Work ceases on the cathedral.

## 1918

Daniel Mary Gorman is appointed bishop of Idaho.

## 1919

- Work resumes on finishing the cathedral.
- Church of the Good Shepherd is dedicated.

## 1921

- The finished cathedral is dedicated on May 30, 1921.
- Old "basement cathedral" is reduced by half with construction of theater and performance areas on November 27, 1921.

## 1927

- Bishop Gorman dies.
- Edward Joseph Kelly is appointed bishop of Idaho.

## 1928

- Church of the Good Shepherd is closed.
- Chancery and bishop's residence is moved from 9th Street to the former Church of the Good Shepherd at 5th and Bannock streets.

## 1929

First parishioner, Linus Dougherty who lived at 815 Hays Street, is ordained in the Cathedral.

## 1941

Old St. John's church/St. Joseph's gymnasium at 8th & Fort streets is demolished.

## 1946

Mortgage for the building of the cathedral is paid off.

**1948**

Gymnasium is built at 8th and Fort Streets.

**1951**

Roof, gutters, and downspouts are redone to eliminate leaking on cathedral walls.

**1952**

Interior walls and ceilings are cleaned.

**1956**

- Bishop Kelly dies.
- James Joseph Byrne is appointed bishop of Idaho.

**1959**

Basement chapel is remodeled.

**1961**

Basement chapel is remodeled, with new altar installed.

**1962**

- Bishop Byrne is appointed bishop of Dubuque, Iowa.
- Sylvester W. Treinan is appointed bishop of Idaho.

**1963**

Organ is rebuilt.

**1964**

New gas-fired boilers are installed as the cathedral heating system.

**1964**

First Mass said in English.

**1965**

First Mass said in Basque.

**1971**

Major sandblasting and cleaning done to the exterior.

**1973**

- New hand carved doors are installed.
- Elevator is installed.

## Appendix F

**1974**

Statue of St. John at apex of roofline is replaced.

**1975**

Speaker system is installed.

**1976**

Cathedral is placed on the National Register of Historic Places.

**1976**

Consideration is given to splitting Idaho into two dioceses.

**1977**

Recommendation is made to retain present structure of diocese.

**1978–79**

Major renovation and remodeling:
- Old "high altar" is decommissioned.
- Side altars and altar rail are removed.
- Tabernacle, baptismal font, cathedra, and ambo are relocated.
- Stained glass window is added to the central location in the apse.
- Interior decorations are cleaned.
- Lighting and electrical work is upgraded.

**1982**

Major renovation is given to the organ.

**1988**

- Bishop Treinan retires.
- Tod David Brown is appointed bishop of Idaho.

**1994**

Organ is restored and upgraded with electronic enhancements.

**1995**

Exterior steps are redone.

**1998**

Bishop Brown is appointed bishop of Orange, California.

**1999**

Michael Patrick Driscoll is appointed bishop of Idaho.

**2002**

Emergency exit is added to choir loft.

**2006**

Organ is renovated and upgraded.

**2007**

Lower level and chapel are remodeled.

**2014**

- Bishop Driscoll retires.
- Peter Forsyth Christensen is appointed bishop of Idaho.

# End Notes

1. *The Rites of the Catholic Church as Revised by the Second Vatican Ecumenical Council, Volume Two*, (Collegeville, The Liturgical Press, 1991) p.355.

2. National Compensation Survey. U.S. Department of Labor. Hilda L. Solis, Secretary U.S. Bureau of Labor Statistics Keith Hall, Commissioner.

3. *Documents of the Liturgy 1963–1979 Conciliar, Papal and Curial Texts.* International Commission on English in the Liturgy, A Joint Commission of Catholic Bishops Conference. (The Liturgical Press, Collegeville. 1982.) #4371.

4. Letter, April 27, 1937. *Bishop of Boise to Very Rev. J.P. O'Toole*, St. Johns Cathedral file, Diocese of Boise.

5. Bradley, Cyprian O.S.B. and Kelly, Edward D.D. Ph.D. *History of the Diocese of Boise, 1863–1953* (Caldwell, The Caxton Printers, 1953) p.105.

6. Bradley, Cyprian O.S.B. and Kelly, Edward D.D. Ph.D. *History of the Diocese of Boise, 1863–1953* (Caldwell, The Caxton Printers, 1953) p.114.

7. Ibid p.261.

8. Smith, S. B. (Sebastian Bach), *Notes on the Second Plenary council of Baltimore* (New York, 1874).

9. Bradley, Cyprian O.S.B. and Kelly, Edward D.D. Ph.D. *History of the Diocese of Boise, 1863–1953* (Caldwell, The Caxton Printers, 1953) p.315.

10. *Northwest Magazine*, November 1906, Vol. II No. 5. P. 13.

11. *Idaho Daily Statesman* August 24th, 1905. P.1.

12. Ibid May 3rd, 1905 P. 3.

13. Ibid September 3, 1906.

14. Ibid November 10, 1906.

15. Ibid. April 26, 1907.

16. Ibid September 19th, 1917.

17. Letter *B. E. Hyatt, Secretary Boise Commercial Club,* October 19, 1917, Archives Diocese of Boise. Boise Catholic Monthly, December 1927.

18. *General Instruction for the Roman Missal Third Edition,* United States Conference of Catholic Bishops 2003. Paragraph 315.

19. *Built of Living Stones: Art, Architecture and Worship,* United States Conference of Catholic Bishops. November, 2000. Section 80.

20. *Built of Living Stones: Art, Architecture and Worship,* United States Conference of Catholic Bishops. November, 2000. Section 74.

21. Bradley, Cyprian O.S.B. and Kelly, Edward D.D. Ph.D. *History of the Diocese of Boise, 1863–1953* (Caldwell, The Caxton Printers, 1953) p.336.

22. Financial Statement and Envelope Contributions for St. John's Cathedral for the year 1945.

23. *The Caldwell Tribune.* Caldwell, July 17, 1909.

24. Bradley, Cyprian O.S.B. and Kelly, Edward D.D. Ph.D. *History of the Diocese of Boise, 1863–1953* (Caldwell, The Caxton Printers, 1953) p. 360.

25. Letter, August 20, 1922, *Brother Z. Joseph, Brothers of the Christian Schools, Martinez California to Right Reverend Daniel M. Gorman, D.D.* Diocese of Boise. Archives of the Diocese of Boise.

26. Bradley, Cyprian O.S.B. and Kelly, Edward D.D. Ph.D. *History of the Diocese of Boise, 1863–1953* (Caldwell, The Caxton Printers, 1953) p. 368.

27. Letter, March 6, 1924. *Brother Z. Joseph, Brothers of the Christian Schools, Martinez California to Right Reverend Daniel M. Gorman, D.D.* Diocese of Boise. Archives of the Diocese of Boise.

28. Bradley, Cyprian O.S.B. and Kelly, Edward D.D. Ph.D. *History of the Diocese of Boise, 1863–1953*

## End Notes

(Caldwell, The Caxton Printers, 1953) p. 375.

29. *Idaho Statesman* May 29th, 1921 p.1.

30. *Boise Catholic Monthly, Vol. II #4* January 1928.

31. Paul Burns, *Butler's Lives of the Saints, New Concise Edition*. Copyright 2003 by Order of Saint Benedict. Published by Liturgical Press, Collegeville, Minnesota. Reprinted with permission.

32. *General Instruction for the Roman Missal Third Edition*, United States Conference of Catholic Bishops 2010 P. 90 #295.

33. Statement signed by Rev. Andrew Schumacher, August 17, 1979, Document Dated May 6, 1921, Father Augustinus Zampini. Archives Cathedral of St. John the Evangelist.

34. *General Instruction for the Roman Missal Third Edition*, United States Conference of Catholic Bishops 2003. P.90 Paragraph 296.

35. Ibid P. 90 Paragraph 299.

36. *Documents on the Liturgy 1963–1979 Conciliar, Papa, and Curial Texts*, Thomas C. O'Brien, Editor and Translator, (Collegeville, The Liturgical Press, 1982) p. 10 para. 26 & 30.

37. *General Instruction for the Roman Missal Third Edition*, United States Conference of Catholic Bishops 2003. Paragraph 299.

38. *Idaho Statesman* April 8th, 1978.

39. St. John's Cathedral Restoration Report and Recommendation of the Committee for the Restoration of St. Johns Cathedral, July 1978 p.2.

40. *Idaho Statesman* September 23, 1978.

41. *Repair, Renovation plans for Cathedral announced*. Judy Steele, Idaho Statesman, September 23, 1978.

42. *Idaho Statesman* October 13, 1979.

43. Letter. *Frederic Fleming Beale to Bishop Gorman*, May 1, 1920. St. Johns Cathedral File, Archives Diocese of Boise.

44. Letter. August 2, 1921. *Allerd P. Kent to Bishop Gorman*, St. Johns File, Archives Diocese of Boise.

45. Letter. April 6, 1922 F.F. Beale to R. Rev. Bishop Gorman. Robert S. Smylie Archives, College of Idaho.

46. Ibid.

47. Letter, October 21st, *Teresa to Dear Professor,* Archives the Diocese of Boise.

48. Undated Letter *Lenore Wagrich ? to Mr. Beale* Archives the Diocese of Boise.

49. *Cathedral Directions Given to the Rev. M.J. McGowan . . . June 29th, 1930* and *Cathedral Regulations Given to Father Dougherty, August 1931.* Archives the Diocese of Boise.

50. Letter, January 26, 1933 *Edward Kelly Bishop of Boise to Rev. L.M. Dougherty,* Archives Diocese of Boise.

51. Letter, January 26, 1933 *Rev. L.M. Dougherty, Rector, to Most Rev. E. J. Kelly Bishop of Boise* Archives Diocese of Boise.

52. Letter, April 17, 1933 *Edward Kelly Bishop of Boise to Rev. L.M. Dougherty,* Archives Diocese of Boise.

53. Letter, April 8, 1936 *Chancellor to Most Reverend Joseph B. Ritter, D.D.* Archives, Diocese of Boise.

54. Letter, August 13, 1945, *C.M. Verhoeven, D.D. to Most Rev. E.J. Kelly,* Archives, Diocese of Boise.

55. Letter, February 5, 1958 *Sister M. Leonilla C.S.C. to Most Reverend James J. Byrne STD.* Archives, Diocese of Boise.

56. Letter March 2, 1972 *Nicholas V. Hughes to Most Rev. S.W. Treinen, D.D.* Archives, Diocese of Boise.

57. *Language divides Anglo, Hispanic Catholics.* Judy Steele and Ralph Knappenberger Idaho Statesman September 22, 1981.

58. Canon, 1248, 1983 Code of Canon Law.

## About the Author: John J. O'Hagan

John and his wife, Letitia, have been members of St. John's parish for over 25 years. They have served at various times as extraordinary ministers, lectors, and sacristan. John is currently an usher and a member of the Knights of Columbus. Letitia is active in the Saint Vincent de Paul Society, and maintains altar linens and liturgical vestments for the parish.

John has two historical works published by Caxton Press in Caldwell—*Lands Never Trodden: The Franciscans and the California Missions* and *When the Basques Ruled California*.

He also wrote: *The History of the Monastery of the Ascension*, published by the Benedictine Monks of Ascension Monastery.

In addition to these works, John has a series of "mission mysteries," all based on actual historical events. The first, *A Convenient Death at San Diego*, was published by Oak Tree Press in 2015 and the second, *An Incidental Death at Monterey*, was released in 2017. Look for more mission mysteries over the next several years.

John and Letitia are the proud parents of six children, spread all over the United States, and twenty-one grandchildren, equally far flung.

*Stone Wondrously Hewn*